This Book Belongs To

Name: _______________________________________

Address: _______________________________________

Better With A PLAN | BUDGET PLANNER

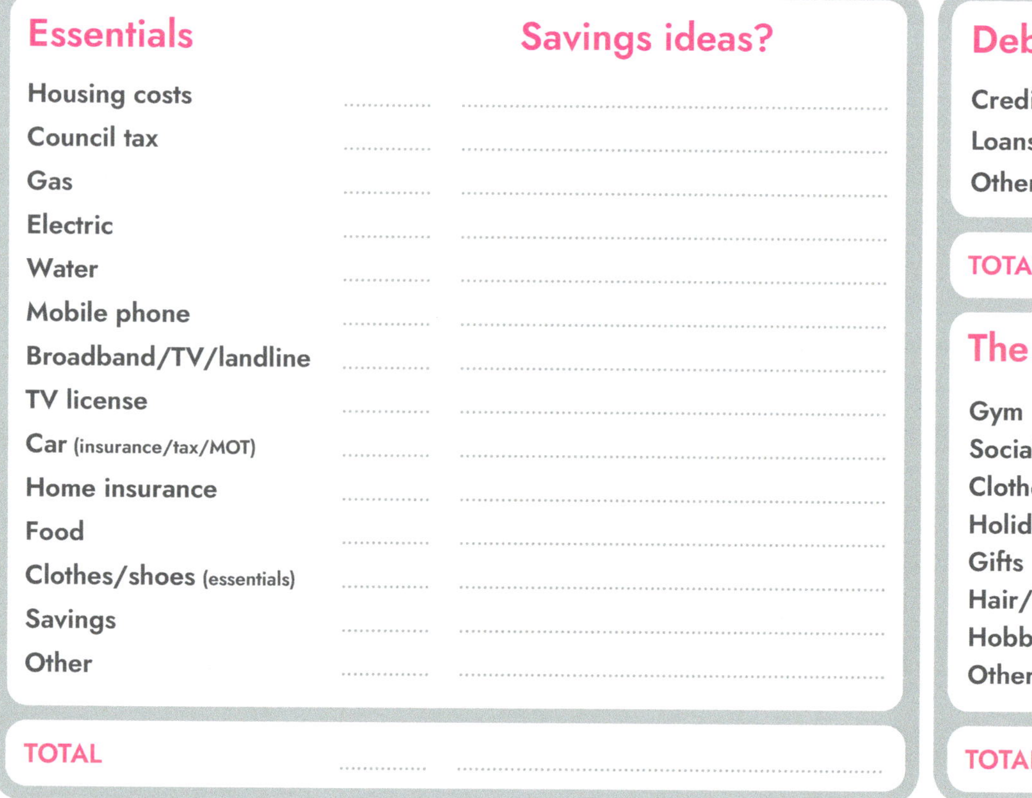

What's coming in?

Salary

Extras

Bank Balance

Total

What's going out?

Essentials

Housing costs
Council tax
Gas
Electric
Water
Mobile phone
Broadband/TV/landline
TV license
Car (insurance/tax/MOT)
Home insurance
Food
Clothes/shoes (essentials)
Savings
Other

TOTAL

Savings ideas?

Debts...

Credit cards
Loans
Other

TOTAL

The Fun Stuff

Gym
Socialising
Clothes
Holidays
Gifts
Hair/beauty
Hobbies
Other

TOTAL

Are you getting the best interest rates?

Day to day costs

Lunch/Food
Travelling
Drinks
Extras

Where are we?

Incomings
Outgoings
What's left

Action plan...

Better With A PLAN | BUDGET PLANNER

What's coming in?

| Salary | Extras | Bank Balance | Total |

What's going out?

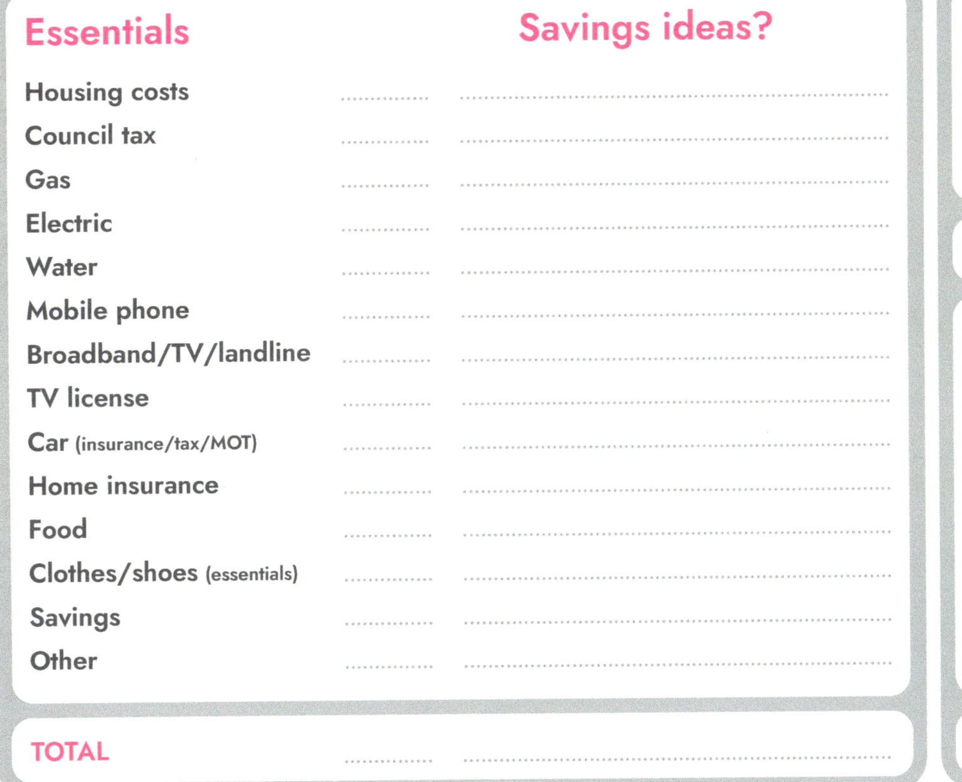

Essentials

Housing costs

Council tax

Gas

Electric

Water

Mobile phone

Broadband/TV/landline

TV license

Car (insurance/tax/MOT)

Home insurance

Food

Clothes/shoes (essentials)

Savings

Other

TOTAL

Savings ideas?

Debts...

Credit cards

Loans

Other

TOTAL

Are you getting the best interest rates?

The Fun Stuff

Gym

Socialising

Clothes

Holidays

Gifts

Hair/beauty

Hobbies

Other

TOTAL

Day to day costs

Lunch/Food

Travelling

Drinks

Extras

Where are we?

Incomings

Outgoings

What's left

Action plan...

Better With A PLAN | BUDGET PLANNER

What's coming in?

Salary	Extras	Bank Balance	Total

What's going out?

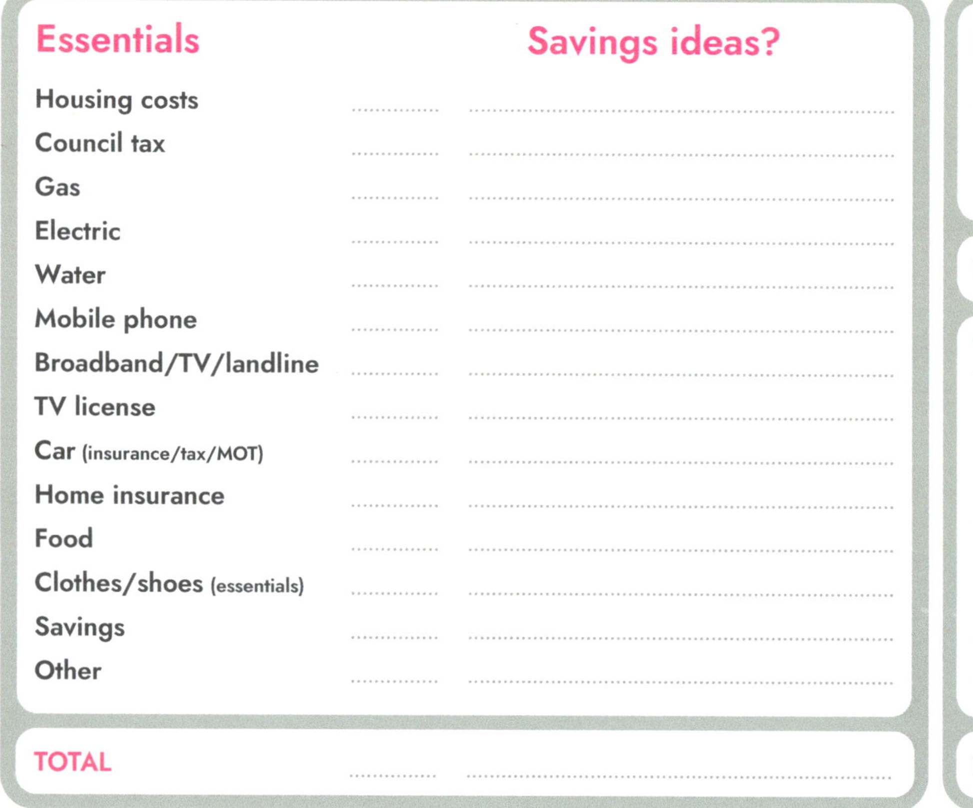

Essentials

Savings ideas?

Housing costs
Council tax
Gas
Electric
Water
Mobile phone
Broadband/TV/landline
TV license
Car (insurance/tax/MOT)
Home insurance
Food
Clothes/shoes (essentials)
Savings
Other

TOTAL

Debts...

Credit cards
Loans
Other

TOTAL

Are you getting the best interest rates?

The Fun Stuff

Gym
Socialising
Clothes
Holidays
Gifts
Hair/beauty
Hobbies
Other

TOTAL

Day to day costs

Lunch/Food
Travelling
Drinks
Extras

Where are we?

Incomings
Outgoings
What's left

Action plan...

Better With A PLAN | BUDGET PLANNER

What's coming in?

Salary	Extras	Bank Balance	Total

What's going out?

Essentials

Savings ideas?

- Housing costs
- Council tax
- Gas
- Electric
- Water
- Mobile phone
- Broadband/TV/landline
- TV license
- Car (insurance/tax/MOT)
- Home insurance
- Food
- Clothes/shoes (essentials)
- Savings
- Other

TOTAL

Day to day costs

- Lunch/Food
- Travelling
- Drinks
- Extras

Debts...

- Credit cards
- Loans
- Other

TOTAL

Are you getting the best interest rates?

The Fun Stuff

- Gym
- Socialising
- Clothes
- Holidays
- Gifts
- Hair/beauty
- Hobbies
- Other

TOTAL

Where are we?

- Incomings
- Outgoings
- What's left

Action plan...

Better With A PLAN | BUDGET PLANNER

What's coming in?

Salary

Extras

Bank Balance

Total

What's going out?

Essentials

Housing costs
Council tax
Gas
Electric
Water
Mobile phone
Broadband/TV/landline
TV license
Car (insurance/tax/MOT)
Home insurance
Food
Clothes/shoes (essentials)
Savings
Other

TOTAL

Savings ideas?

Debts...

Credit cards
Loans
Other

TOTAL

Are you getting the best interest rates?

The Fun Stuff

Gym
Socialising
Clothes
Holidays
Gifts
Hair/beauty
Hobbies
Other

TOTAL

Day to day costs

Lunch/Food
Travelling
Drinks
Extras

Where are we?

Incomings
Outgoings
What's left

Action plan...

BUDGET PLANNER

What's coming in?

Salary

Extras

Bank Balance

Total

What's going out?

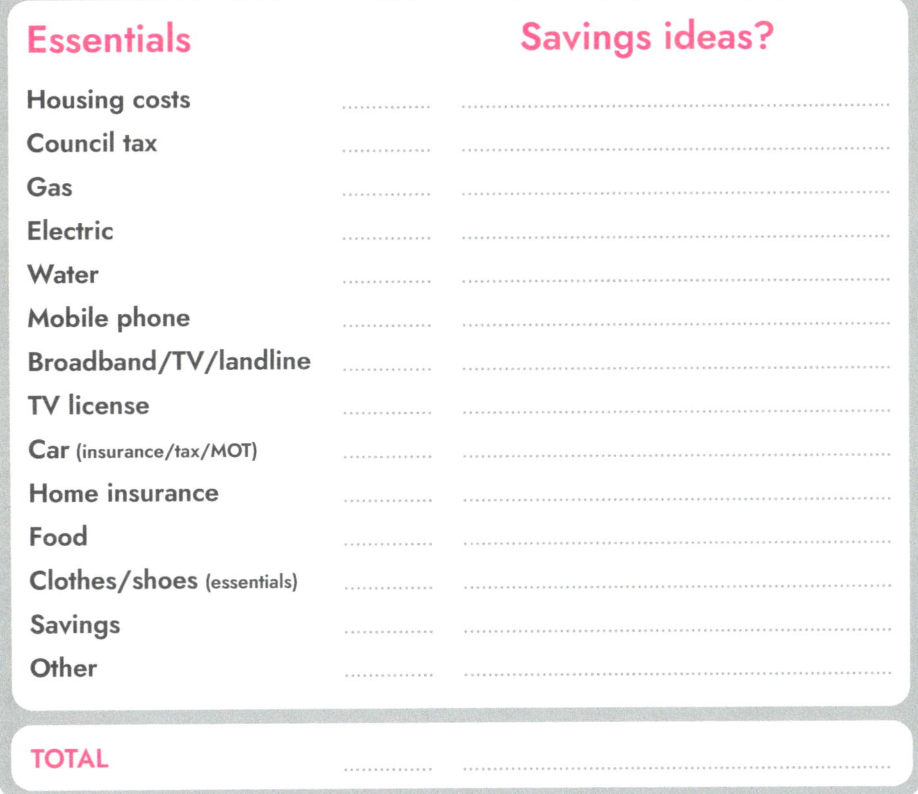

Essentials

Housing costs
Council tax
Gas
Electric
Water
Mobile phone
Broadband/TV/landline
TV license
Car (insurance/tax/MOT)
Home insurance
Food
Clothes/shoes (essentials)
Savings
Other

TOTAL

Savings ideas?

Day to day costs

Lunch/Food
Travelling
Drinks
Extras

Debts...

Credit cards
Loans
Other

TOTAL

The Fun Stuff

Gym
Socialising
Clothes
Holidays
Gifts
Hair/beauty
Hobbies
Other

TOTAL

Where are we?

Incomings
Outgoings
What's left

Action plan...

Better With A
PLAN | BUDGET PLANNER

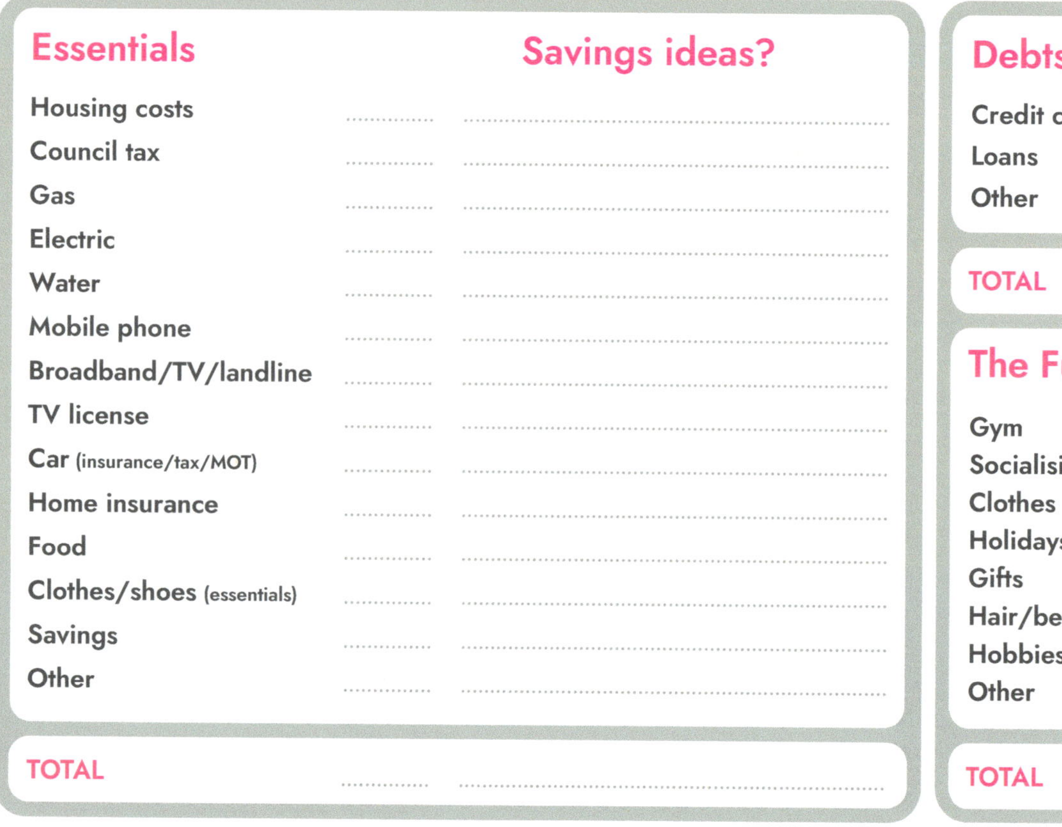

What's coming in?

Salary
Extras
Bank Balance
Total

What's going out?

Essentials

Housing costs
Council tax
Gas
Electric
Water
Mobile phone
Broadband/TV/landline
TV license
Car (insurance/tax/MOT)
Home insurance
Food
Clothes/shoes (essentials)
Savings
Other

Savings ideas?

TOTAL

Debts...

Credit cards
Loans
Other

TOTAL

The Fun Stuff

Gym
Socialising
Clothes
Holidays
Gifts
Hair/beauty
Hobbies
Other

TOTAL

Are you getting the best interest rates?

Day to day costs

Lunch/Food
Travelling
Drinks
Extras

Where are we?

Incomings
Outgoings
What's left

Action plan...

Better With A PLAN | BUDGET PLANNER

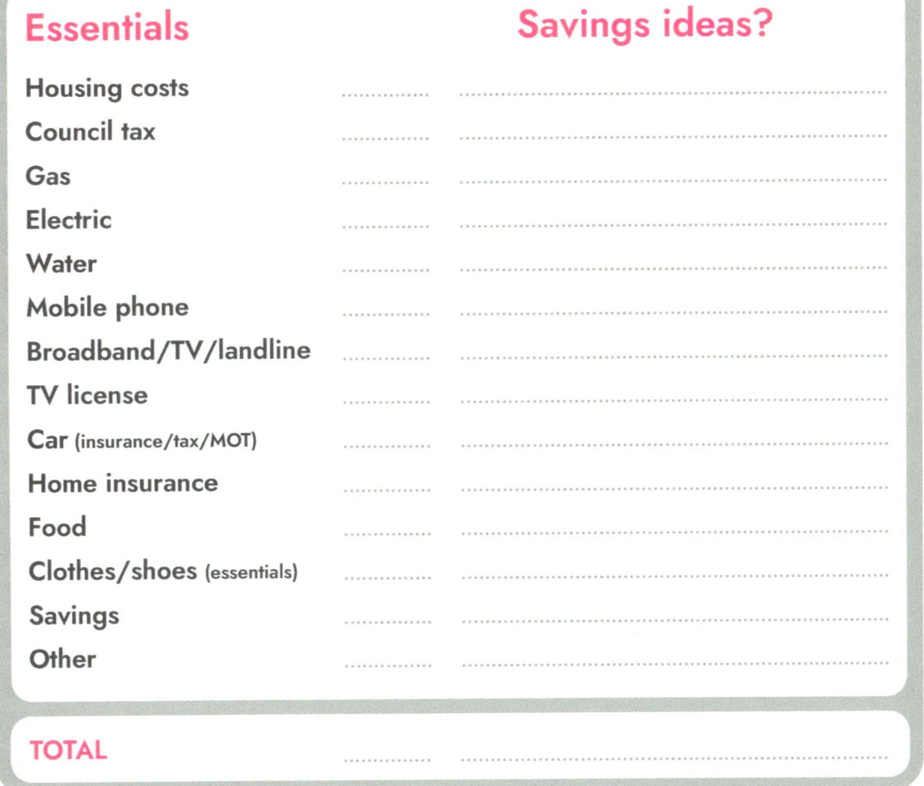

What's coming in?

Salary

Extras

Bank Balance

Total

What's going out?

Essentials

Housing costs
Council tax
Gas
Electric
Water
Mobile phone
Broadband/TV/landline
TV license
Car (insurance/tax/MOT)
Home insurance
Food
Clothes/shoes (essentials)
Savings
Other

TOTAL

Savings ideas?

Debts...

Credit cards
Loans
Other

TOTAL

The Fun Stuff

Gym
Socialising
Clothes
Holidays
Gifts
Hair/beauty
Hobbies
Other

TOTAL

Are you getting the best interest rates?

Day to day costs

Lunch/Food
Travelling
Drinks
Extras

Where are we?

Incomings
Outgoings
What's left

Action plan...

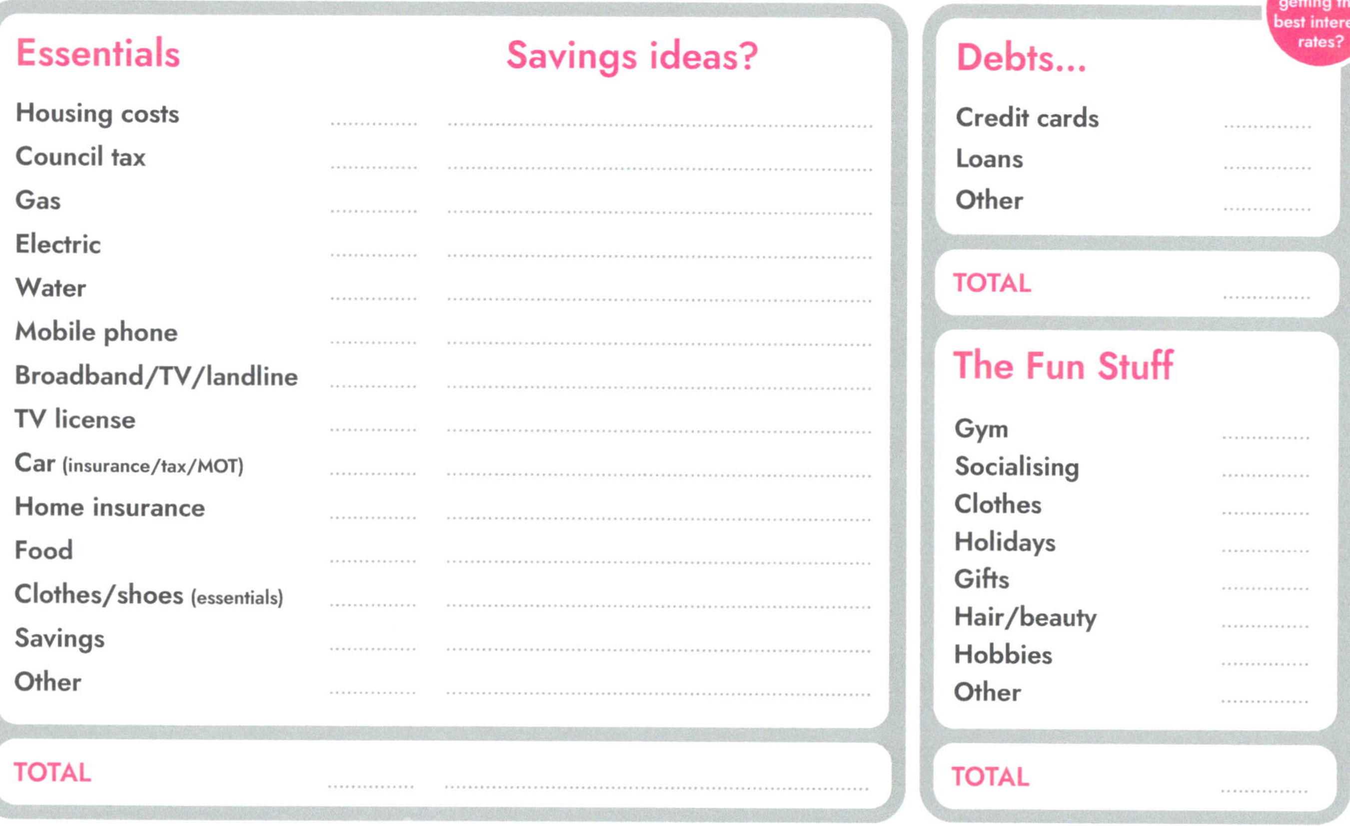

Better With A PLAN | BUDGET PLANNER

What's coming in?

Salary

Extras

Bank Balance

Total

What's going out?

Essentials

Housing costs
Council tax
Gas
Electric
Water
Mobile phone
Broadband/TV/landline
TV license
Car (insurance/tax/MOT)
Home insurance
Food
Clothes/shoes (essentials)
Savings
Other

Savings ideas?

TOTAL

Debts...

Credit cards
Loans
Other

TOTAL

Are you getting the best interest rates?

The Fun Stuff

Gym
Socialising
Clothes
Holidays
Gifts
Hair/beauty
Hobbies
Other

TOTAL

Day to day costs

Lunch/Food
Travelling
Drinks
Extras

Where are we?

Incomings
Outgoings
What's left

Action plan...

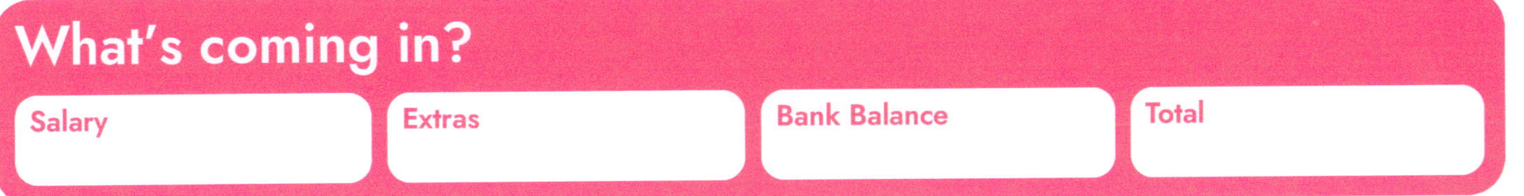

Better With A PLAN | BUDGET PLANNER

What's coming in?

Salary | Extras | Bank Balance | Total

What's going out?

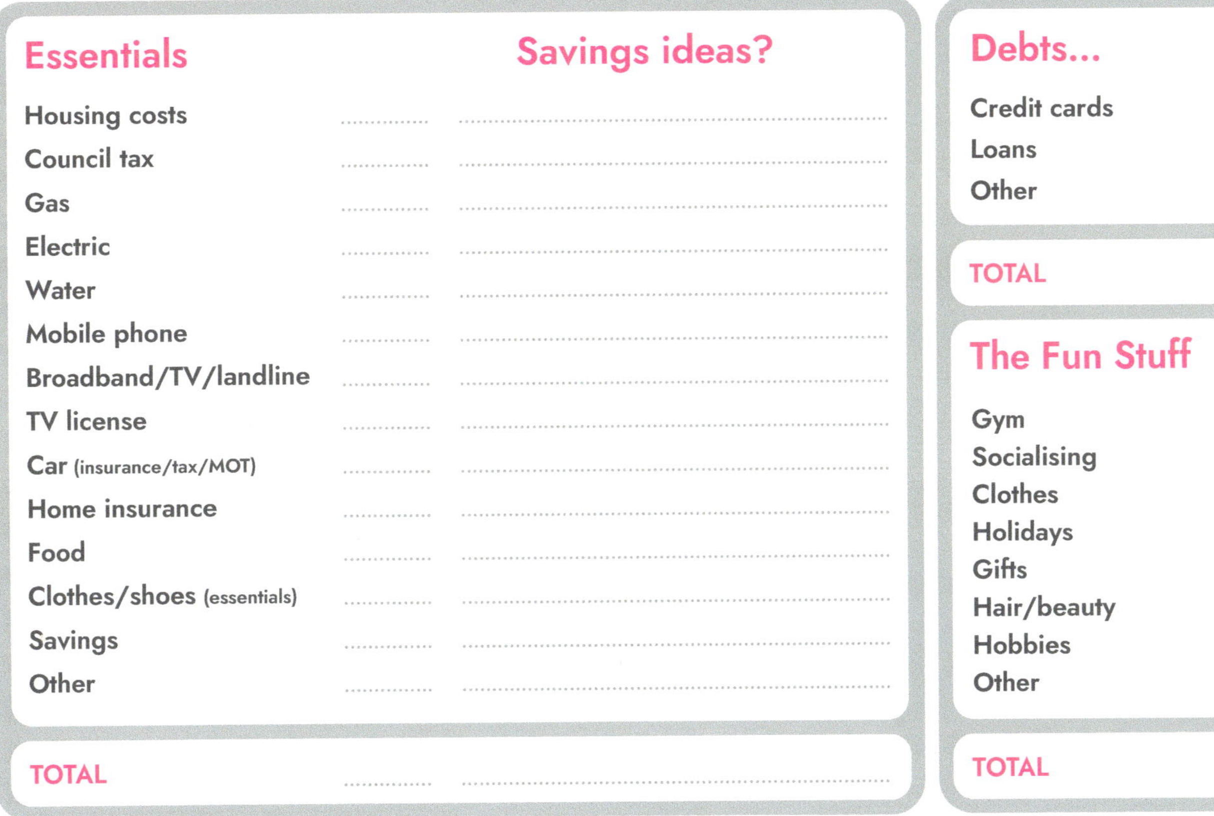

Essentials

Housing costs
Council tax
Gas
Electric
Water
Mobile phone
Broadband/TV/landline
TV license
Car (insurance/tax/MOT)
Home insurance
Food
Clothes/shoes (essentials)
Savings
Other

TOTAL

Savings ideas?

Debts...

Credit cards
Loans
Other

TOTAL

Are you getting the best interest rates?

The Fun Stuff

Gym
Socialising
Clothes
Holidays
Gifts
Hair/beauty
Hobbies
Other

TOTAL

Day to day costs

Lunch/Food
Travelling
Drinks
Extras

Where are we?

Incomings
Outgoings
What's left

Action plan...

Better With A PLAN | BUDGET PLANNER

What's coming in?

Salary

Extras

Bank Balance

Total

What's going out?

Essentials

Housing costs
Council tax
Gas
Electric
Water
Mobile phone
Broadband/TV/landline
TV license
Car (insurance/tax/MOT)
Home insurance
Food
Clothes/shoes (essentials)
Savings
Other

TOTAL

Savings ideas?

Debts...

Credit cards
Loans
Other

TOTAL

Are you getting the best interest rates?

The Fun Stuff

Gym
Socialising
Clothes
Holidays
Gifts
Hair/beauty
Hobbies
Other

TOTAL

Day to day costs

Lunch/Food
Travelling
Drinks
Extras

Where are we?

Incomings
Outgoings
What's left

Action plan...

Better With A PLAN | BUDGET PLANNER

What's coming in?

Salary

Extras

Bank Balance

Total

What's going out?

Essentials

Savings ideas?

Housing costs

Council tax

Gas

Electric

Water

Mobile phone

Broadband/TV/landline

TV license

Car (insurance/tax/MOT)

Home insurance

Food

Clothes/shoes (essentials)

Savings

Other

TOTAL

Debts...

Credit cards

Loans

Other

TOTAL

Are you getting the best interest rates?

The Fun Stuff

Gym

Socialising

Clothes

Holidays

Gifts

Hair/beauty

Hobbies

Other

TOTAL

Day to day costs

Lunch/Food

Travelling

Drinks

Extras

Where are we?

Incomings

Outgoings

What's left

Action plan...

Better With A PLAN | BUDGET PLANNER

What's coming in?

Salary | Extras | Bank Balance | Total

What's going out?

Essentials

Housing costs
Council tax
Gas
Electric
Water
Mobile phone
Broadband/TV/landline
TV license
Car (insurance/tax/MOT)
Home insurance
Food
Clothes/shoes (essentials)
Savings
Other

TOTAL

Savings ideas?

Debts...

Credit cards
Loans
Other

TOTAL

Are you getting the best interest rates?

The Fun Stuff

Gym
Socialising
Clothes
Holidays
Gifts
Hair/beauty
Hobbies
Other

TOTAL

Day to day costs

Lunch/Food
Travelling
Drinks
Extras

Where are we?

Incomings
Outgoings
What's left

Action plan...

Better With A PLAN | BUDGET PLANNER

What's coming in?

Salary

Extras

Bank Balance

Total

What's going out?

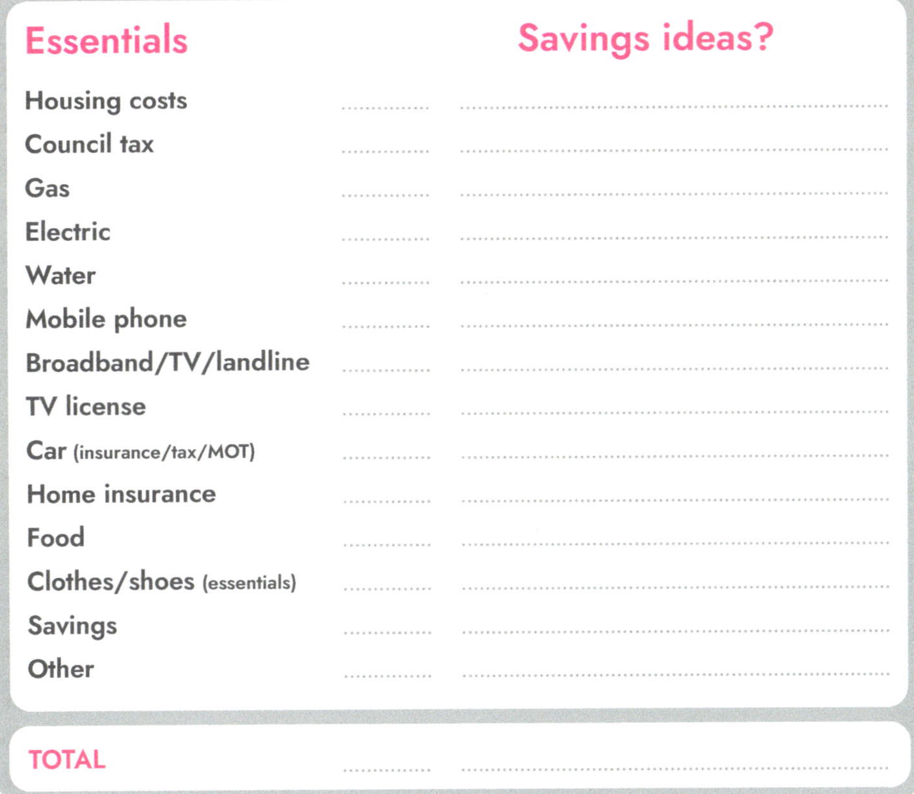

Essentials

Housing costs
Council tax
Gas
Electric
Water
Mobile phone
Broadband/TV/landline
TV license
Car (insurance/tax/MOT)
Home insurance
Food
Clothes/shoes (essentials)
Savings
Other

TOTAL

Savings ideas?

Debts...

Credit cards
Loans
Other

TOTAL

Are you getting the best interest rates?

The Fun Stuff

Gym
Socialising
Clothes
Holidays
Gifts
Hair/beauty
Hobbies
Other

TOTAL

Day to day costs

Lunch/Food
Travelling
Drinks
Extras

Where are we?

Incomings
Outgoings
What's left

Action plan...

Better With A PLAN | BUDGET PLANNER

What's coming in?

| Salary | Extras | Bank Balance | Total |

What's going out?

Essentials

Savings ideas?

Housing costs
Council tax
Gas
Electric
Water
Mobile phone
Broadband/TV/landline
TV license
Car (insurance/tax/MOT)
Home insurance
Food
Clothes/shoes (essentials)
Savings
Other

TOTAL

Debts...

Credit cards
Loans
Other

TOTAL

The Fun Stuff

Gym
Socialising
Clothes
Holidays
Gifts
Hair/beauty
Hobbies
Other

TOTAL

Are you getting the best interest rates?

Day to day costs

Lunch/Food
Travelling
Drinks
Extras

Where are we?

Incomings
Outgoings
What's left

Action plan...

Better With A PLAN | BUDGET PLANNER

What's coming in?

Salary	Extras	Bank Balance	Total

What's going out?

Essentials | Savings ideas?

Housing costs

Council tax

Gas

Electric

Water

Mobile phone

Broadband/TV/landline

TV license

Car (insurance/tax/MOT)

Home insurance

Food

Clothes/shoes (essentials)

Savings

Other

TOTAL

Day to day costs

Lunch/Food

Travelling

Drinks

Extras

Debts...

Are you getting the best interest rates?

Credit cards

Loans

Other

TOTAL

The Fun Stuff

Gym

Socialising

Clothes

Holidays

Gifts

Hair/beauty

Hobbies

Other

TOTAL

Where are we?

Incomings

Outgoings

What's left

Action plan...

Better With A PLAN | BUDGET PLANNER

What's coming in?

Salary	Extras	Bank Balance	Total

What's going out?

Day to day costs

Lunch/Food ....
Travelling ....
Drinks ....
Extras ....

Essentials / Savings ideas?

Housing costs ....
Council tax ....
Gas ....
Electric ....
Water ....
Mobile phone ....
Broadband/TV/landline ....
TV license ....
Car (insurance/tax/MOT) ....
Home insurance ....
Food ....
Clothes/shoes (essentials) ....
Savings ....
Other ....

TOTAL ....

Debts...

Are you getting the best interest rates?

Credit cards ....
Loans ....
Other ....

TOTAL ....

The Fun Stuff

Gym ....
Socialising ....
Clothes ....
Holidays ....
Gifts ....
Hair/beauty ....
Hobbies ....
Other ....

TOTAL ....

Where are we?

Incomings ....
Outgoings ....
What's left ....

Action plan...

....
....
....
....
....
....
....
....
....
....

Better With A PLAN | BUDGET PLANNER

What's coming in?

Salary	Extras	Bank Balance	Total

What's going out?

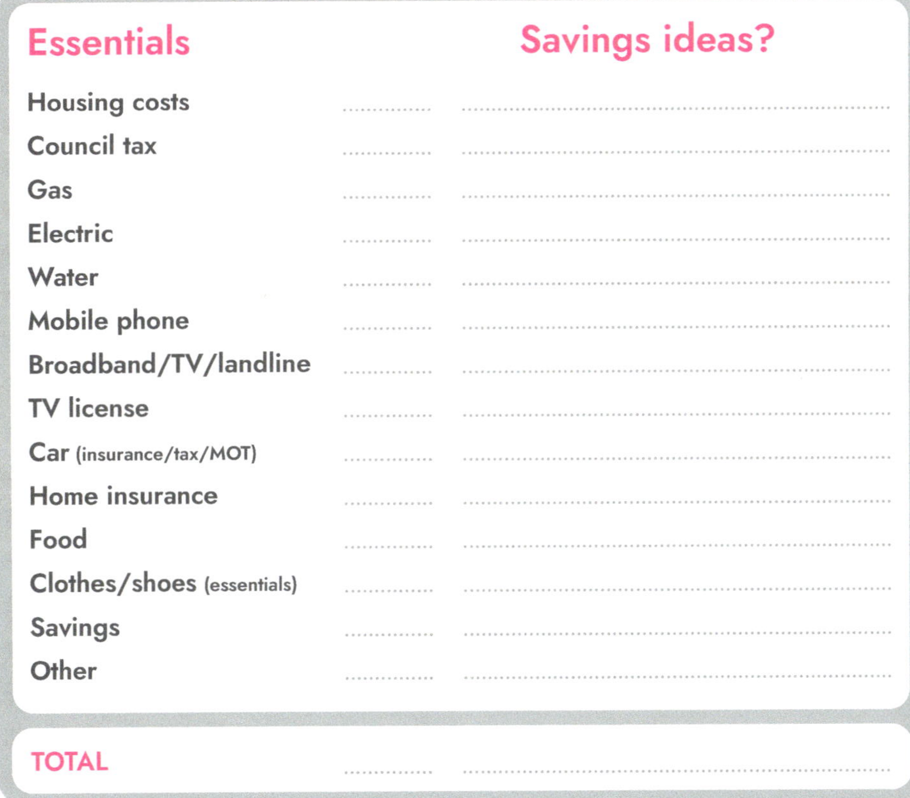

Essentials

- Housing costs
- Council tax
- Gas
- Electric
- Water
- Mobile phone
- Broadband/TV/landline
- TV license
- Car (insurance/tax/MOT)
- Home insurance
- Food
- Clothes/shoes (essentials)
- Savings
- Other

TOTAL

Savings ideas?

Debts...

- Credit cards
- Loans
- Other

TOTAL

Are you getting the best interest rates?

The Fun Stuff

- Gym
- Socialising
- Clothes
- Holidays
- Gifts
- Hair/beauty
- Hobbies
- Other

TOTAL

Day to day costs

- Lunch/Food
- Travelling
- Drinks
- Extras

Where are we?

- Incomings
- Outgoings
- What's left

Action plan...

Better With A PLAN | BUDGET PLANNER

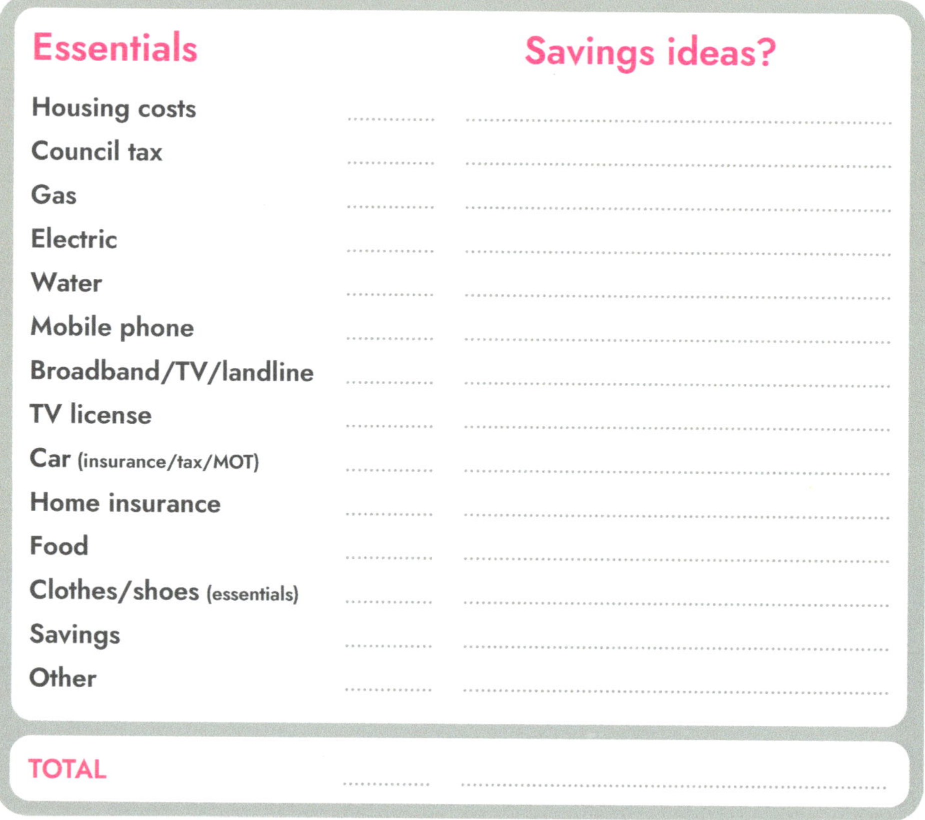

What's coming in?

Salary	Extras	Bank Balance	Total

What's going out?

Essentials

Housing costs
Council tax
Gas
Electric
Water
Mobile phone
Broadband/TV/landline
TV license
Car (insurance/tax/MOT)
Home insurance
Food
Clothes/shoes (essentials)
Savings
Other

Savings ideas?

TOTAL

Debts...

Credit cards
Loans
Other

TOTAL

The Fun Stuff

Gym
Socialising
Clothes
Holidays
Gifts
Hair/beauty
Hobbies
Other

TOTAL

Are you getting the best interest rates?

Day to day costs

Lunch/Food
Travelling
Drinks
Extras

Where are we?

Incomings
Outgoings
What's left

Action plan...

Better With A PLAN | BUDGET PLANNER

What's coming in?

Salary

Extras

Bank Balance

Total

What's going out?

Essentials

Housing costs
Council tax
Gas
Electric
Water
Mobile phone
Broadband/TV/landline
TV license
Car (insurance/tax/MOT)
Home insurance
Food
Clothes/shoes (essentials)
Savings
Other

Savings ideas?

TOTAL

Debts...

Credit cards
Loans
Other

TOTAL

The Fun Stuff

Gym
Socialising
Clothes
Holidays
Gifts
Hair/beauty
Hobbies
Other

TOTAL

Day to day costs

Lunch/Food
Travelling
Drinks
Extras

Where are we?

Incomings
Outgoings
What's left

Action plan...

Better With A PLAN | BUDGET PLANNER

What's coming in?

Salary

Extras

Bank Balance

Total

What's going out?

Essentials

Housing costs

Council tax

Gas

Electric

Water

Mobile phone

Broadband/TV/landline

TV license

Car (insurance/tax/MOT)

Home insurance

Food

Clothes/shoes (essentials)

Savings

Other

TOTAL

Savings ideas?

Debts...

Credit cards

Loans

Other

TOTAL

Are you getting the best interest rates?

The Fun Stuff

Gym

Socialising

Clothes

Holidays

Gifts

Hair/beauty

Hobbies

Other

TOTAL

Day to day costs

Lunch/Food

Travelling

Drinks

Extras

Where are we?

Incomings

Outgoings

What's left

Action plan...

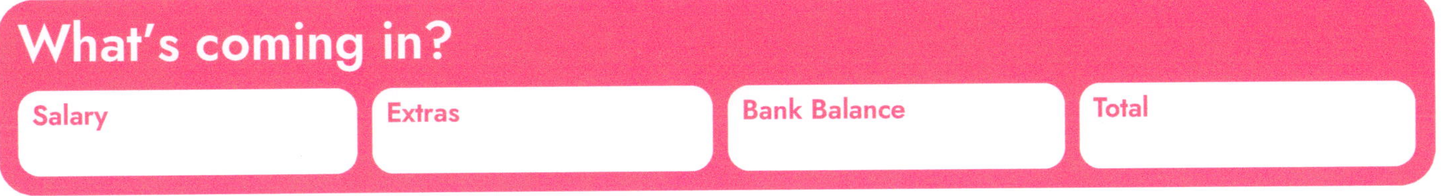

What's coming in?

Salary

Extras

Bank Balance

Total

What's going out?

Day to day costs

Lunch/Food ....
Travelling ....
Drinks ....
Extras ....

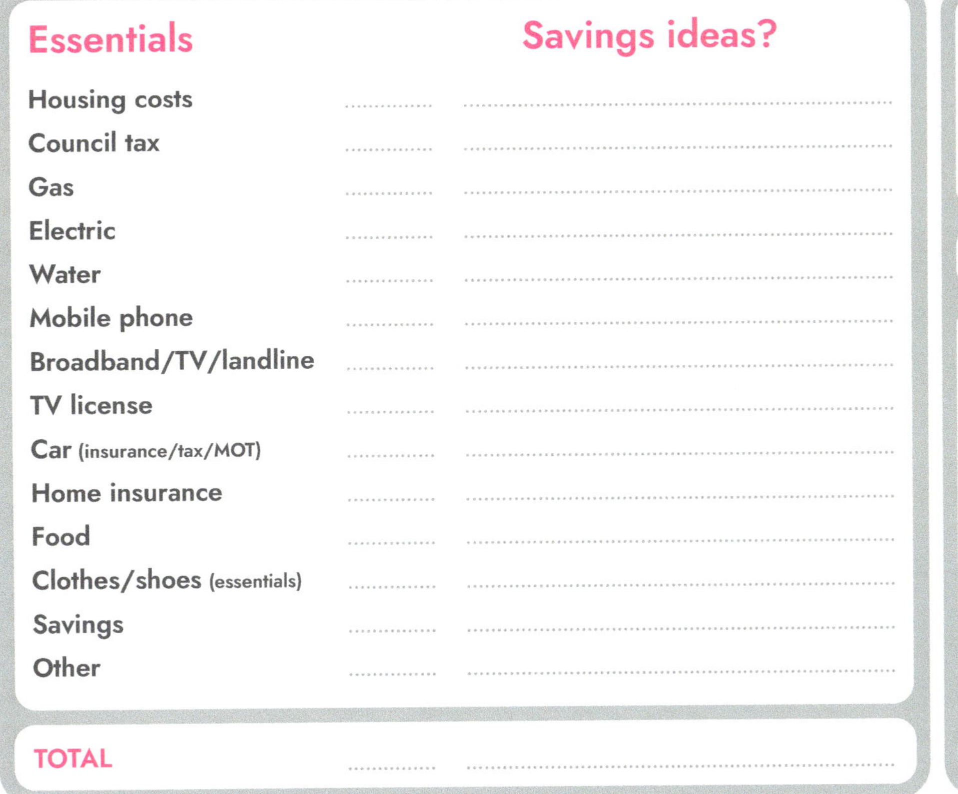

Essentials

Savings ideas?

Housing costs ....
Council tax ....
Gas
Electric ....
Water ....
Mobile phone ....
Broadband/TV/landline
TV license ....
Car (insurance/tax/MOT) ....
Home insurance
Food ....
Clothes/shoes (essentials) ....
Savings ....
Other ....

TOTAL ....

Debts...

Credit cards ....
Loans ....
Other ....

TOTAL ....

The Fun Stuff

Gym ....
Socialising ....
Clothes ....
Holidays ....
Gifts ....
Hair/beauty ....
Hobbies ....
Other ....

TOTAL ....

Where are we?

Incomings ....
Outgoings ....
What's left ....

Action plan...

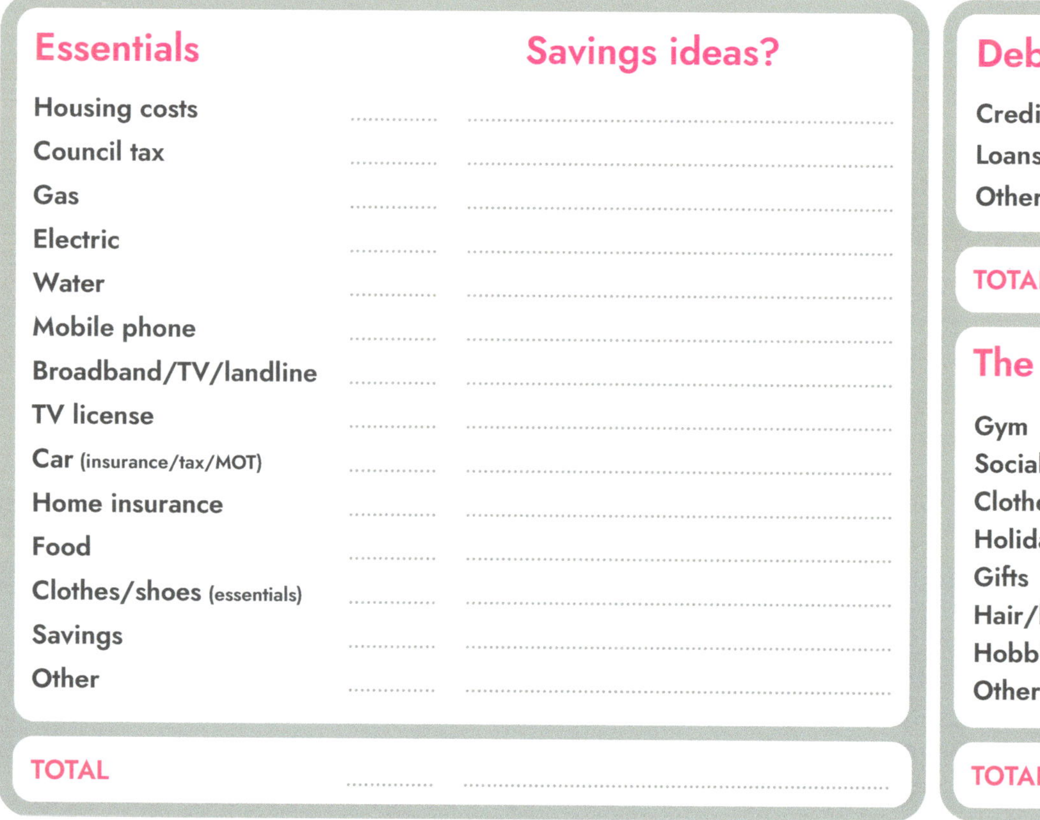

Better With A PLAN | BUDGET PLANNER

What's coming in?

Salary

Extras

Bank Balance

Total

What's going out?

Essentials

Housing costs
Council tax
Gas
Electric
Water
Mobile phone
Broadband/TV/landline
TV license
Car (insurance/tax/MOT)
Home insurance
Food
Clothes/shoes (essentials)
Savings
Other

TOTAL

Savings ideas?

Debts...

Credit cards
Loans
Other

TOTAL

The Fun Stuff

Gym
Socialising
Clothes
Holidays
Gifts
Hair/beauty
Hobbies
Other

TOTAL

Are you getting the best interest rates?

Day to day costs

Lunch/Food
Travelling
Drinks
Extras

Where are we?

Incomings
Outgoings
What's left

Action plan...

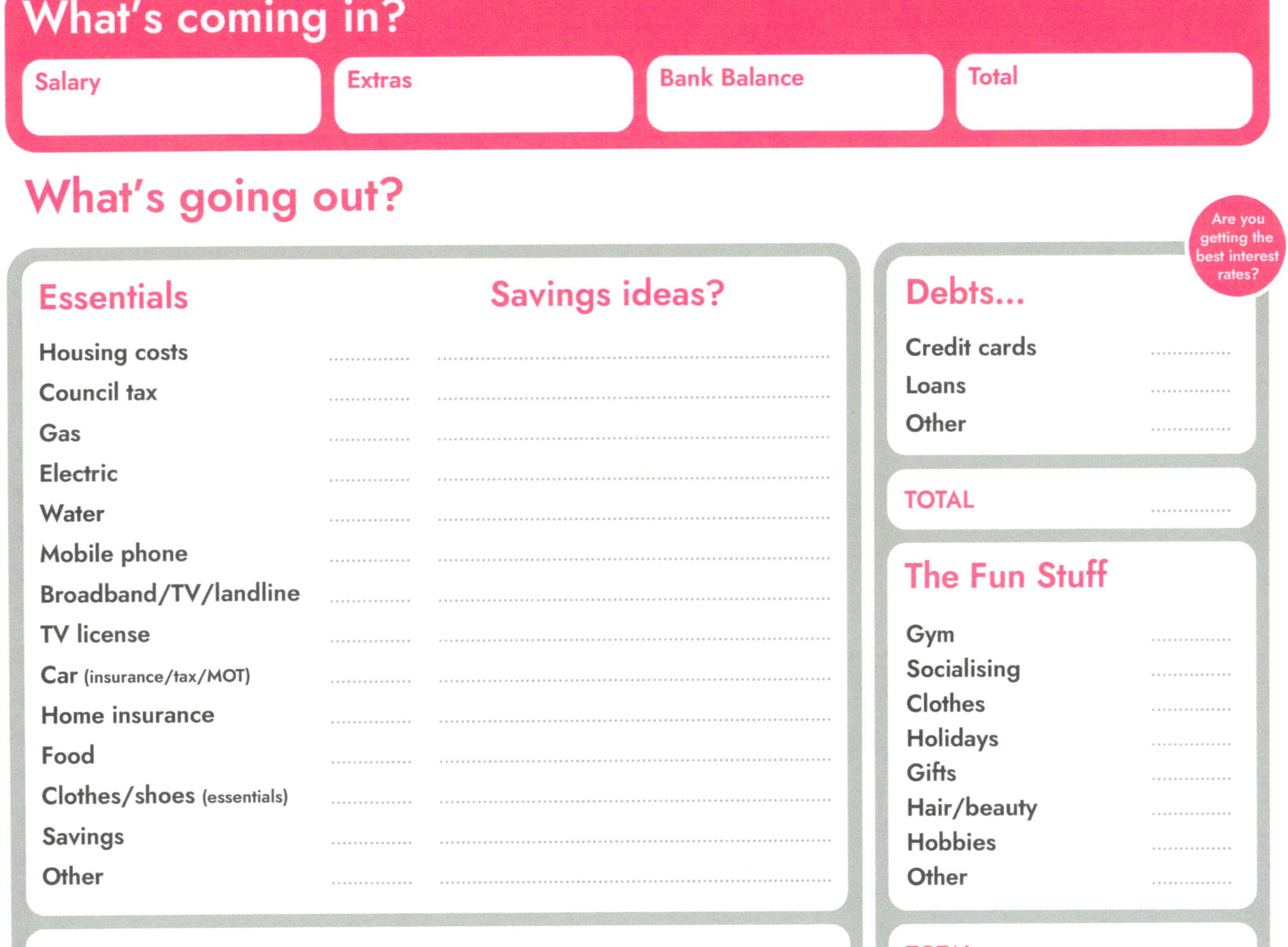

Better With A **PLAN** | **BUDGET PLANNER**

What's coming in?

| Salary | Extras | Bank Balance | Total |

What's going out?

Essentials

Housing costs
Council tax
Gas
Electric
Water
Mobile phone
Broadband/TV/landline
TV license
Car (insurance/tax/MOT)
Home insurance
Food
Clothes/shoes (essentials)
Savings
Other

TOTAL

Savings ideas?

Debts...

Credit cards
Loans
Other

TOTAL

The Fun Stuff

Gym
Socialising
Clothes
Holidays
Gifts
Hair/beauty
Hobbies
Other

TOTAL

Are you getting the best interest rates?

Day to day costs

Lunch/Food
Travelling
Drinks
Extras

Where are we?

Incomings
Outgoings
What's left

Action plan...

Better With A PLAN | BUDGET PLANNER

What's coming in?

Salary

Extras

Bank Balance

Total

What's going out?

Essentials

Housing costs
Council tax
Gas
Electric
Water
Mobile phone
Broadband/TV/landline
TV license
Car (insurance/tax/MOT)
Home insurance
Food
Clothes/shoes (essentials)
Savings
Other

TOTAL

Savings ideas?

Debts...

Credit cards
Loans
Other

TOTAL

The Fun Stuff

Gym
Socialising
Clothes
Holidays
Gifts
Hair/beauty
Hobbies
Other

TOTAL

Are you getting the best interest rates?

Day to day costs

Lunch/Food
Travelling
Drinks
Extras

Where are we?

Incomings
Outgoings
What's left

Action plan...

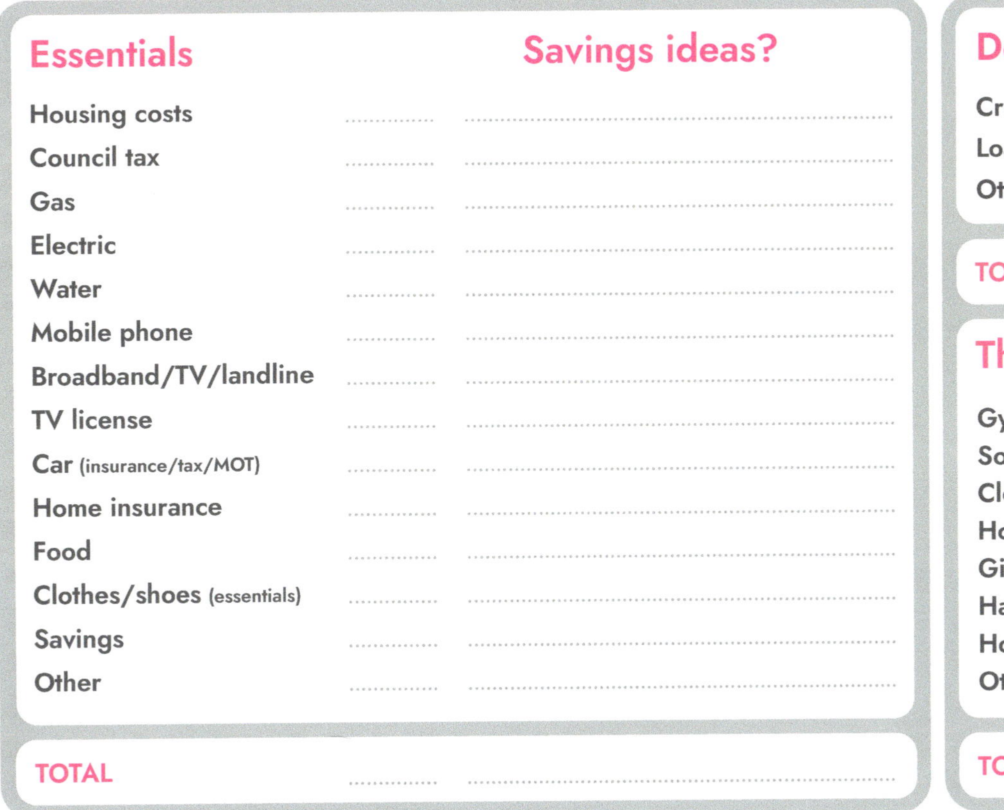

Better With A PLAN | BUDGET PLANNER

Better With A PLAN | BUDGET PLANNER

What's coming in?

Salary	Extras	Bank Balance	Total

What's going out?

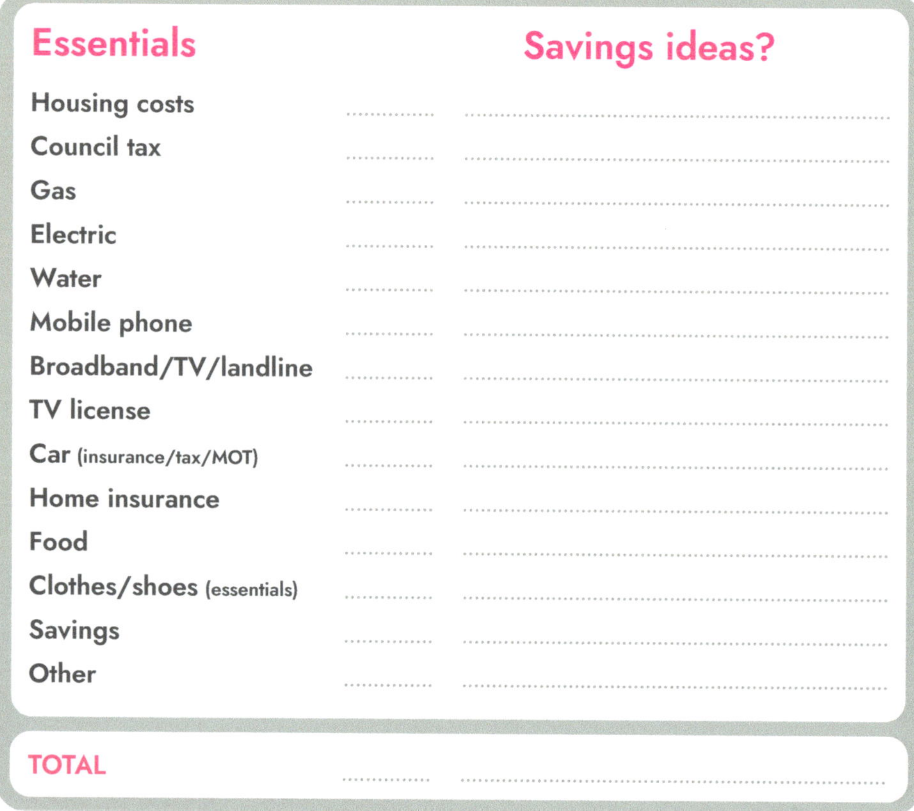

Essentials

Housing costs
Council tax
Gas
Electric
Water
Mobile phone
Broadband/TV/landline
TV license
Car (insurance/tax/MOT)
Home insurance
Food
Clothes/shoes (essentials)
Savings
Other

TOTAL

Savings ideas?

Debts...

Credit cards
Loans
Other

TOTAL

Are you getting the best interest rates?

The Fun Stuff

Gym
Socialising
Clothes
Holidays
Gifts
Hair/beauty
Hobbies
Other

TOTAL

Day to day costs

Lunch/Food
Travelling
Drinks
Extras

Where are we?

Incomings
Outgoings
What's left

Action plan...

Better With A PLAN | BUDGET PLANNER

What's coming in?

Salary | **Extras** | **Bank Balance** | **Total**

What's going out?

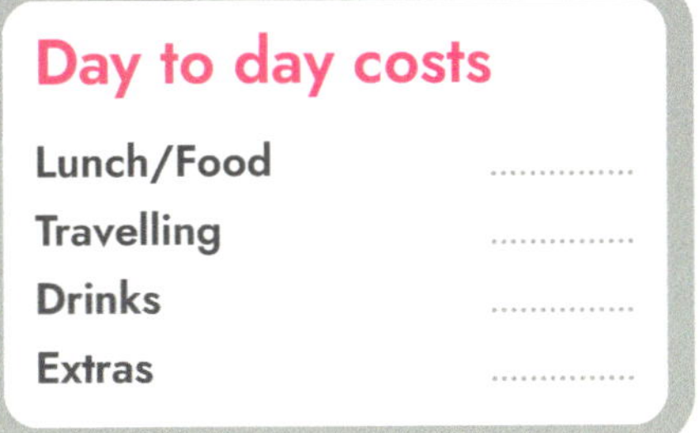

Essentials

Housing costs
Council tax
Gas
Electric
Water
Mobile phone
Broadband/TV/landline
TV license
Car (insurance/tax/MOT)
Home insurance
Food
Clothes/shoes (essentials)
Savings
Other

TOTAL

Savings ideas?

Debts...

Credit cards
Loans
Other

TOTAL

The Fun Stuff

Gym
Socialising
Clothes
Holidays
Gifts
Hair/beauty
Hobbies
Other

TOTAL

Day to day costs

Lunch/Food
Travelling
Drinks
Extras

Where are we?

Incomings
Outgoings
What's left

Action plan...

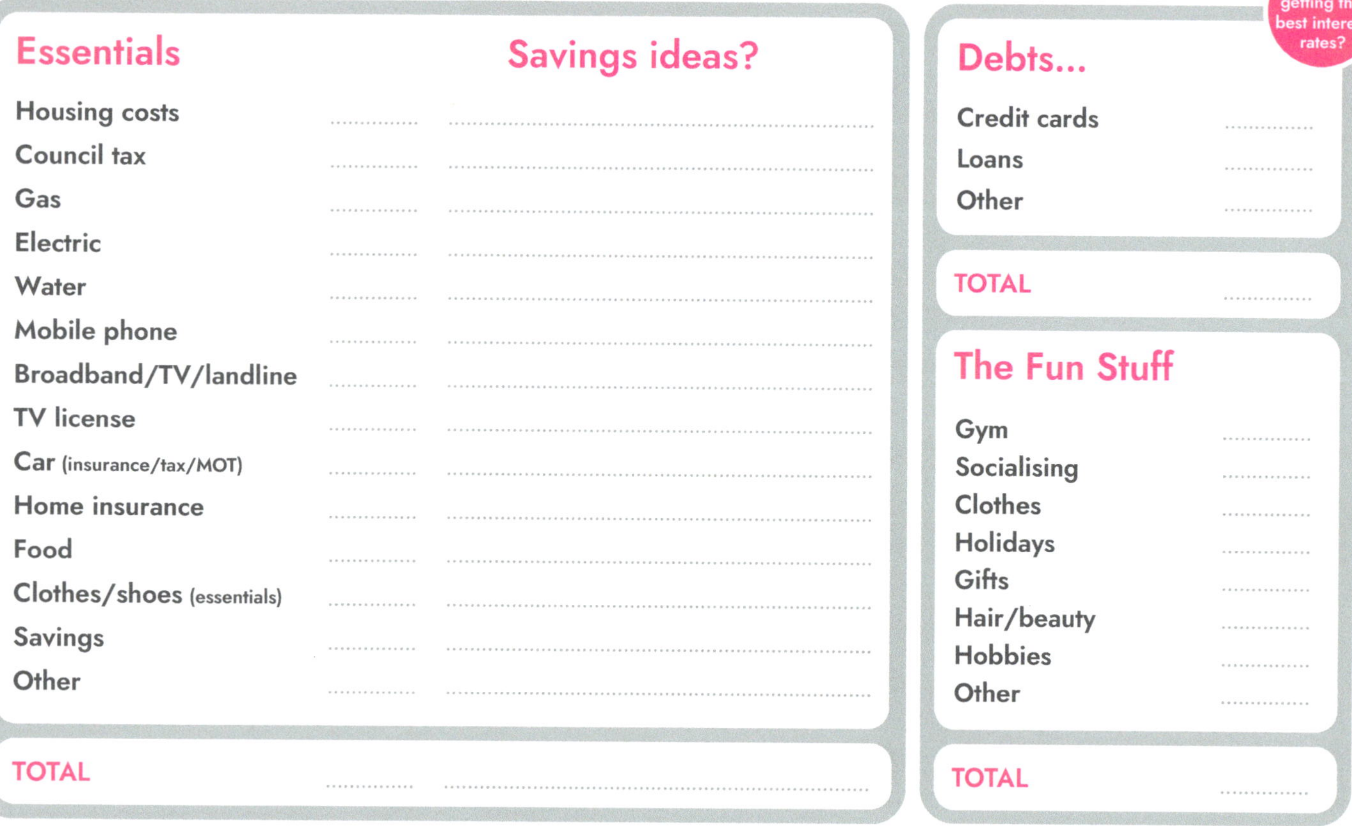

Better With A PLAN | BUDGET PLANNER

What's coming in?

Salary

Extras

Bank Balance

Total

Day to day costs

Lunch/Food

Travelling

Drinks

Extras

What's going out?

Essentials

Housing costs

Council tax

Gas

Electric

Water

Mobile phone

Broadband/TV/landline

TV license

Car (insurance/tax/MOT)

Home insurance

Food

Clothes/shoes (essentials)

Savings

Other

TOTAL

Savings ideas?

Debts...

Credit cards

Loans

Other

TOTAL

The Fun Stuff

Gym

Socialising

Clothes

Holidays

Gifts

Hair/beauty

Hobbies

Other

TOTAL

Where are we?

Incomings

Outgoings

What's left

Action plan...

Better With A PLAN | BUDGET PLANNER

What's coming in?

Salary	Extras	Bank Balance	Total

What's going out?

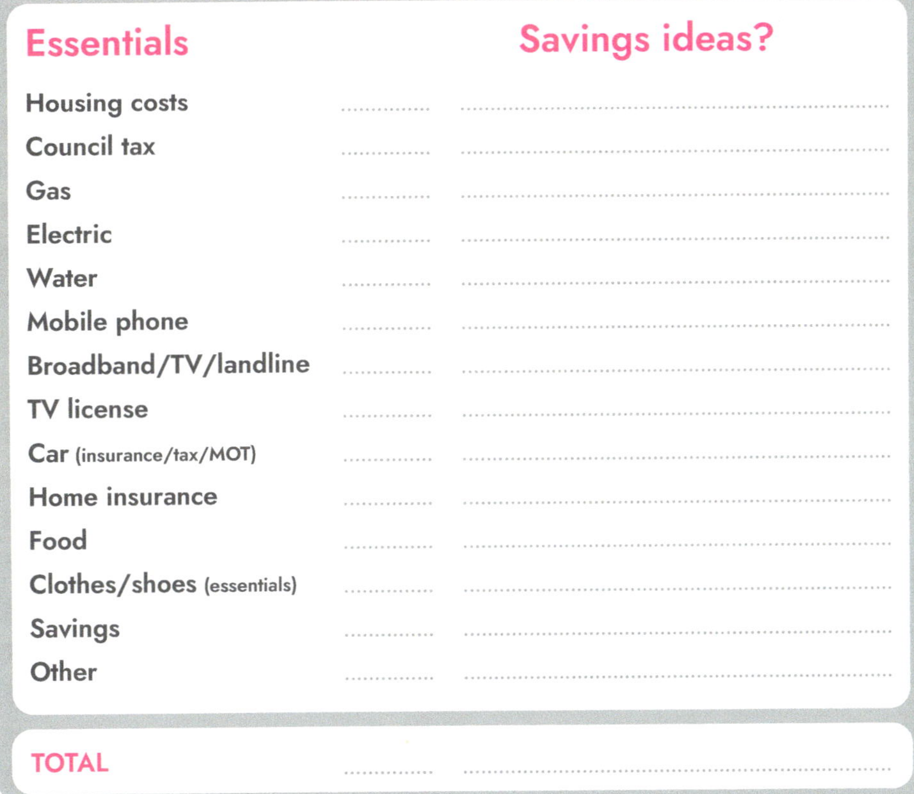

Essentials

Savings ideas?

Housing costs

Council tax

Gas

Electric

Water

Mobile phone

Broadband/TV/landline

TV license

Car (insurance/tax/MOT)

Home insurance

Food

Clothes/shoes (essentials)

Savings

Other

TOTAL

Debts...

Credit cards

Loans

Other

TOTAL

The Fun Stuff

Gym

Socialising

Clothes

Holidays

Gifts

Hair/beauty

Hobbies

Other

TOTAL

Are you getting the best interest rates?

Day to day costs

Lunch/Food

Travelling

Drinks

Extras

Where are we?

Incomings

Outgoings

What's left

Action plan...

30

Better With A PLAN | BUDGET PLANNER

What's coming in?

Salary

Extras

Bank Balance

Total

What's going out?

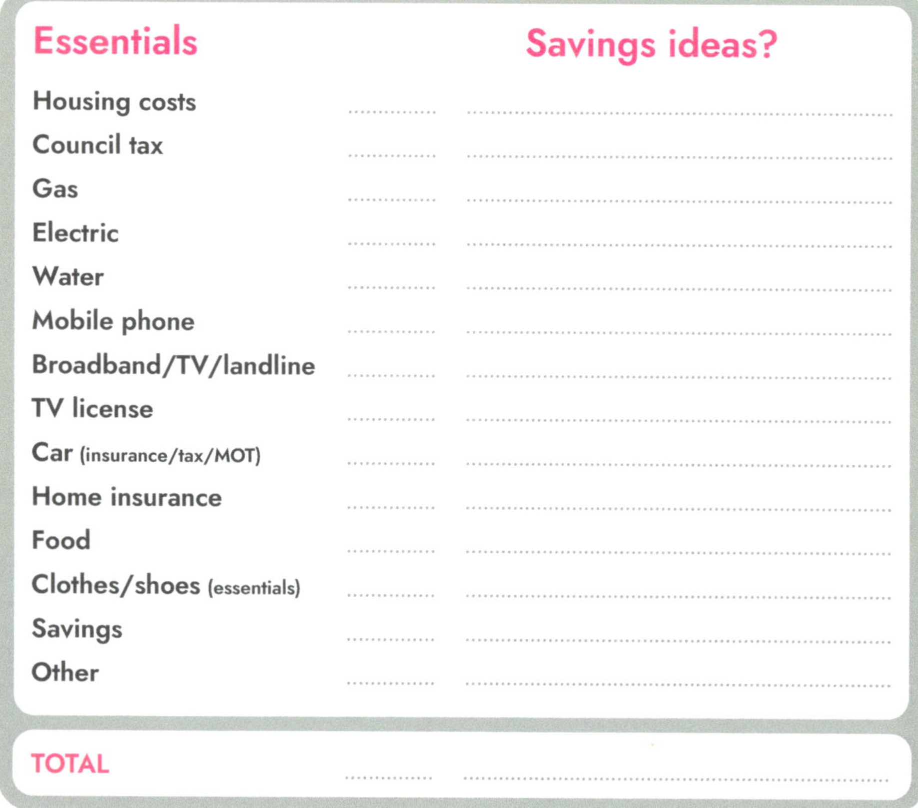

Essentials

Housing costs
Council tax
Gas
Electric
Water
Mobile phone
Broadband/TV/landline
TV license
Car (insurance/tax/MOT)
Home insurance
Food
Clothes/shoes (essentials)
Savings
Other

TOTAL

Savings ideas?

Debts...

Credit cards
Loans
Other

TOTAL

The Fun Stuff

Gym
Socialising
Clothes
Holidays
Gifts
Hair/beauty
Hobbies
Other

TOTAL

Are you getting the best interest rates?

Day to day costs

Lunch/Food
Travelling
Drinks
Extras

Where are we?

Incomings
Outgoings
What's left

Action plan...

Better With A PLAN | BUDGET PLANNER

What's coming in?

Salary

Extras

Bank Balance

Total

Day to day costs

Lunch/Food ....
Travelling ....
Drinks ....
Extras ....

What's going out?

Are you getting the best interest rates?

Essentials

Housing costs ....
Council tax ....
Gas ....
Electric ....
Water ....
Mobile phone ....
Broadband/TV/landline ....
TV license ....
Car (insurance/tax/MOT) ....
Home insurance ....
Food ....
Clothes/shoes (essentials) ....
Savings ....
Other ....

Savings ideas?

TOTAL ....

Debts...

Credit cards ....
Loans ....
Other ....

TOTAL ....

The Fun Stuff

Gym ....
Socialising ....
Clothes ....
Holidays ....
Gifts ....
Hair/beauty ....
Hobbies ....
Other ....

TOTAL ....

Where are we?

Incomings ....
Outgoings ....
What's left ....

Action plan...

Better With A PLAN | BUDGET PLANNER

What's coming in?

Salary

Extras

Bank Balance

Total

What's going out?

Essentials

Housing costs
Council tax
Gas
Electric
Water
Mobile phone
Broadband/TV/landline
TV license
Car (insurance/tax/MOT)
Home insurance
Food
Clothes/shoes (essentials)
Savings
Other

TOTAL

Savings ideas?

Debts...

Credit cards
Loans
Other

TOTAL

Are you getting the best interest rates?

The Fun Stuff

Gym
Socialising
Clothes
Holidays
Gifts
Hair/beauty
Hobbies
Other

TOTAL

Day to day costs

Lunch/Food
Travelling
Drinks
Extras

Where are we?

Incomings
Outgoings
What's left

Action plan...

Better With A PLAN | BUDGET PLANNER

What's coming in?

Salary Extras Bank Balance Total

What's going out?

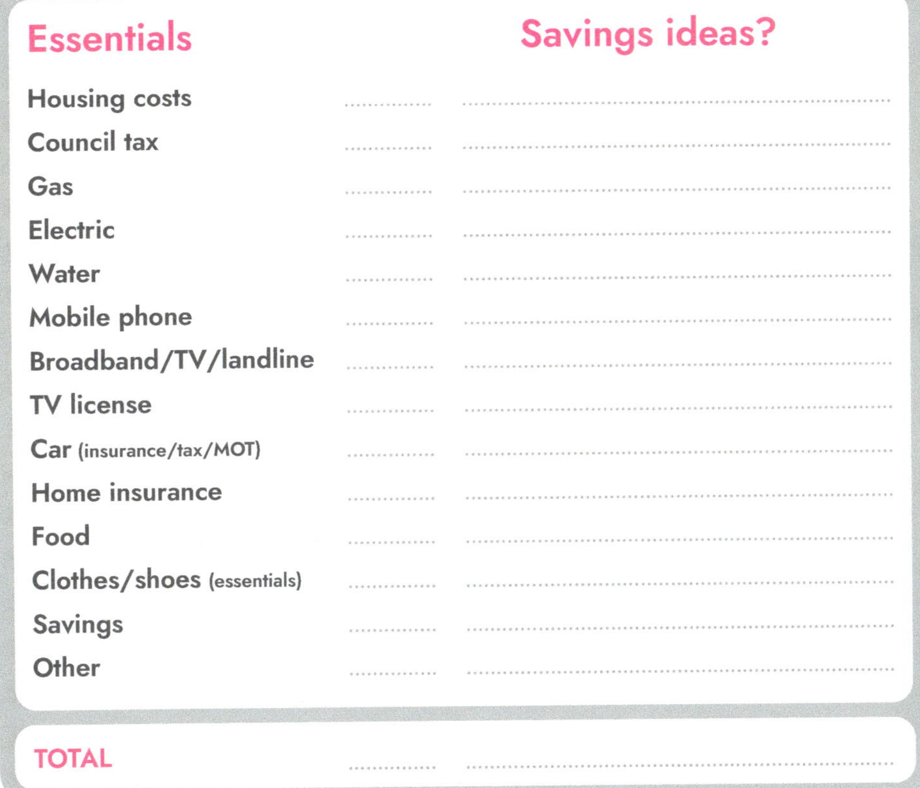

Essentials

Housing costs
Council tax
Gas
Electric
Water
Mobile phone
Broadband/TV/landline
TV license
Car (insurance/tax/MOT)
Home insurance
Food
Clothes/shoes (essentials)
Savings
Other

Savings ideas?

TOTAL

Debts...

Credit cards
Loans
Other

TOTAL

Are you getting the best interest rates?

The Fun Stuff

Gym
Socialising
Clothes
Holidays
Gifts
Hair/beauty
Hobbies
Other

TOTAL

Day to day costs

Lunch/Food
Travelling
Drinks
Extras

Where are we?

Incomings
Outgoings
What's left

Action plan...

Better With A PLAN | BUDGET PLANNER

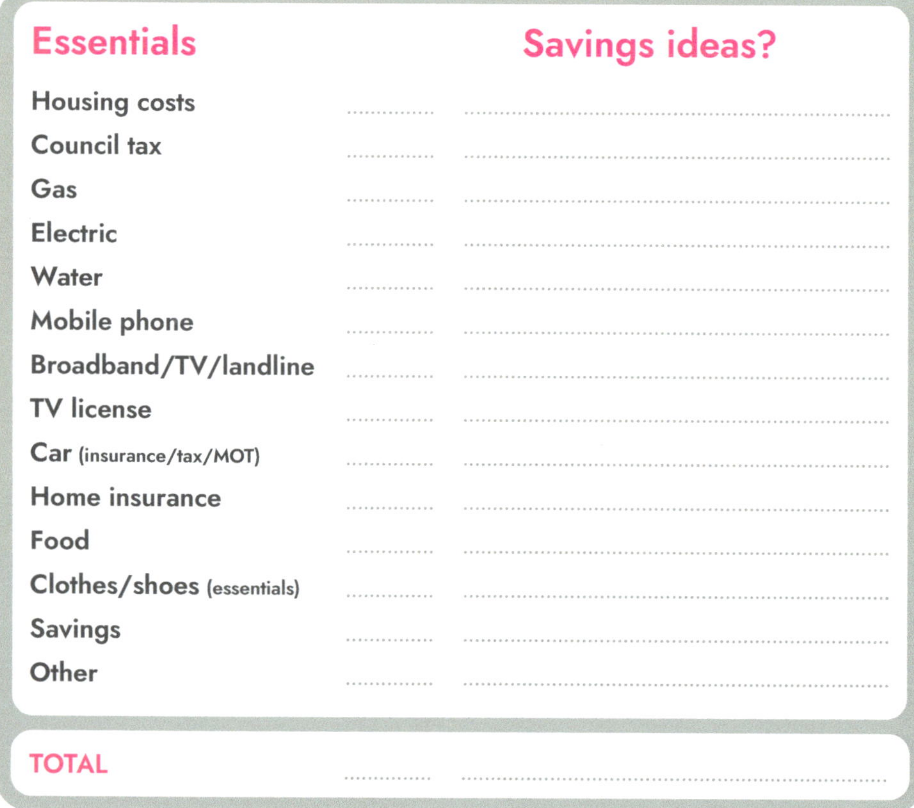

What's coming in?

Salary	Extras	Bank Balance	Total

What's going out?

Essentials

Housing costs
Council tax
Gas
Electric
Water
Mobile phone
Broadband/TV/landline
TV license
Car (insurance/tax/MOT)
Home insurance
Food
Clothes/shoes (essentials)
Savings
Other

Savings ideas?

TOTAL

Debts...

Credit cards
Loans
Other

TOTAL

The Fun Stuff

Gym
Socialising
Clothes
Holidays
Gifts
Hair/beauty
Hobbies
Other

TOTAL

Are you getting the best interest rates?

Day to day costs

Lunch/Food
Travelling
Drinks
Extras

Where are we?

Incomings
Outgoings
What's left

Action plan...

Better With A PLAN | BUDGET PLANNER

What's coming in?

Salary	Extras	Bank Balance	Total

What's going out?

Essentials | Savings ideas?

Housing costs
Council tax
Gas
Electric
Water
Mobile phone
Broadband/TV/landline
TV license
Car (insurance/tax/MOT)
Home insurance
Food
Clothes/shoes (essentials)
Savings
Other

TOTAL

Debts...

Credit cards
Loans
Other

TOTAL

Are you getting the best interest rates?

The Fun Stuff

Gym
Socialising
Clothes
Holidays
Gifts
Hair/beauty
Hobbies
Other

TOTAL

Day to day costs

Lunch/Food
Travelling
Drinks
Extras

Where are we?

Incomings
Outgoings
What's left

Action plan...

Better With A PLAN | BUDGET PLANNER

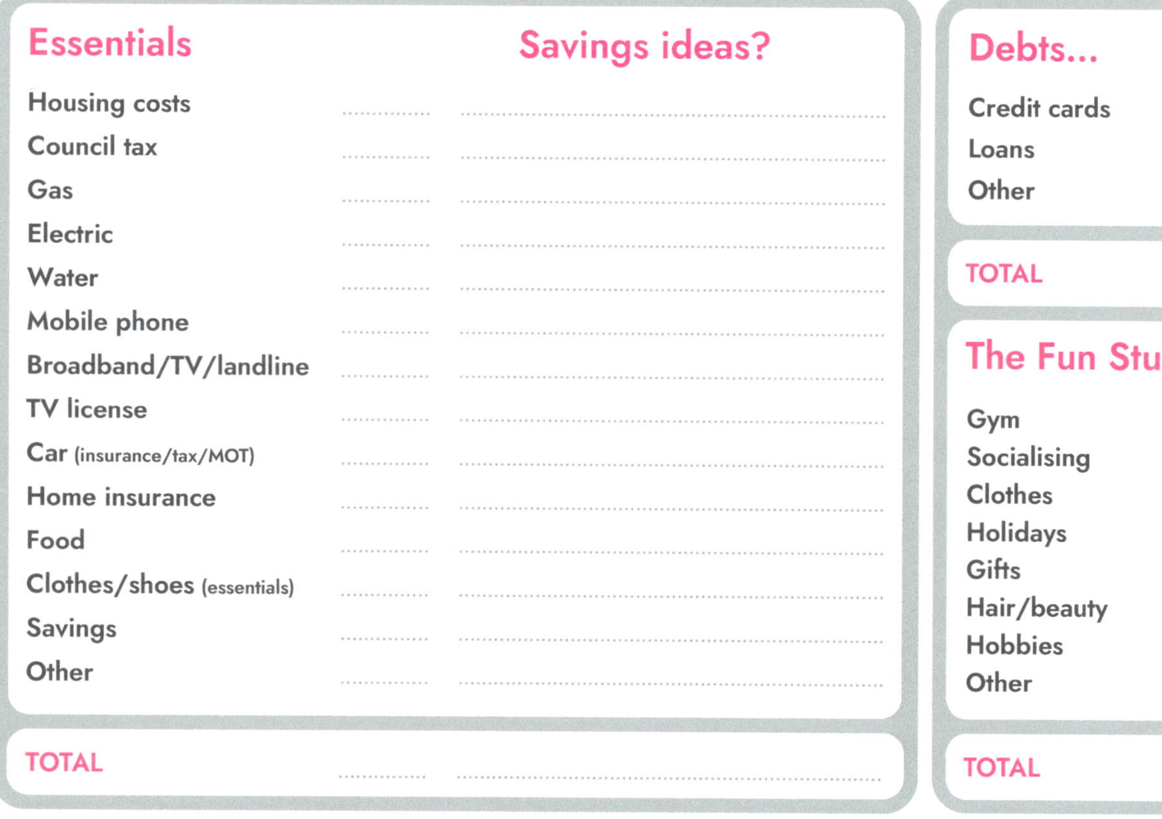

What's coming in?

Salary

Extras

Bank Balance

Total

What's going out?

Essentials

Housing costs

Council tax

Gas

Electric

Water

Mobile phone

Broadband/TV/landline

TV license

Car (insurance/tax/MOT)

Home insurance

Food

Clothes/shoes (essentials)

Savings

Other

TOTAL

Savings ideas?

Debts...

Credit cards

Loans

Other

TOTAL

Are you getting the best interest rates?

The Fun Stuff

Gym

Socialising

Clothes

Holidays

Gifts

Hair/beauty

Hobbies

Other

TOTAL

Day to day costs

Lunch/Food

Travelling

Drinks

Extras

Where are we?

Incomings

Outgoings

What's left

Action plan...

Better With A PLAN | BUDGET PLANNER

What's coming in?

Salary

Extras

Bank Balance

Total

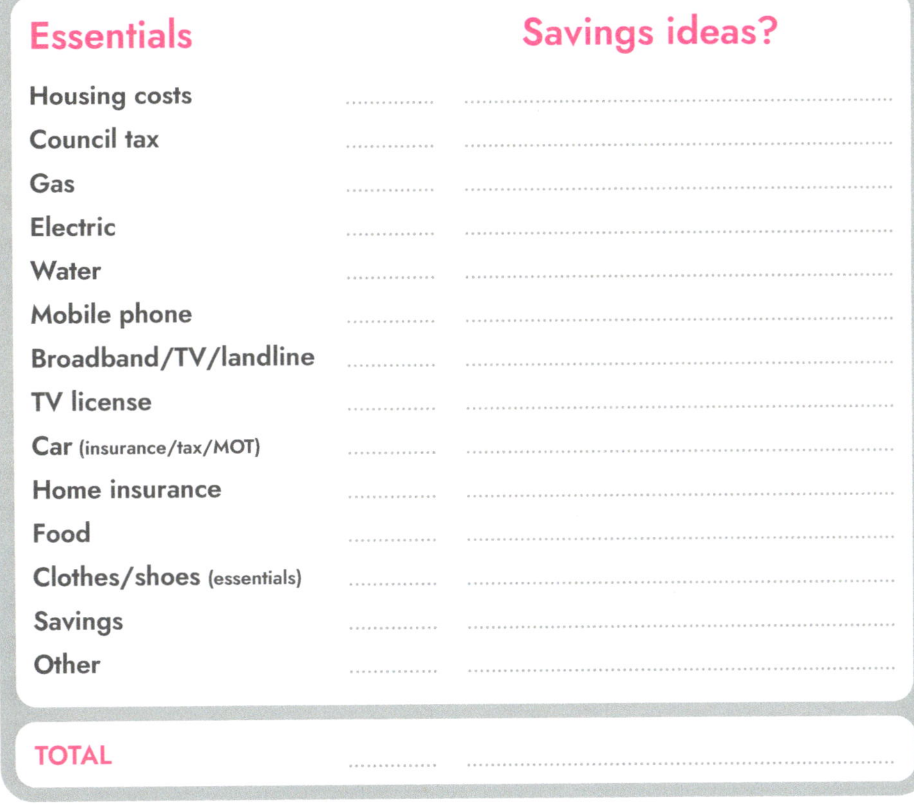

What's going out?

Are you getting the best interest rates?

Essentials

Housing costs
Council tax
Gas
Electric
Water
Mobile phone
Broadband/TV/landline
TV license
Car (insurance/tax/MOT)
Home insurance
Food
Clothes/shoes (essentials)
Savings
Other

TOTAL

Savings ideas?

Debts...

Credit cards
Loans
Other

TOTAL

The Fun Stuff

Gym
Socialising
Clothes
Holidays
Gifts
Hair/beauty
Hobbies
Other

TOTAL

Day to day costs

Lunch/Food
Travelling
Drinks
Extras

Where are we?

Incomings
Outgoings
What's left

Action plan...

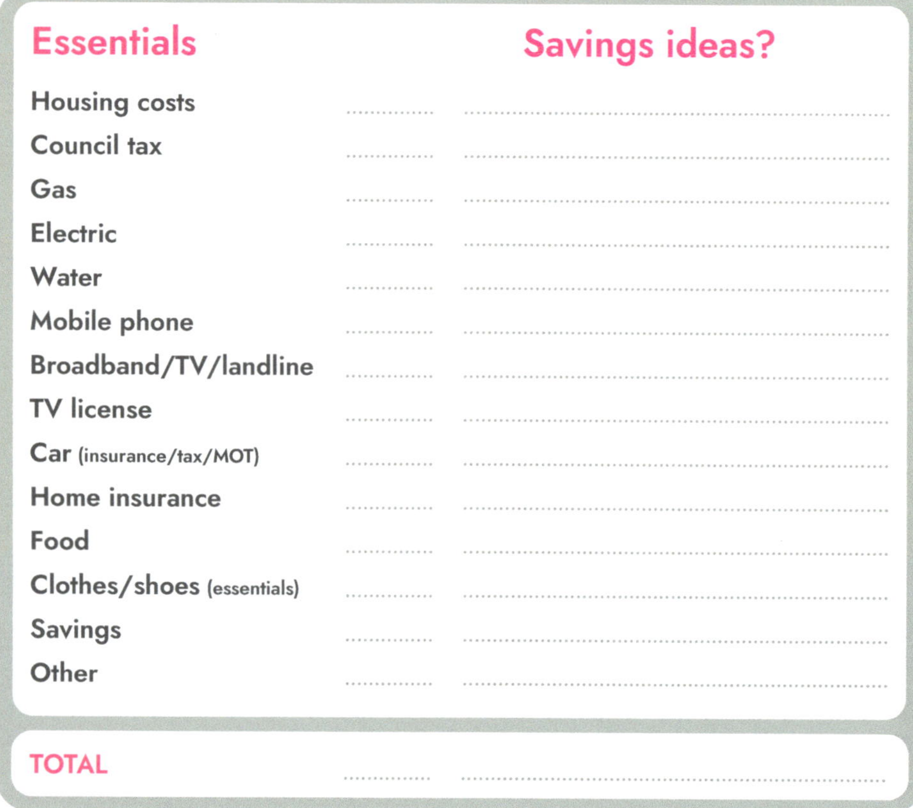

Day to day costs
Lunch/Food
Travelling
Drinks
Extras

Are you getting the best interest rates?

Debts...
Credit cards
Loans
Other

TOTAL

The Fun Stuff
Gym
Socialising
Clothes
Holidays
Gifts
Hair/beauty
Hobbies
Other

TOTAL

Where are we?
Incomings
Outgoings
What's left

Action plan...

Better With A PLAN | BUDGET PLANNER

What's coming in?

Salary

Extras

Bank Balance

Total

What's going out?

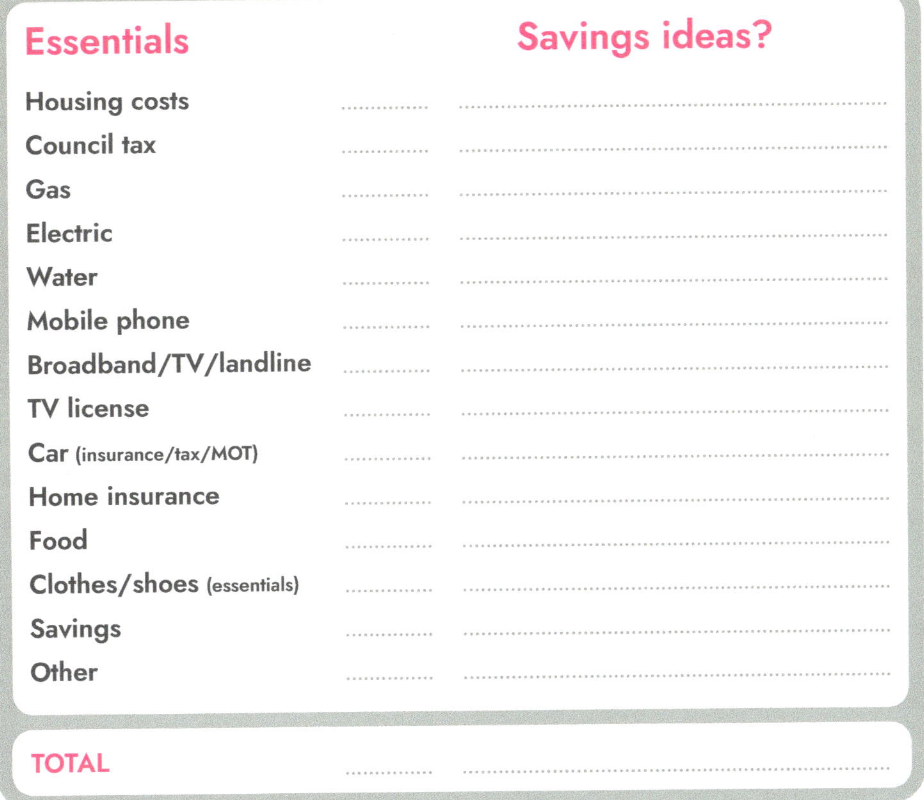

Essentials

Savings ideas?

Housing costs

Council tax

Gas

Electric

Water

Mobile phone

Broadband/TV/landline

TV license

Car (insurance/tax/MOT)

Home insurance

Food

Clothes/shoes (essentials)

Savings

Other

TOTAL

Day to day costs

Lunch/Food

Travelling

Drinks

Extras

Debts...

Credit cards

Loans

Other

TOTAL

The Fun Stuff

Gym

Socialising

Clothes

Holidays

Gifts

Hair/beauty

Hobbies

Other

TOTAL

Where are we?

Incomings

Outgoings

What's left

Action plan...

What's coming in?

Salary

Extras

Bank Balance

Total

What's going out?

Essentials

Housing costs
Council tax
Gas
Electric
Water
Mobile phone
Broadband/TV/landline
TV license
Car (insurance/tax/MOT)
Home insurance
Food
Clothes/shoes (essentials)
Savings
Other

TOTAL

Savings ideas?

Debts...

Credit cards
Loans
Other

TOTAL

The Fun Stuff

Gym
Socialising
Clothes
Holidays
Gifts
Hair/beauty
Hobbies
Other

TOTAL

Are you getting the best interest rates?

Day to day costs

Lunch/Food
Travelling
Drinks
Extras

Where are we?

Incomings
Outgoings
What's left

Action plan...

Better With A PLAN | BUDGET PLANNER

What's coming in?

Salary

Extras

Bank Balance

Total

What's going out?

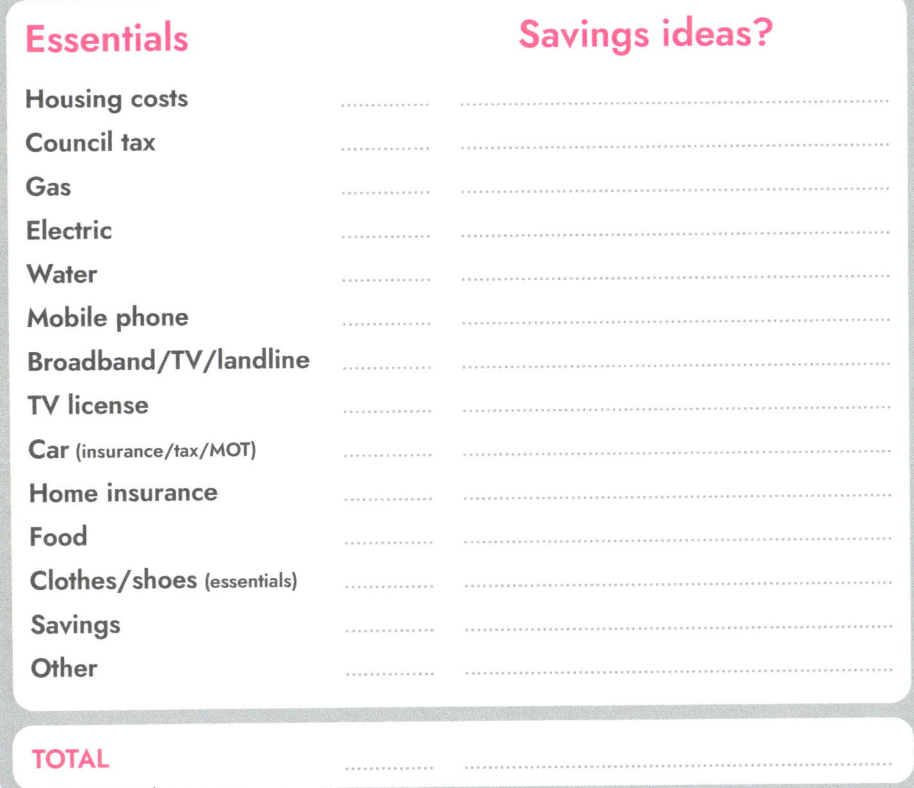

Essentials

Housing costs
Council tax
Gas
Electric
Water
Mobile phone
Broadband/TV/landline
TV license
Car (insurance/tax/MOT)
Home insurance
Food
Clothes/shoes (essentials)
Savings
Other

TOTAL

Savings ideas?

Debts...

Are you getting the best interest rates?

Credit cards
Loans
Other

TOTAL

The Fun Stuff

Gym
Socialising
Clothes
Holidays
Gifts
Hair/beauty
Hobbies
Other

TOTAL

Day to day costs

Lunch/Food
Travelling
Drinks
Extras

Where are we?

Incomings
Outgoings
What's left

Action plan...

What's coming in?

Salary

Extras

Bank Balance

Total

What's going out?

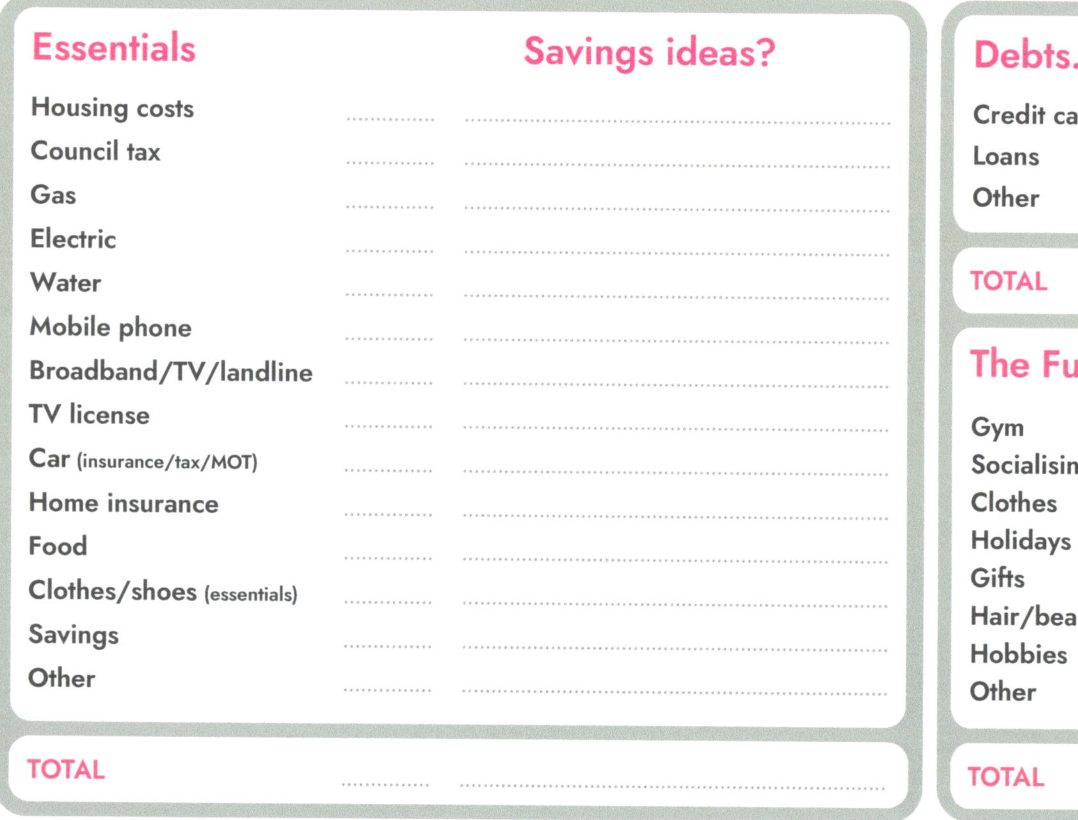

Essentials

Housing costs
Council tax
Gas
Electric
Water
Mobile phone
Broadband/TV/landline
TV license
Car (insurance/tax/MOT)
Home insurance
Food
Clothes/shoes (essentials)
Savings
Other

TOTAL

Savings ideas?

Debts...

Credit cards
Loans
Other

TOTAL

Are you getting the best interest rates?

The Fun Stuff

Gym
Socialising
Clothes
Holidays
Gifts
Hair/beauty
Hobbies
Other

TOTAL

Day to day costs

Lunch/Food
Travelling
Drinks
Extras

Where are we?

Incomings
Outgoings
What's left

Action plan...

Better With A PLAN | BUDGET PLANNER

What's coming in?

Salary	Extras	Bank Balance	Total

What's going out?

Essentials

	Savings ideas?
Housing costs	
Council tax	
Gas	
Electric	
Water	
Mobile phone	
Broadband/TV/landline	
TV license	
Car (insurance/tax/MOT)	
Home insurance	
Food	
Clothes/shoes (essentials)	
Savings	
Other	

TOTAL

Debts...

Credit cards	
Loans	
Other	

TOTAL

The Fun Stuff

Gym	
Socialising	
Clothes	
Holidays	
Gifts	
Hair/beauty	
Hobbies	
Other	

TOTAL

Day to day costs

Lunch/Food	
Travelling	
Drinks	
Extras	

Where are we?

Incomings	
Outgoings	
What's left	

Action plan...

Better With A PLAN | BUDGET PLANNER

What's coming in?

Salary

Extras

Bank Balance

Total

What's going out?

Essentials

Housing costs

Council tax

Gas

Electric

Water

Mobile phone

Broadband/TV/landline

TV license

Car (insurance/tax/MOT)

Home insurance

Food

Clothes/shoes (essentials)

Savings

Other

TOTAL

Savings ideas?

Debts...

Credit cards

Loans

Other

TOTAL

The Fun Stuff

Gym

Socialising

Clothes

Holidays

Gifts

Hair/beauty

Hobbies

Other

TOTAL

Day to day costs

Lunch/Food

Travelling

Drinks

Extras

Where are we?

Incomings

Outgoings

What's left

Action plan...

Better With A PLAN | BUDGET PLANNER

What's coming in?

Salary	Extras	Bank Balance	Total

What's going out?

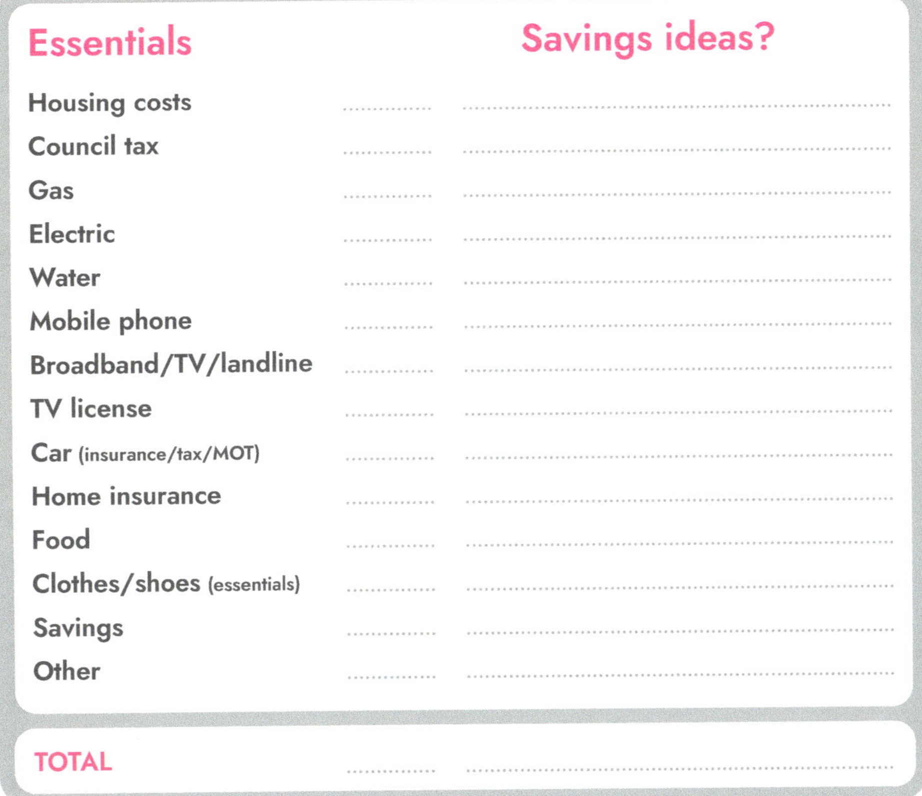

Essentials

	Savings ideas?
Housing costs	
Council tax	
Gas	
Electric	
Water	
Mobile phone	
Broadband/TV/landline	
TV license	
Car (insurance/tax/MOT)	
Home insurance	
Food	
Clothes/shoes (essentials)	
Savings	
Other	

TOTAL

Day to day costs

Lunch/Food
Travelling
Drinks
Extras

Debts...

Credit cards
Loans
Other

TOTAL

Are you getting the best interest rates?

The Fun Stuff

Gym
Socialising
Clothes
Holidays
Gifts
Hair/beauty
Hobbies
Other

TOTAL

Where are we?

Incomings
Outgoings
What's left

Action plan...

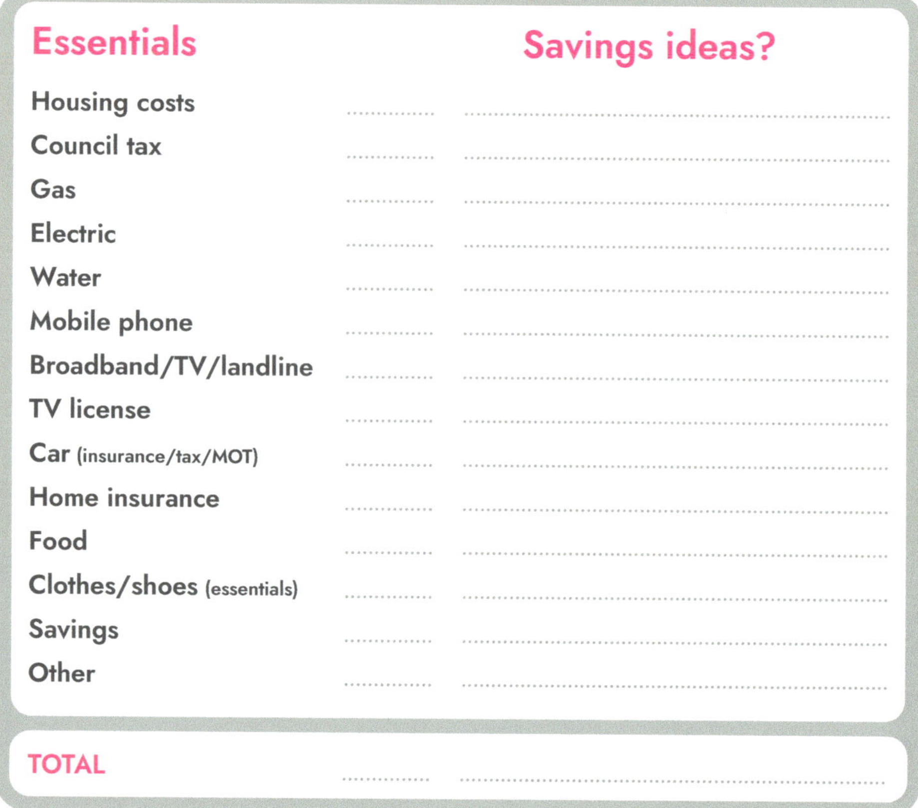

Better With A PLAN | BUDGET PLANNER

What's coming in?

| Salary | Extras | Bank Balance | Total |

What's going out?

Essentials

Housing costs
Council tax
Gas
Electric
Water
Mobile phone
Broadband/TV/landline
TV license
Car (insurance/tax/MOT)
Home insurance
Food
Clothes/shoes (essentials)
Savings
Other

TOTAL

Savings ideas?

Debts...

Credit cards
Loans
Other

TOTAL

The Fun Stuff

Gym
Socialising
Clothes
Holidays
Gifts
Hair/beauty
Hobbies
Other

TOTAL

Day to day costs

Lunch/Food
Travelling
Drinks
Extras

Where are we?

Incomings
Outgoings
What's left

Action plan...

BUDGET PLANNER

What's coming in?

Salary

Extras

Bank Balance

Total

What's going out?

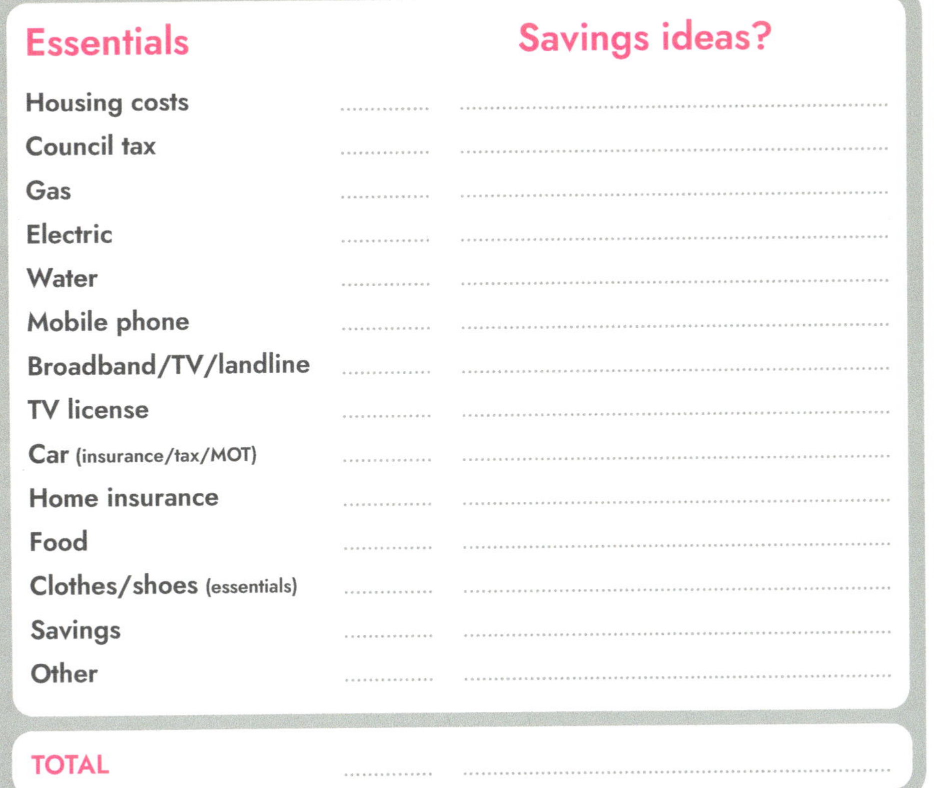

Essentials

Housing costs
Council tax
Gas
Electric
Water
Mobile phone
Broadband/TV/landline
TV license
Car (insurance/tax/MOT)
Home insurance
Food
Clothes/shoes (essentials)
Savings
Other

TOTAL

Savings ideas?

Day to day costs

Lunch/Food
Travelling
Drinks
Extras

Are you getting the best interest rates?

Debts...

Credit cards
Loans
Other

TOTAL

The Fun Stuff

Gym
Socialising
Clothes
Holidays
Gifts
Hair/beauty
Hobbies
Other

TOTAL

Where are we?

Incomings
Outgoings
What's left

Action plan...

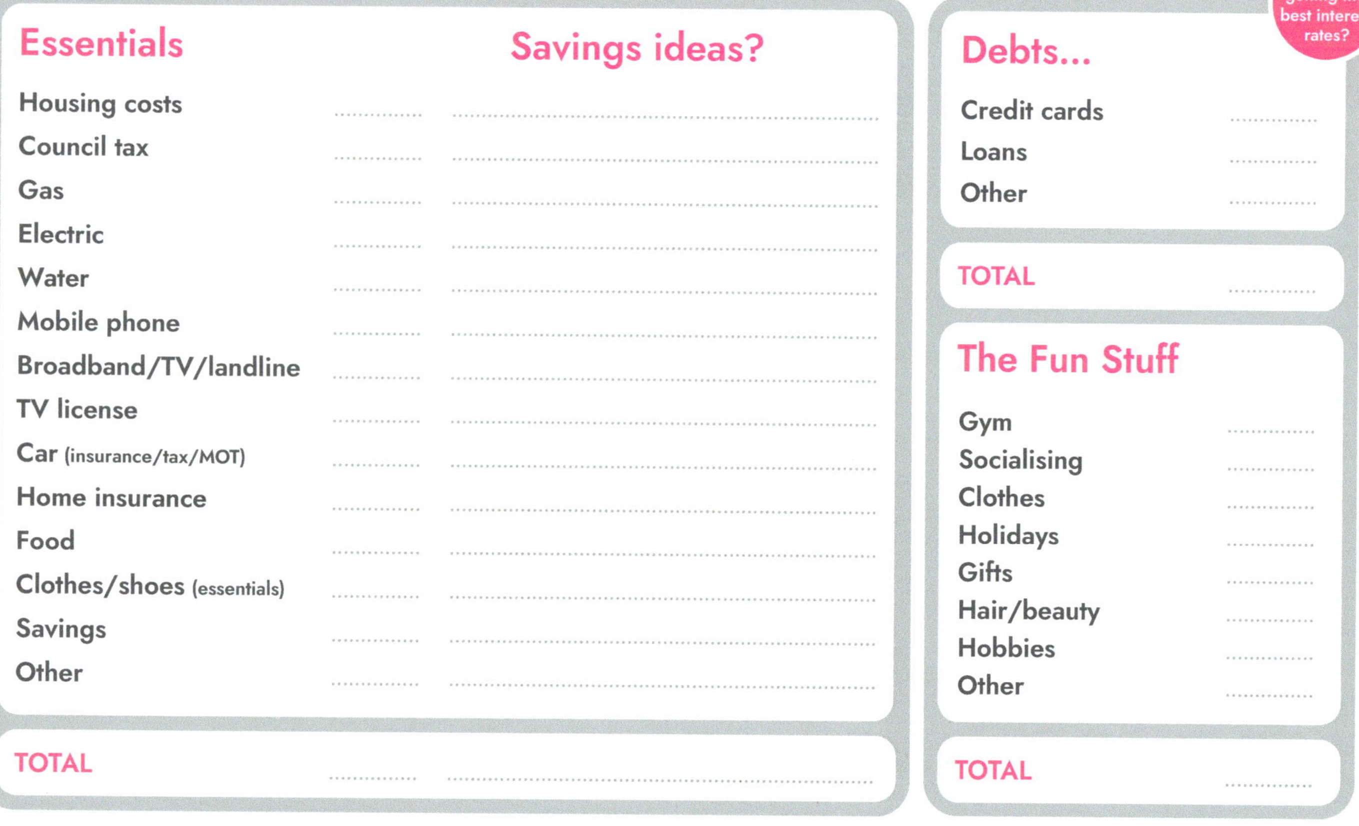

Better With A PLAN | BUDGET PLANNER

What's coming in?

| Salary | Extras | Bank Balance | Total |

What's going out?

Day to day costs

Lunch/Food
Travelling
Drinks
Extras

Essentials

Savings ideas?

Housing costs
Council tax
Gas
Electric
Water
Mobile phone
Broadband/TV/landline
TV license
Car (insurance/tax/MOT)
Home insurance
Food
Clothes/shoes (essentials)
Savings
Other

TOTAL

Debts...

Credit cards
Loans
Other

TOTAL

Are you getting the best interest rates?

The Fun Stuff

Gym
Socialising
Clothes
Holidays
Gifts
Hair/beauty
Hobbies
Other

TOTAL

Where are we?

Incomings
Outgoings
What's left

Action plan...

PLAN | BUDGET PLANNER

What's coming in?

| Salary | Extras | Bank Balance | Total |

What's going out?

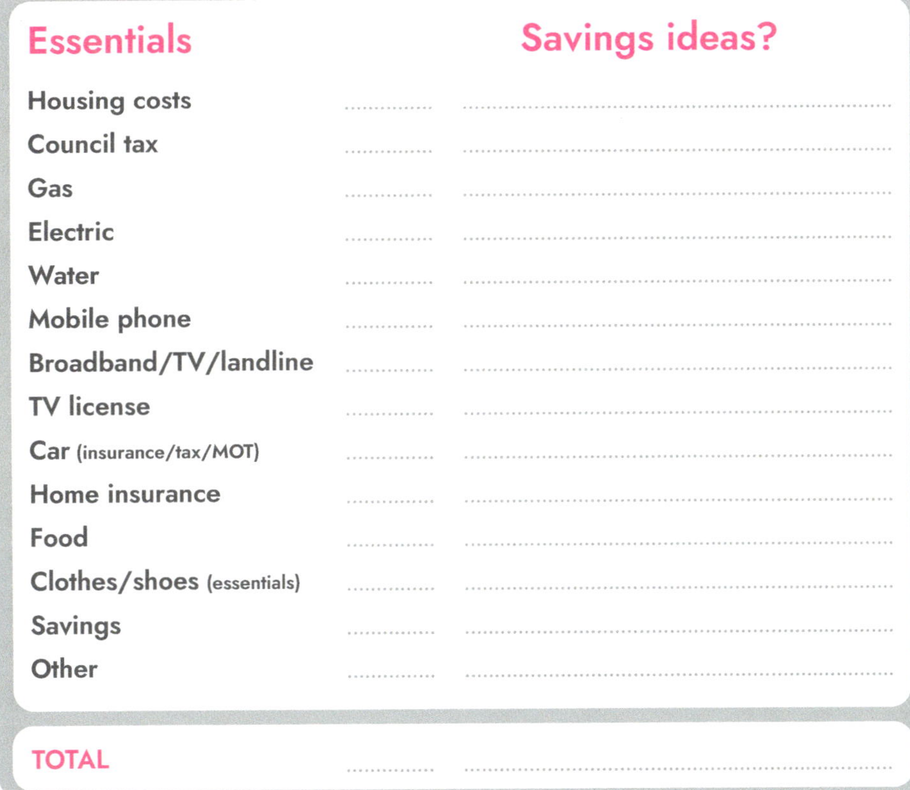

Essentials

Housing costs
Council tax
Gas
Electric
Water
Mobile phone
Broadband/TV/landline
TV license
Car (insurance/tax/MOT)
Home insurance
Food
Clothes/shoes (essentials)
Savings
Other

TOTAL

Savings ideas?

Debts...

Credit cards
Loans
Other

TOTAL

Are you getting the best interest rates?

The Fun Stuff

Gym
Socialising
Clothes
Holidays
Gifts
Hair/beauty
Hobbies
Other

TOTAL

Day to day costs

Lunch/Food
Travelling
Drinks
Extras

Where are we?

Incomings
Outgoings
What's left

Action plan...

Better With A PLAN | BUDGET PLANNER

What's coming in?

Salary	Extras	Bank Balance	Total

What's going out?

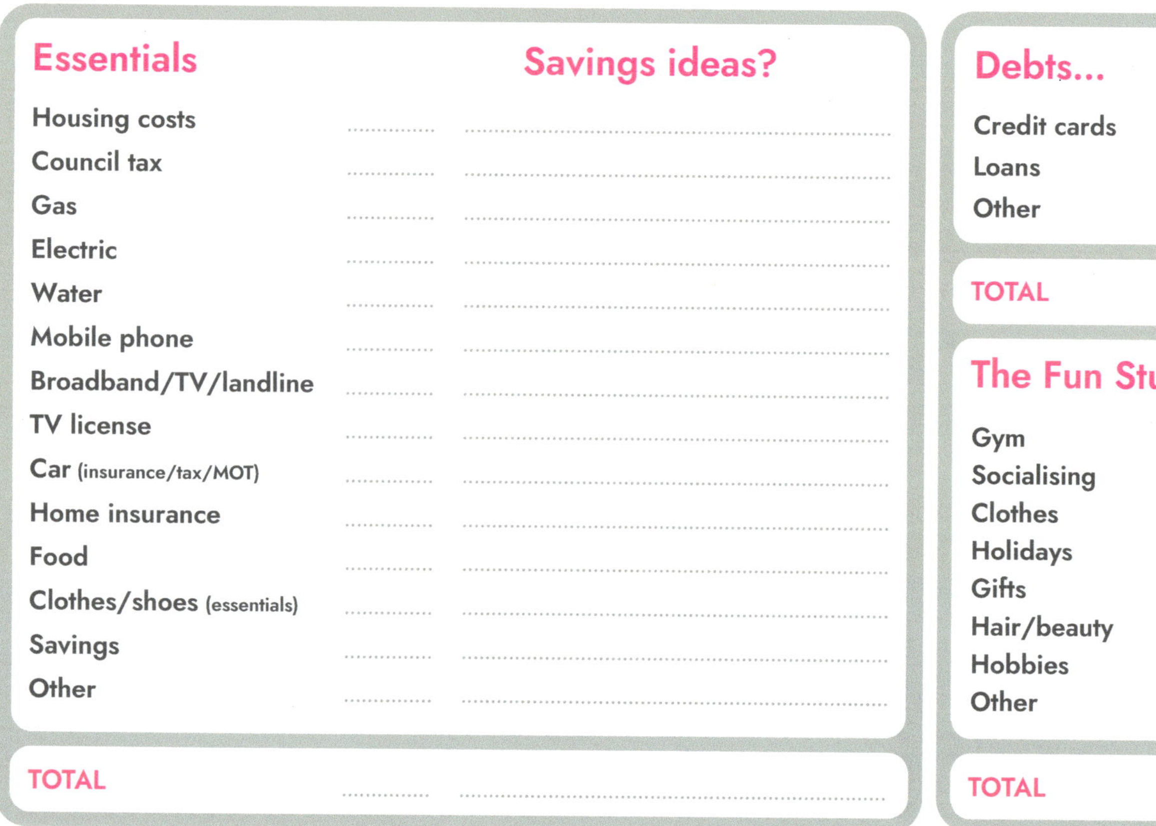

Essentials

Housing costs
Council tax
Gas
Electric
Water
Mobile phone
Broadband/TV/landline
TV license
Car (insurance/tax/MOT)
Home insurance
Food
Clothes/shoes (essentials)
Savings
Other

TOTAL

Savings ideas?

Debts...

Credit cards
Loans
Other

TOTAL

Are you getting the best interest rates?

The Fun Stuff

Gym
Socialising
Clothes
Holidays
Gifts
Hair/beauty
Hobbies
Other

TOTAL

Day to day costs

Lunch/Food
Travelling
Drinks
Extras

Where are we?

Incomings
Outgoings
What's left

Action plan...

Better With A PLAN | BUDGET PLANNER

What's coming in?

Salary	Extras	Bank Balance	Total

What's going out?

Essentials   Savings ideas?

Housing costs ....
Council tax ....
Gas ....
Electric ....
Water ....
Mobile phone ....
Broadband/TV/landline ....
TV license ....
Car (insurance/tax/MOT) ....
Home insurance ....
Food ....
Clothes/shoes (essentials) ....
Savings ....
Other ....

TOTAL ....

Debts...

Credit cards ....
Loans ....
Other ....

TOTAL ....

Are you getting the best interest rates?

The Fun Stuff

Gym ....
Socialising ....
Clothes ....
Holidays ....
Gifts ....
Hair/beauty ....
Hobbies ....
Other ....

TOTAL ....

Day to day costs

Lunch/Food ....
Travelling ....
Drinks ....
Extras ....

Where are we?

Incomings ....
Outgoings ....
What's left ....

Action plan...

....
....
....
....
....
....
....
....
....
....

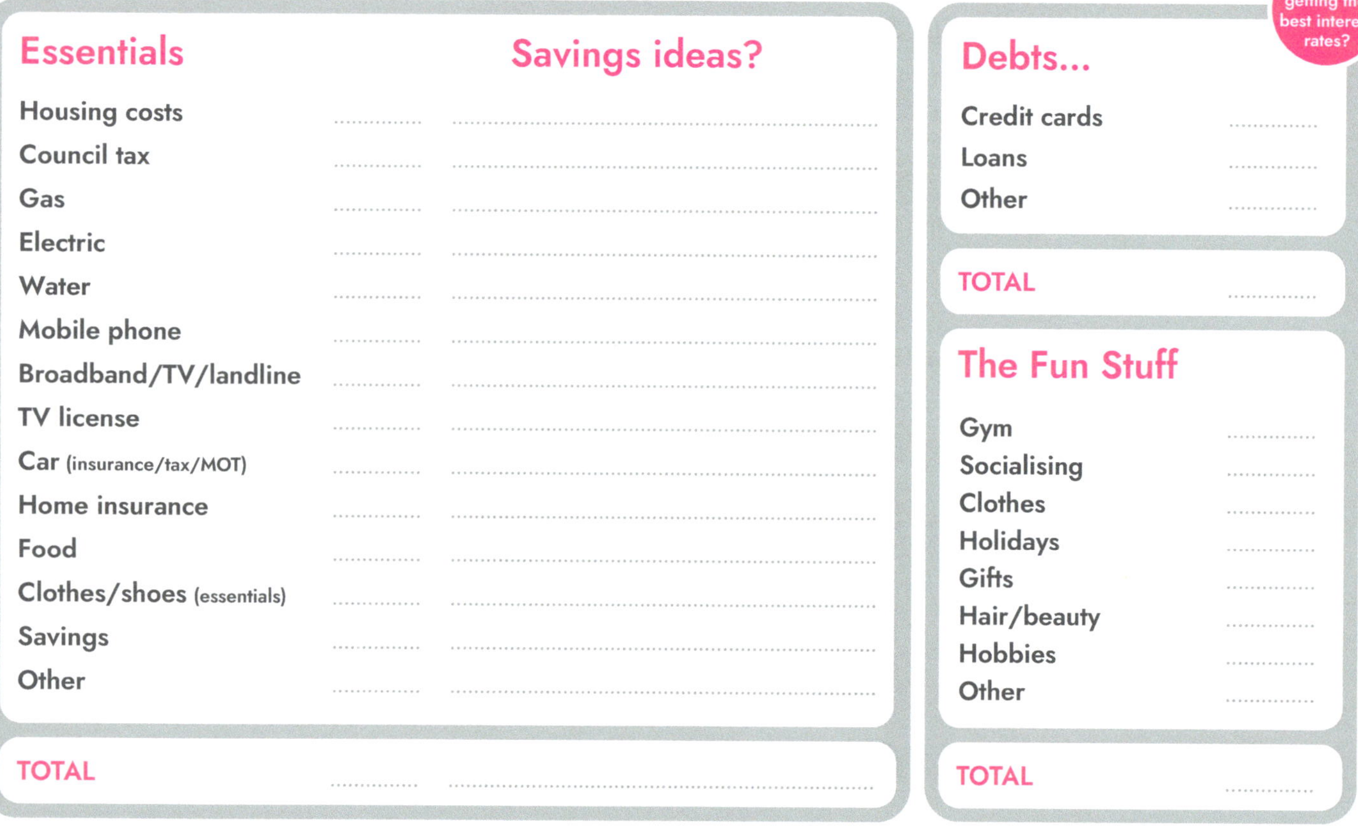

Better With A PLAN | BUDGET PLANNER

What's coming in?

| Salary | Extras | Bank Balance | Total |

What's going out?

Essentials

Housing costs
Council tax
Gas
Electric
Water
Mobile phone
Broadband/TV/landline
TV license
Car (insurance/tax/MOT)
Home insurance
Food
Clothes/shoes (essentials)
Savings
Other

Savings ideas?

TOTAL

Debts...

Credit cards
Loans
Other

TOTAL

Are you getting the best interest rates?

The Fun Stuff

Gym
Socialising
Clothes
Holidays
Gifts
Hair/beauty
Hobbies
Other

TOTAL

Day to day costs

Lunch/Food
Travelling
Drinks
Extras

Where are we?

Incomings
Outgoings
What's left

Action plan...

Better With A PLAN | BUDGET PLANNER

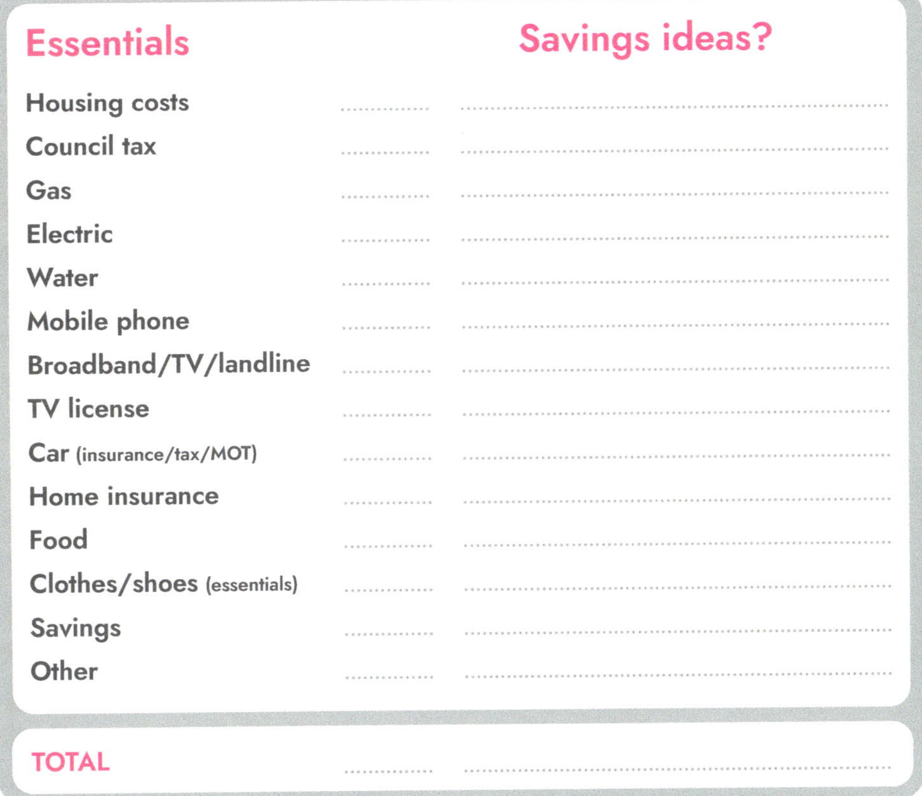

What's coming in?

Salary

Extras

Bank Balance

Total

What's going out?

Are you getting the best interest rates?

Essentials

Savings ideas?

Housing costs

Council tax

Gas

Electric

Water

Mobile phone

Broadband/TV/landline

TV license

Car (insurance/tax/MOT)

Home insurance

Food

Clothes/shoes (essentials)

Savings

Other

TOTAL

Debts...

Credit cards

Loans

Other

TOTAL

The Fun Stuff

Gym

Socialising

Clothes

Holidays

Gifts

Hair/beauty

Hobbies

Other

TOTAL

Day to day costs

Lunch/Food

Travelling

Drinks

Extras

Where are we?

Incomings

Outgoings

What's left

Action plan...

Better With A PLAN | BUDGET PLANNER

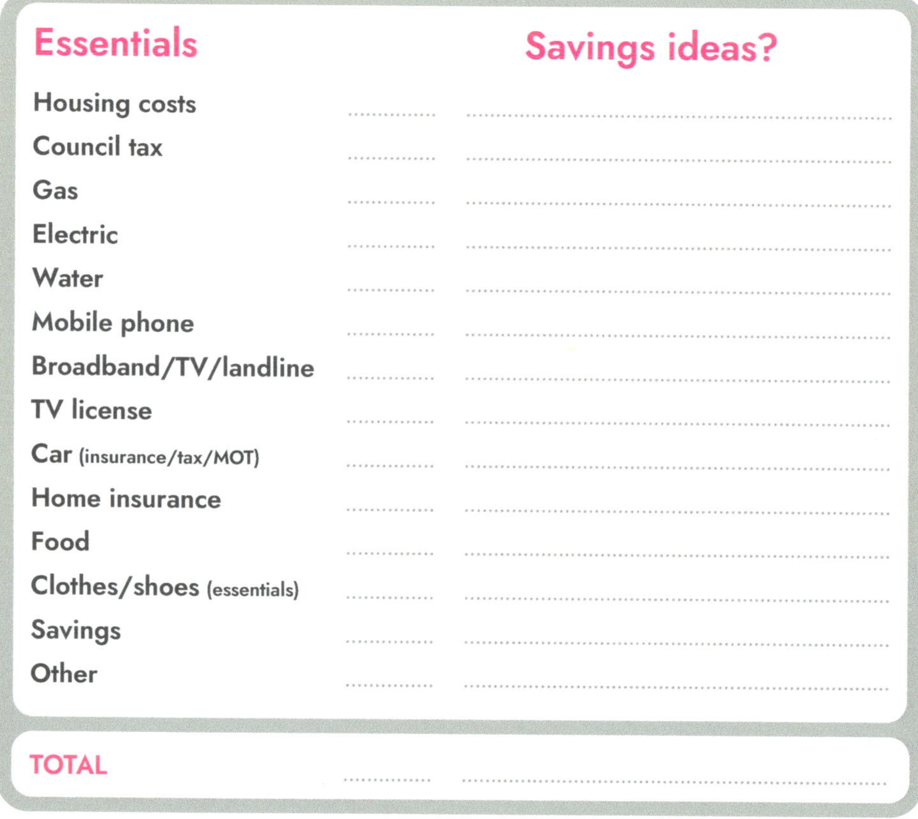

What's coming in?

Salary	Extras	Bank Balance	Total

What's going out?

Essentials

Housing costs
Council tax
Gas
Electric
Water
Mobile phone
Broadband/TV/landline
TV license
Car (insurance/tax/MOT)
Home insurance
Food
Clothes/shoes (essentials)
Savings
Other

TOTAL

Savings ideas?

Debts...

Credit cards
Loans
Other

TOTAL

Are you getting the best interest rates?

The Fun Stuff

Gym
Socialising
Clothes
Holidays
Gifts
Hair/beauty
Hobbies
Other

TOTAL

Day to day costs

Lunch/Food
Travelling
Drinks
Extras

Where are we?

Incomings
Outgoings
What's left

Action plan...

What's coming in?

Salary

Extras

Bank Balance

Total

Day to day costs

Lunch/Food

Travelling

Drinks

Extras

What's going out?

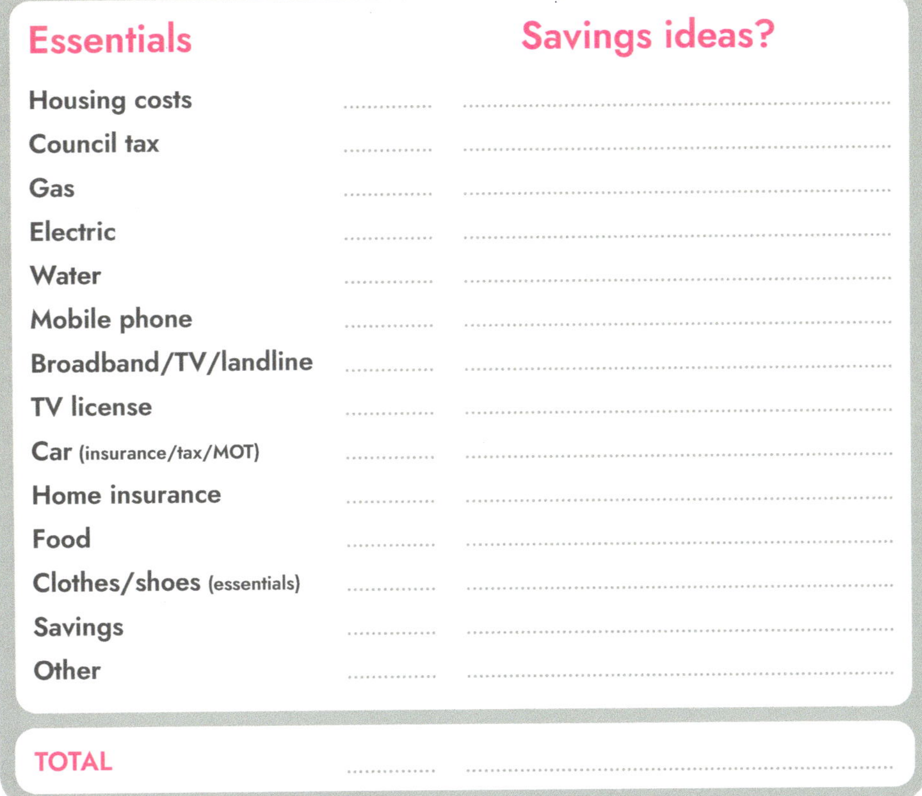

Essentials

Housing costs

Council tax

Gas

Electric

Water

Mobile phone

Broadband/TV/landline

TV license

Car (insurance/tax/MOT)

Home insurance

Food

Clothes/shoes (essentials)

Savings

Other

TOTAL

Savings ideas?

Are you getting the best interest rates?

Debts...

Credit cards

Loans

Other

TOTAL

The Fun Stuff

Gym

Socialising

Clothes

Holidays

Gifts

Hair/beauty

Hobbies

Other

TOTAL

Where are we?

Incomings

Outgoings

What's left

Action plan...

Better With A PLAN | BUDGET PLANNER

What's coming in?

Salary

Extras

Bank Balance

Total

What's going out?

Essentials

Housing costs

Council tax

Gas

Electric

Water

Mobile phone

Broadband/TV/landline

TV license

Car (insurance/tax/MOT)

Home insurance

Food

Clothes/shoes (essentials)

Savings

Other

TOTAL

Savings ideas?

Debts...

Credit cards

Loans

Other

TOTAL

Are you getting the best interest rates?

The Fun Stuff

Gym

Socialising

Clothes

Holidays

Gifts

Hair/beauty

Hobbies

Other

TOTAL

Day to day costs

Lunch/Food

Travelling

Drinks

Extras

Where are we?

Incomings

Outgoings

What's left

Action plan...

Better With A PLAN | BUDGET PLANNER

What's coming in?

| Salary | Extras | Bank Balance | Total |

What's going out?

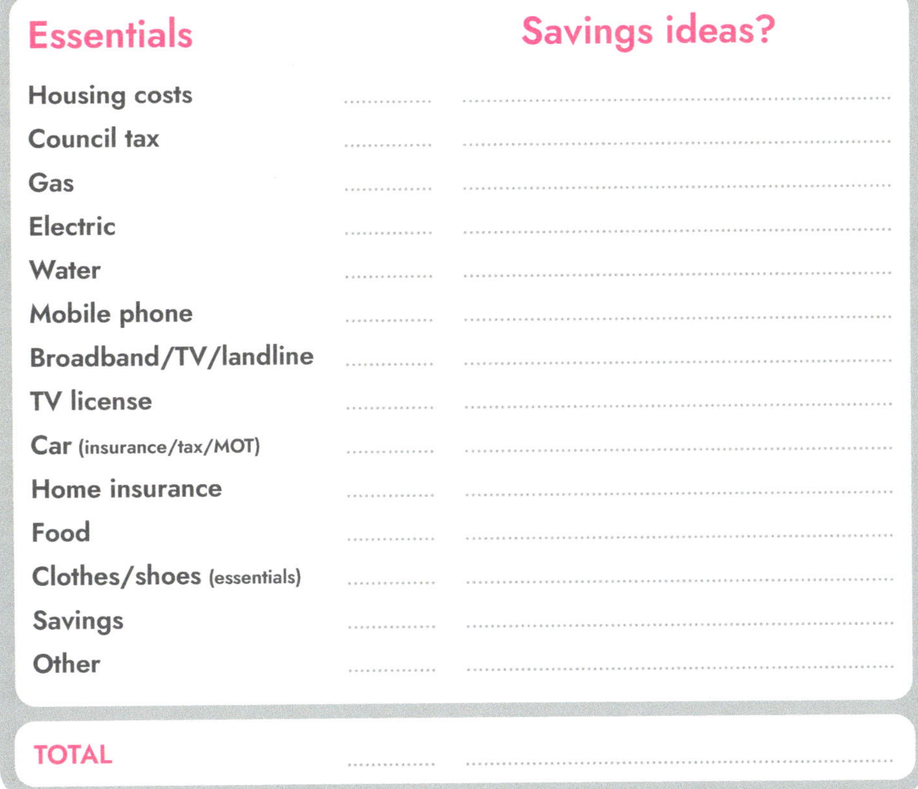

Essentials

Housing costs

Council tax

Gas

Electric

Water

Mobile phone

Broadband/TV/landline

TV license

Car (insurance/tax/MOT)

Home insurance

Food

Clothes/shoes (essentials)

Savings

Other

TOTAL

Savings ideas?

Debts...

Credit cards

Loans

Other

TOTAL

The Fun Stuff

Gym

Socialising

Clothes

Holidays

Gifts

Hair/beauty

Hobbies

Other

TOTAL

Are you getting the best interest rates?

Day to day costs

Lunch/Food

Travelling

Drinks

Extras

Where are we?

Incomings

Outgoings

What's left

Action plan...

Better With A PLAN | BUDGET PLANNER

What's coming in?

Salary | Extras | Bank Balance | Total

What's going out?

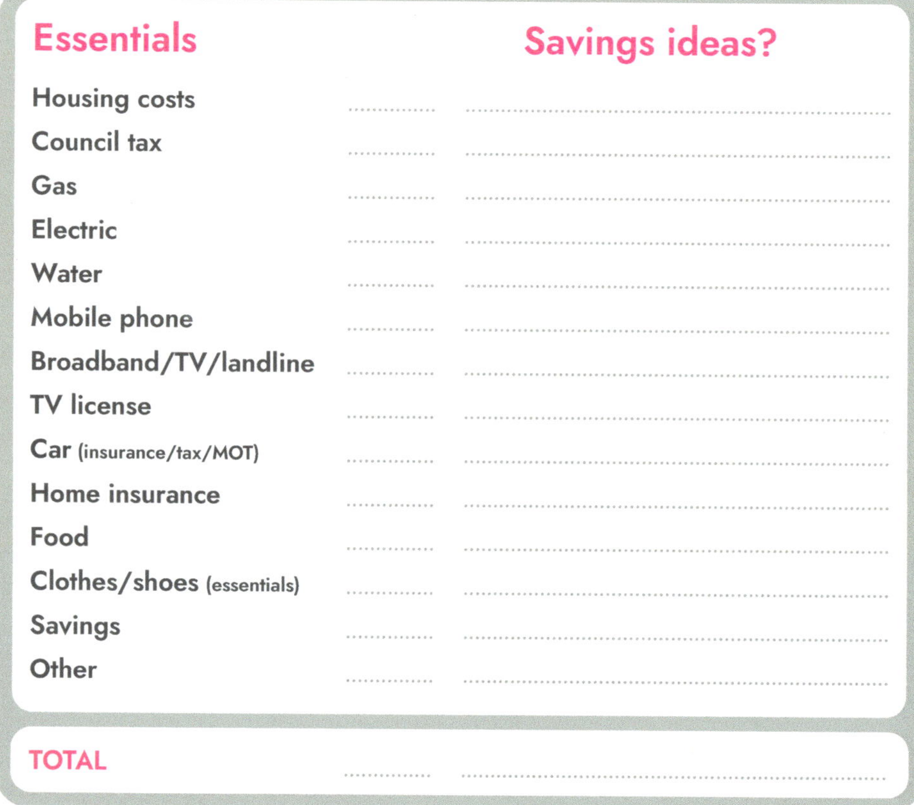

Essentials

Housing costs
Council tax
Gas
Electric
Water
Mobile phone
Broadband/TV/landline
TV license
Car (insurance/tax/MOT)
Home insurance
Food
Clothes/shoes (essentials)
Savings
Other

TOTAL

Savings ideas?

Debts...

Credit cards
Loans
Other

TOTAL

The Fun Stuff

Gym
Socialising
Clothes
Holidays
Gifts
Hair/beauty
Hobbies
Other

TOTAL

Are you getting the best interest rates?

Day to day costs

Lunch/Food
Travelling
Drinks
Extras

Where are we?

Incomings
Outgoings
What's left

Action plan...

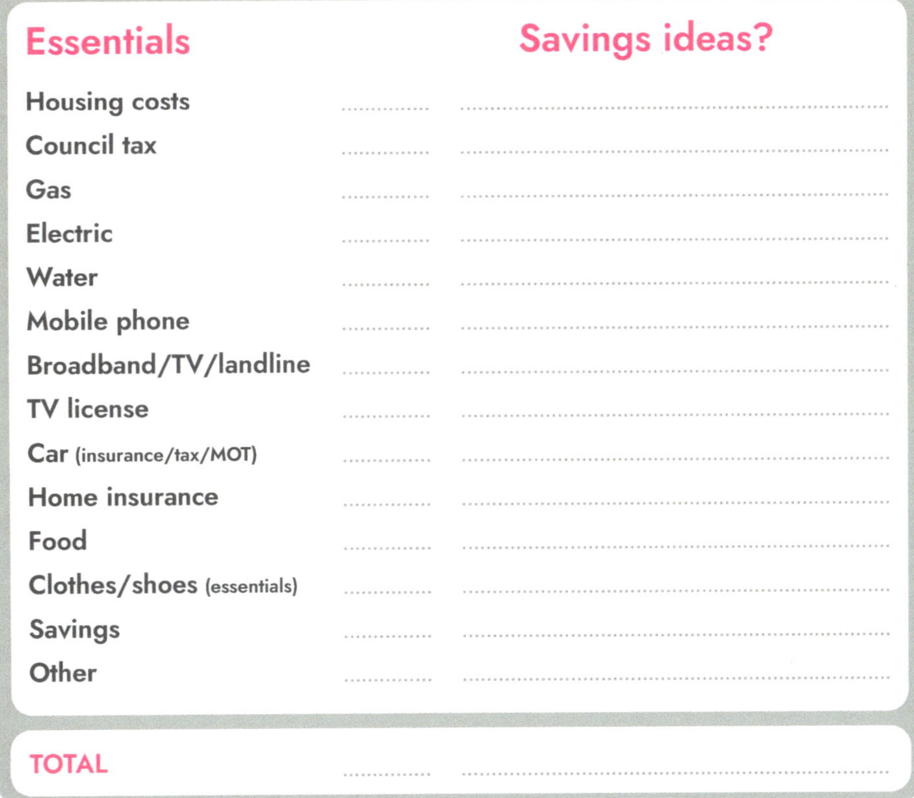

Better With A PLAN | BUDGET PLANNER

What's coming in?

| Salary | Extras | Bank Balance | Total |

What's going out?

Essentials

Housing costs
Council tax
Gas
Electric
Water
Mobile phone
Broadband/TV/landline
TV license
Car (insurance/tax/MOT)
Home insurance
Food
Clothes/shoes (essentials)
Savings
Other

TOTAL

Savings ideas?

Day to day costs

Lunch/Food
Travelling
Drinks
Extras

Debts...

Credit cards
Loans
Other

TOTAL

Are you getting the best interest rates?

The Fun Stuff

Gym
Socialising
Clothes
Holidays
Gifts
Hair/beauty
Hobbies
Other

TOTAL

Where are we?

Incomings
Outgoings
What's left

Action plan...

Better With A PLAN | BUDGET PLANNER

What's coming in?

Salary	Extras	Bank Balance	Total

What's going out?

Essentials · Savings ideas?

- Housing costs
- Council tax
- Gas
- Electric
- Water
- Mobile phone
- Broadband/TV/landline
- TV license
- Car (insurance/tax/MOT)
- Home insurance
- Food
- Clothes/shoes (essentials)
- Savings
- Other

TOTAL

Debts...

- Credit cards
- Loans
- Other

TOTAL

Are you getting the best interest rates?

The Fun Stuff

- Gym
- Socialising
- Clothes
- Holidays
- Gifts
- Hair/beauty
- Hobbies
- Other

TOTAL

Day to day costs

- Lunch/Food
- Travelling
- Drinks
- Extras

Where are we?

- Incomings
- Outgoings
- What's left

Action plan...

BUDGET PLANNER

What's coming in?

Salary | Extras | Bank Balance | Total

What's going out?

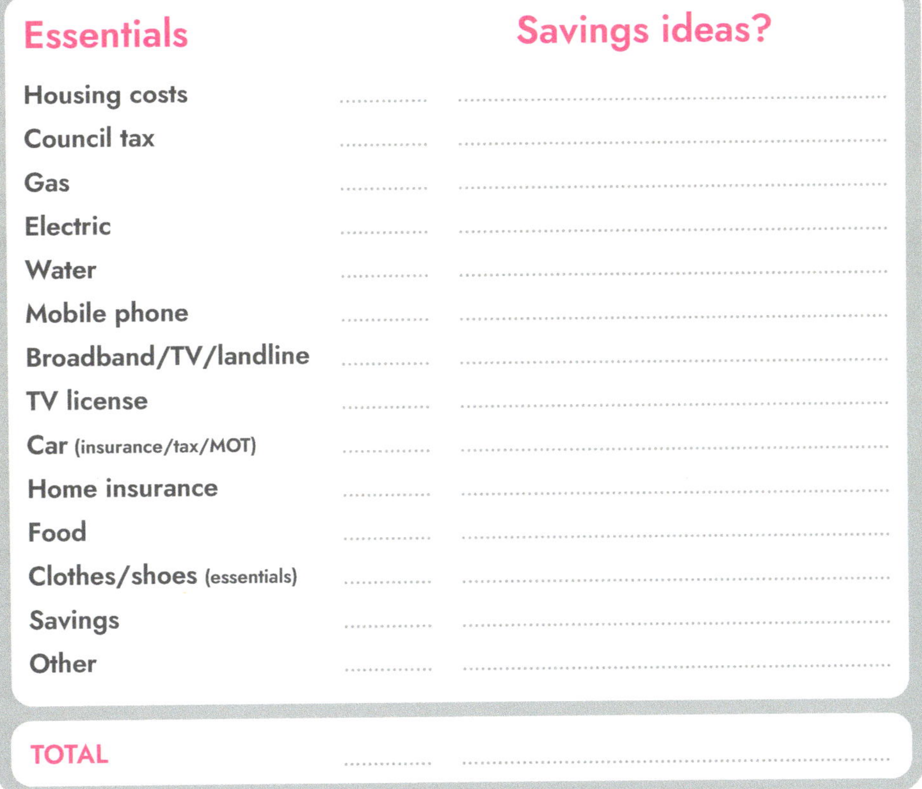

Essentials

	Savings ideas?
Housing costs	
Council tax	
Gas	
Electric	
Water	
Mobile phone	
Broadband/TV/landline	
TV license	
Car (insurance/tax/MOT)	
Home insurance	
Food	
Clothes/shoes (essentials)	
Savings	
Other	

TOTAL

Debts...

Credit cards
Loans
Other

TOTAL

Are you getting the best interest rates?

The Fun Stuff

Gym
Socialising
Clothes
Holidays
Gifts
Hair/beauty
Hobbies
Other

TOTAL

Day to day costs

Lunch/Food
Travelling
Drinks
Extras

Where are we?

Incomings
Outgoings
What's left

Action plan...

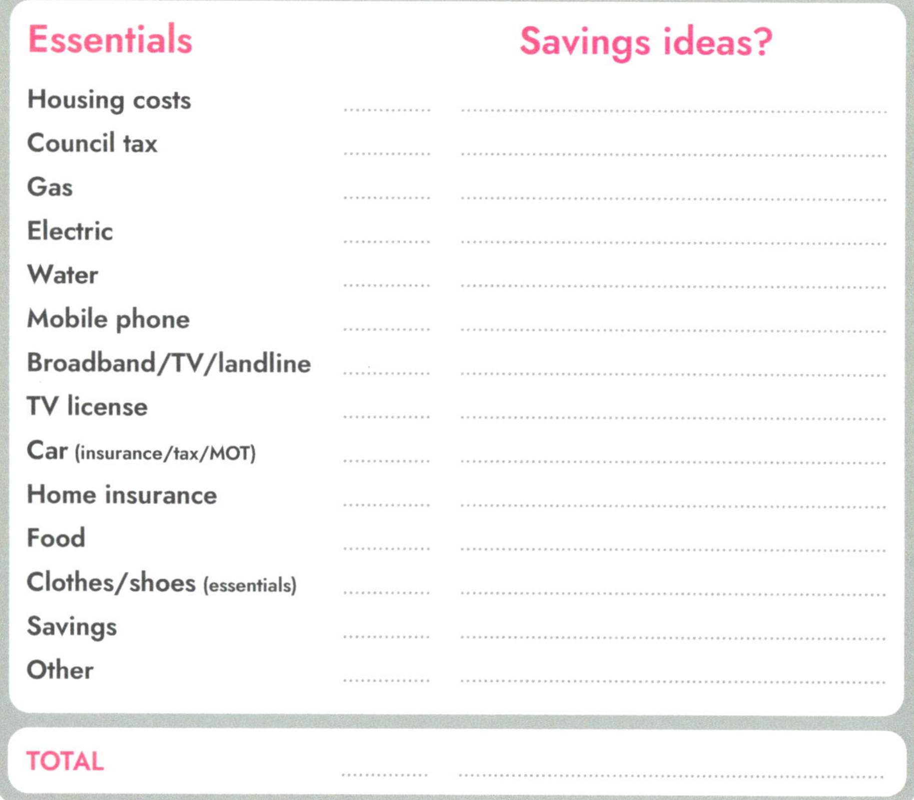

Better With A PLAN | BUDGET PLANNER

What's coming in?

| Salary | Extras | Bank Balance | Total |

What's going out?

Are you getting the best interest rates?

Essentials

Housing costs
Council tax
Gas
Electric
Water
Mobile phone
Broadband/TV/landline
TV license
Car (insurance/tax/MOT)
Home insurance
Food
Clothes/shoes (essentials)
Savings
Other

TOTAL

Savings ideas?

Debts...

Credit cards
Loans
Other

TOTAL

The Fun Stuff

Gym
Socialising
Clothes
Holidays
Gifts
Hair/beauty
Hobbies
Other

TOTAL

Day to day costs

Lunch/Food
Travelling
Drinks
Extras

Where are we?

Incomings
Outgoings
What's left

Action plan...

BUDGET PLANNER

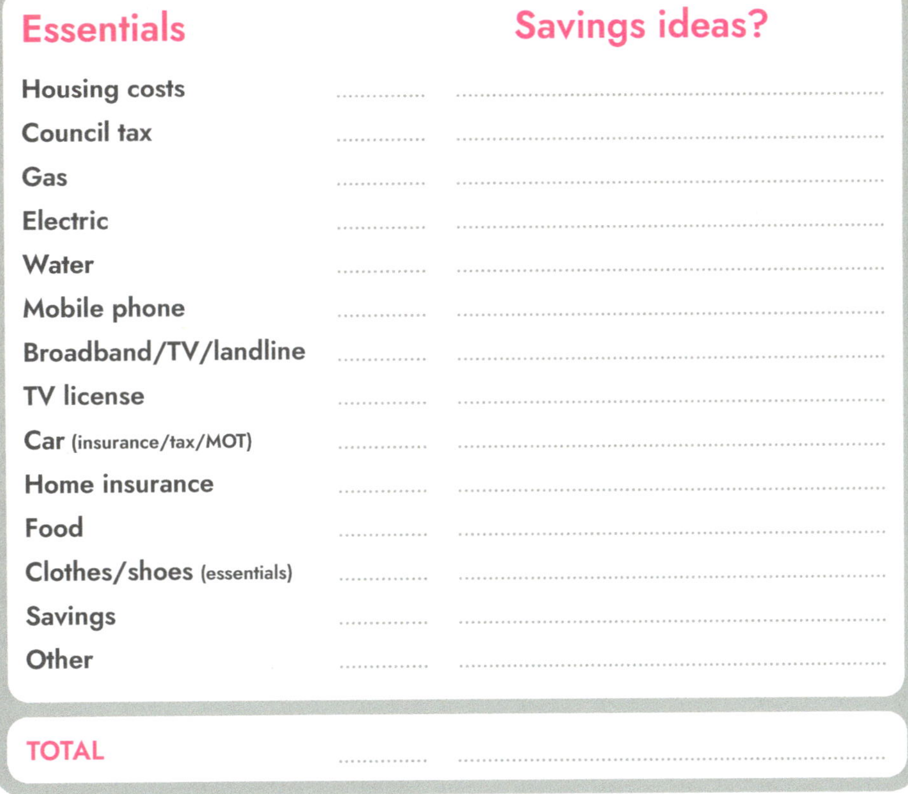

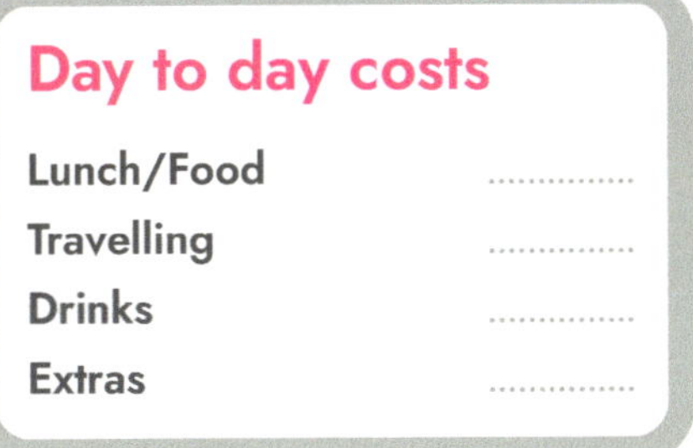

Better With A PLAN | BUDGET PLANNER

What's coming in?

Salary	Extras	Bank Balance	Total

What's going out?

Day to day costs

Lunch/Food ....
Travelling ....
Drinks ....
Extras ....

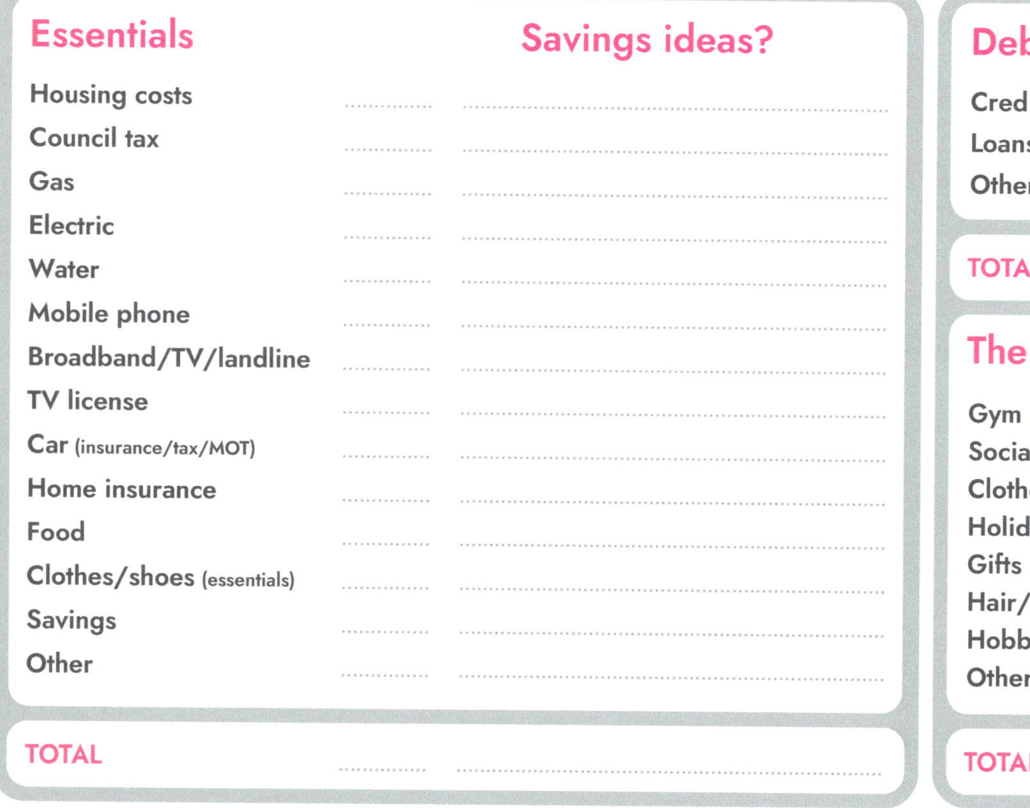

Essentials

Housing costs ....
Council tax ....
Gas ....
Electric ....
Water ....
Mobile phone ....
Broadband/TV/landline ....
TV license ....
Car (insurance/tax/MOT) ....
Home insurance ....
Food ....
Clothes/shoes (essentials) ....
Savings ....
Other ....

TOTAL

Savings ideas?

Are you getting the best interest rates?

Debts...

Credit cards ....
Loans ....
Other ....

TOTAL

The Fun Stuff

Gym ....
Socialising ....
Clothes ....
Holidays ....
Gifts ....
Hair/beauty ....
Hobbies ....
Other ....

TOTAL

Where are we?

Incomings ....
Outgoings ....
What's left ....

Action plan...

Better With A PLAN | BUDGET PLANNER

What's coming in?

Salary | Extras | Bank Balance | Total

What's going out?

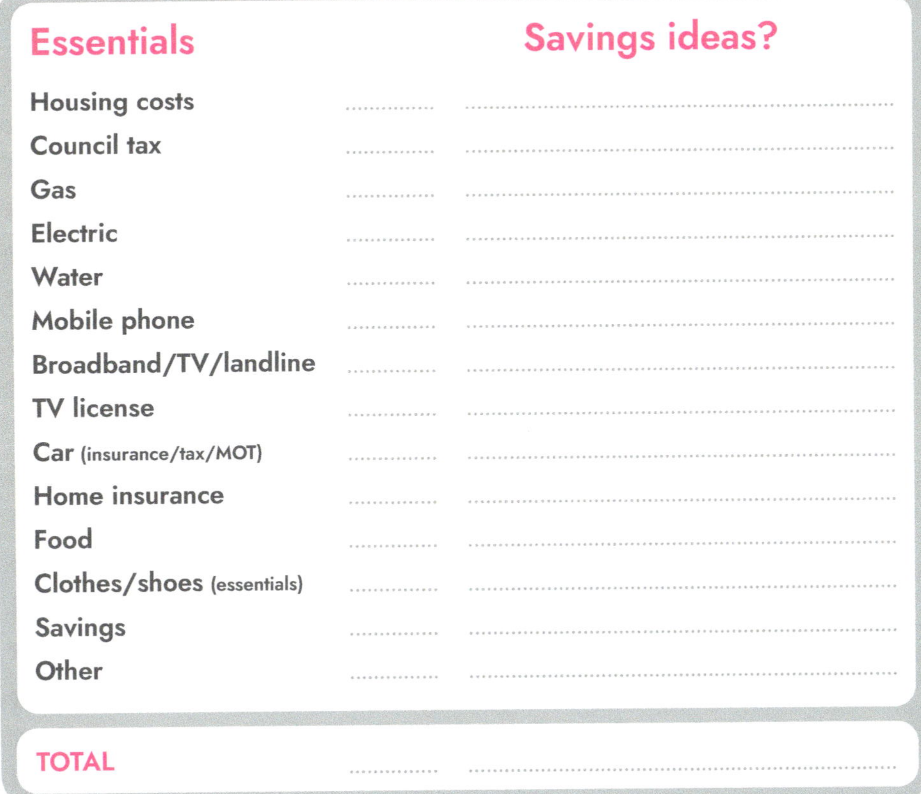

Essentials

Savings ideas?

Housing costs
Council tax
Gas
Electric
Water
Mobile phone
Broadband/TV/landline
TV license
Car (insurance/tax/MOT)
Home insurance
Food
Clothes/shoes (essentials)
Savings
Other

TOTAL

Debts...

Credit cards
Loans
Other

TOTAL

Are you getting the best interest rates?

The Fun Stuff

Gym
Socialising
Clothes
Holidays
Gifts
Hair/beauty
Hobbies
Other

TOTAL

Day to day costs

Lunch/Food
Travelling
Drinks
Extras

Where are we?

Incomings
Outgoings
What's left

Action plan...

Better With A PLAN | BUDGET PLANNER

What's coming in?

Salary

Extras

Bank Balance

Total

What's going out?

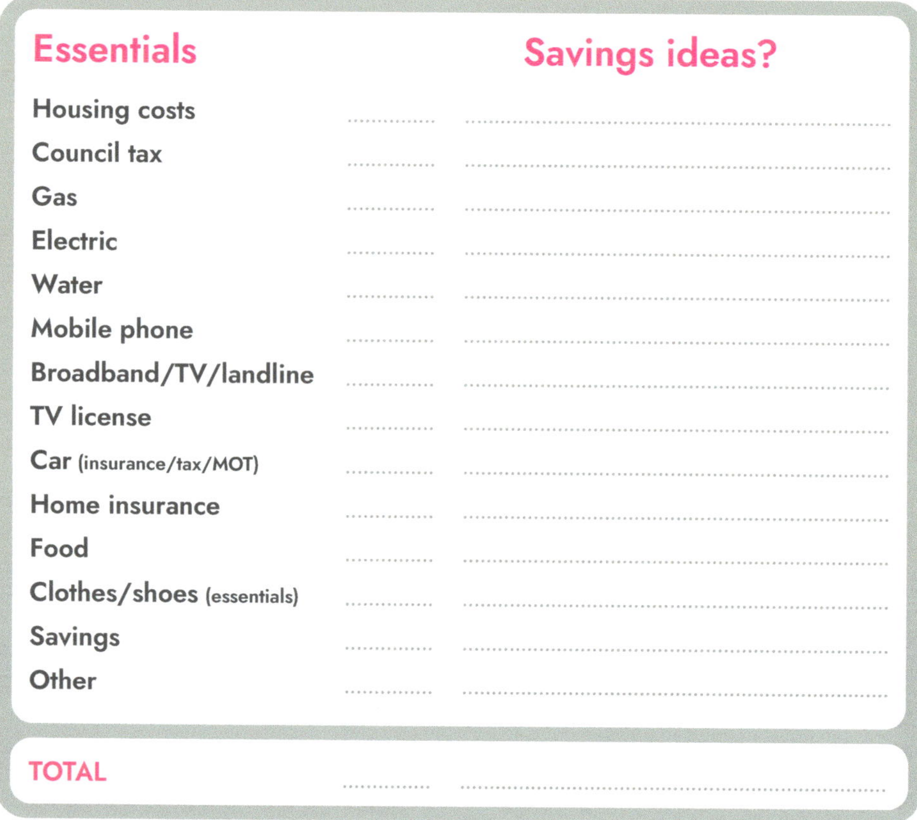

Essentials

Housing costs
Council tax
Gas
Electric
Water
Mobile phone
Broadband/TV/landline
TV license
Car (insurance/tax/MOT)
Home insurance
Food
Clothes/shoes (essentials)
Savings
Other

TOTAL

Savings ideas?

Debts...

Credit cards
Loans
Other

TOTAL

The Fun Stuff

Gym
Socialising
Clothes
Holidays
Gifts
Hair/beauty
Hobbies
Other

TOTAL

Are you getting the best interest rates?

Day to day costs

Lunch/Food
Travelling
Drinks
Extras

Where are we?

Incomings
Outgoings
What's left

Action plan...

Better With A PLAN | BUDGET PLANNER

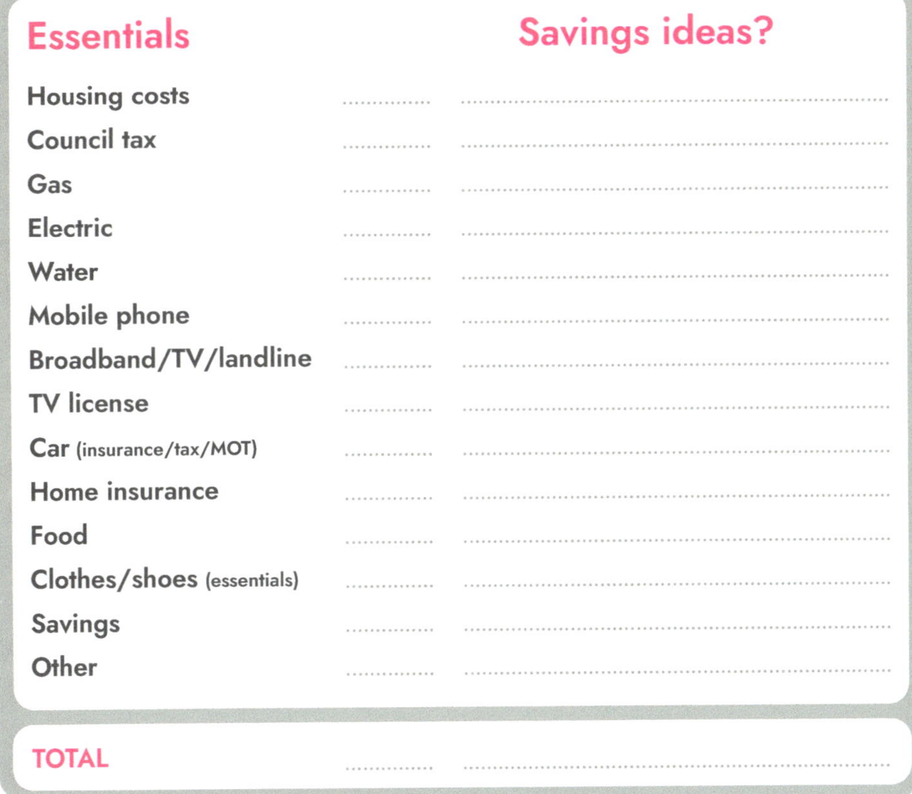

What's coming in?

Salary	Extras	Bank Balance	Total

What's going out?

Essentials

	Savings ideas?
Housing costs	
Council tax	
Gas	
Electric	
Water	
Mobile phone	
Broadband/TV/landline	
TV license	
Car (insurance/tax/MOT)	
Home insurance	
Food	
Clothes/shoes (essentials)	
Savings	
Other	

TOTAL

Debts...

Credit cards	
Loans	
Other	

TOTAL

The Fun Stuff

Gym	
Socialising	
Clothes	
Holidays	
Gifts	
Hair/beauty	
Hobbies	
Other	

TOTAL

Are you getting the best interest rates?

Day to day costs

Lunch/Food	
Travelling	
Drinks	
Extras	

Where are we?

Incomings	
Outgoings	
What's left	

Action plan...

Better With A PLAN | BUDGET PLANNER

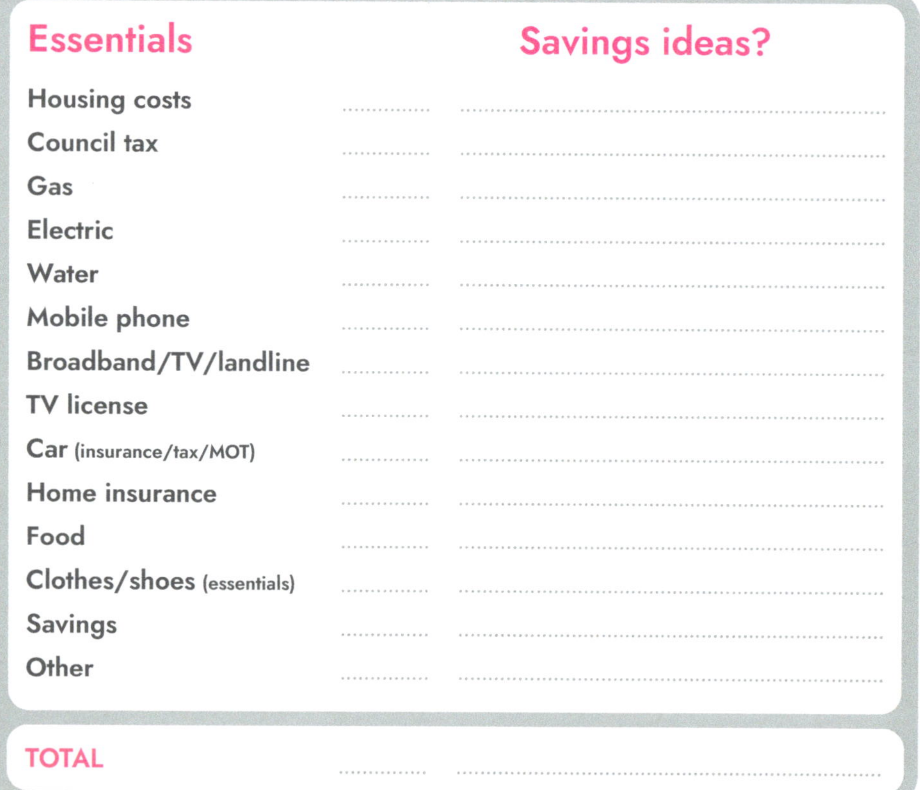

What's coming in?

Salary	Extras	Bank Balance	Total

What's going out?

Essentials / Savings ideas?

Housing costs
Council tax
Gas
Electric
Water
Mobile phone
Broadband/TV/landline
TV license
Car (insurance/tax/MOT)
Home insurance
Food
Clothes/shoes (essentials)
Savings
Other

TOTAL

Day to day costs

Lunch/Food
Travelling
Drinks
Extras

Debts...

Credit cards
Loans
Other

TOTAL

Are you getting the best interest rates?

The Fun Stuff

Gym
Socialising
Clothes
Holidays
Gifts
Hair/beauty
Hobbies
Other

TOTAL

Where are we?

Incomings
Outgoings
What's left

Action plan...

Better With A PLAN | BUDGET PLANNER

What's coming in?

Salary

Extras

Bank Balance

Total

Day to day costs

Lunch/Food ....
Travelling ....
Drinks ....
Extras ....

What's going out?

Are you getting the best interest rates?

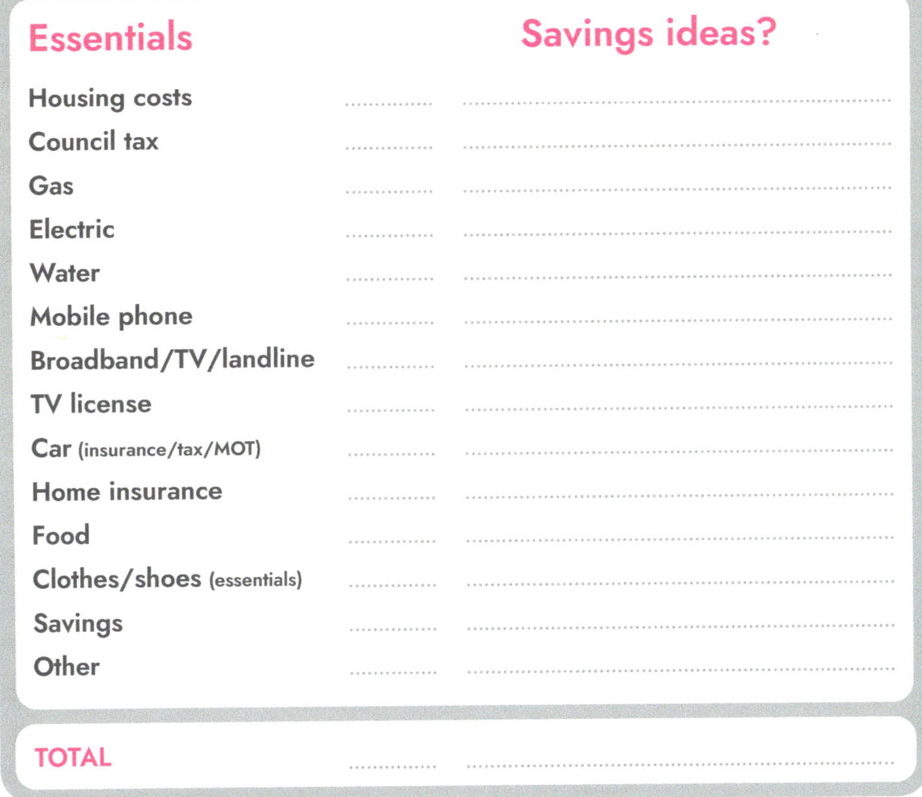

Essentials

Housing costs ....
Council tax ....
Gas ....
Electric ....
Water ....
Mobile phone ....
Broadband/TV/landline ....
TV license ....
Car (insurance/tax/MOT) ....
Home insurance ....
Food ....
Clothes/shoes (essentials) ....
Savings ....
Other ....

Savings ideas?

TOTAL ....

Debts...

Credit cards ....
Loans ....
Other ....

TOTAL ....

The Fun Stuff

Gym ....
Socialising ....
Clothes ....
Holidays ....
Gifts ....
Hair/beauty ....
Hobbies ....
Other ....

TOTAL ....

Where are we?

Incomings ....
Outgoings ....
What's left ....

Action plan...

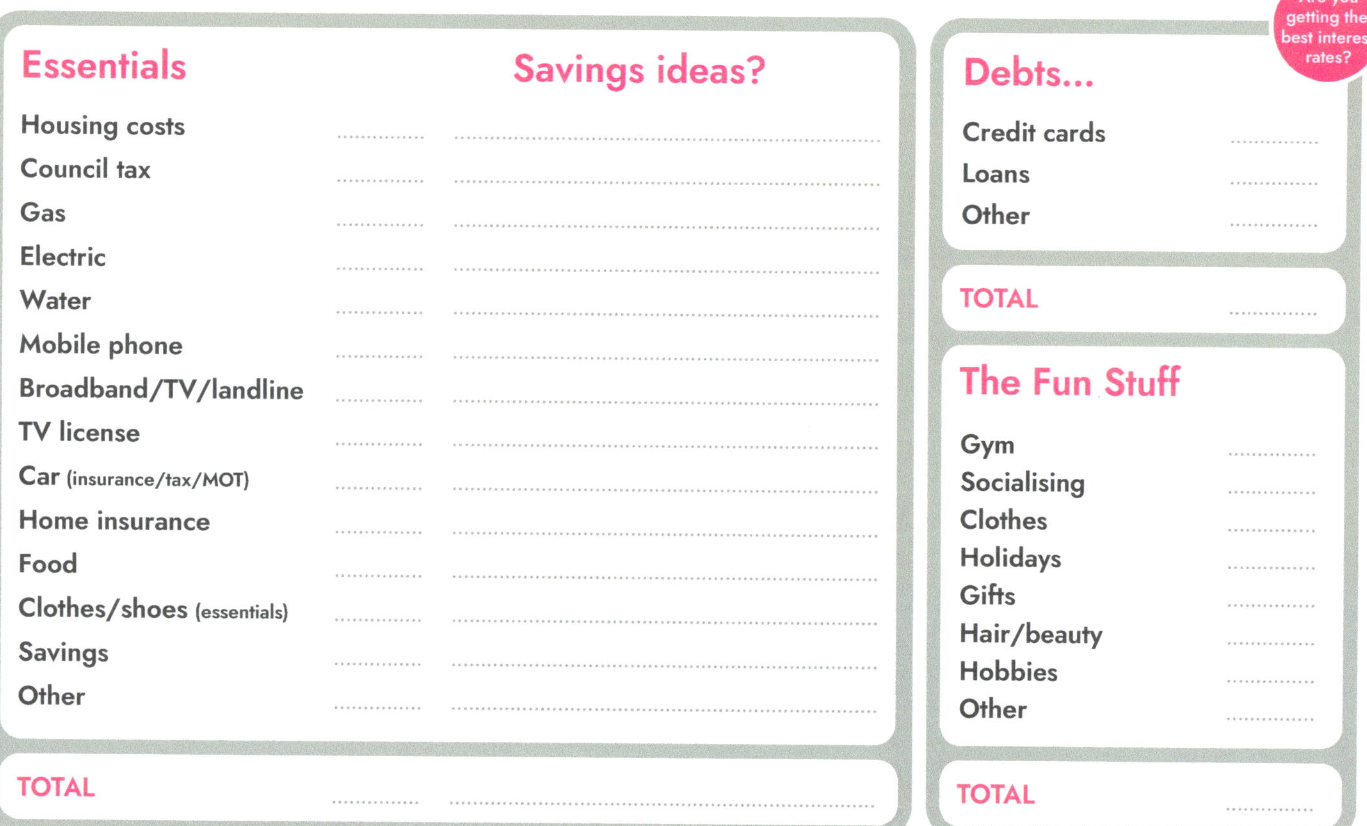

Better With A PLAN | BUDGET PLANNER

What's coming in?

Salary	Extras	Bank Balance	Total

What's going out?

Essentials

Housing costs
Council tax
Gas
Electric
Water
Mobile phone
Broadband/TV/landline
TV license
Car (insurance/tax/MOT)
Home insurance
Food
Clothes/shoes (essentials)
Savings
Other

Savings ideas?

TOTAL

Debts...

Credit cards
Loans
Other

TOTAL

Are you getting the best interest rates?

The Fun Stuff

Gym
Socialising
Clothes
Holidays
Gifts
Hair/beauty
Hobbies
Other

TOTAL

Day to day costs

Lunch/Food
Travelling
Drinks
Extras

Where are we?

Incomings
Outgoings
What's left

Action plan...

Better With A PLAN | BUDGET PLANNER

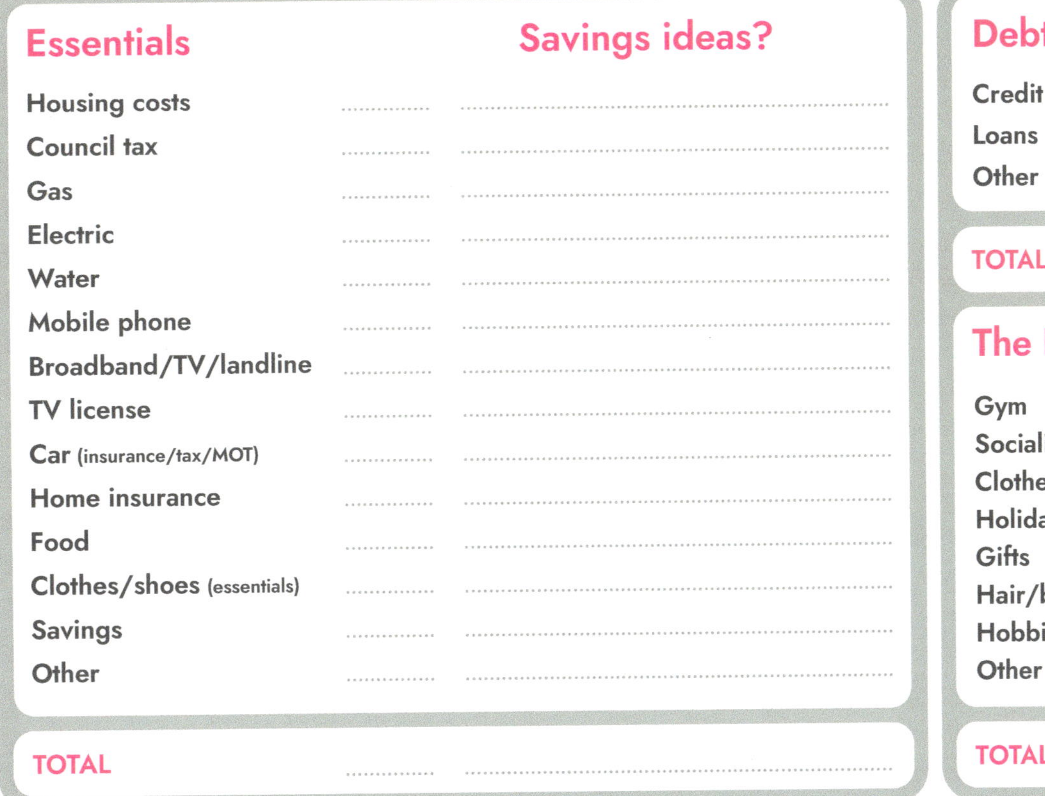

What's coming in?

Salary	Extras	Bank Balance	Total

What's going out?

Day to day costs

Lunch/Food ....
Travelling ....
Drinks ....
Extras ....

Essentials

Housing costs ....
Council tax ....
Gas ....
Electric ....
Water ....
Mobile phone ....
Broadband/TV/landline ....
TV license ....
Car (insurance/tax/MOT) ....
Home insurance ....
Food ....
Clothes/shoes (essentials) ....
Savings ....
Other ....

TOTAL ....

Savings ideas?

Debts...

Are you getting the best interest rates?

Credit cards ....
Loans ....
Other ....

TOTAL ....

The Fun Stuff

Gym ....
Socialising ....
Clothes ....
Holidays ....
Gifts ....
Hair/beauty ....
Hobbies ....
Other ....

TOTAL ....

Where are we?

Incomings ....
Outgoings ....
What's left ....

Action plan...

Better With A PLAN | BUDGET PLANNER

What's coming in?

| Salary | Extras | Bank Balance | Total |

What's going out?

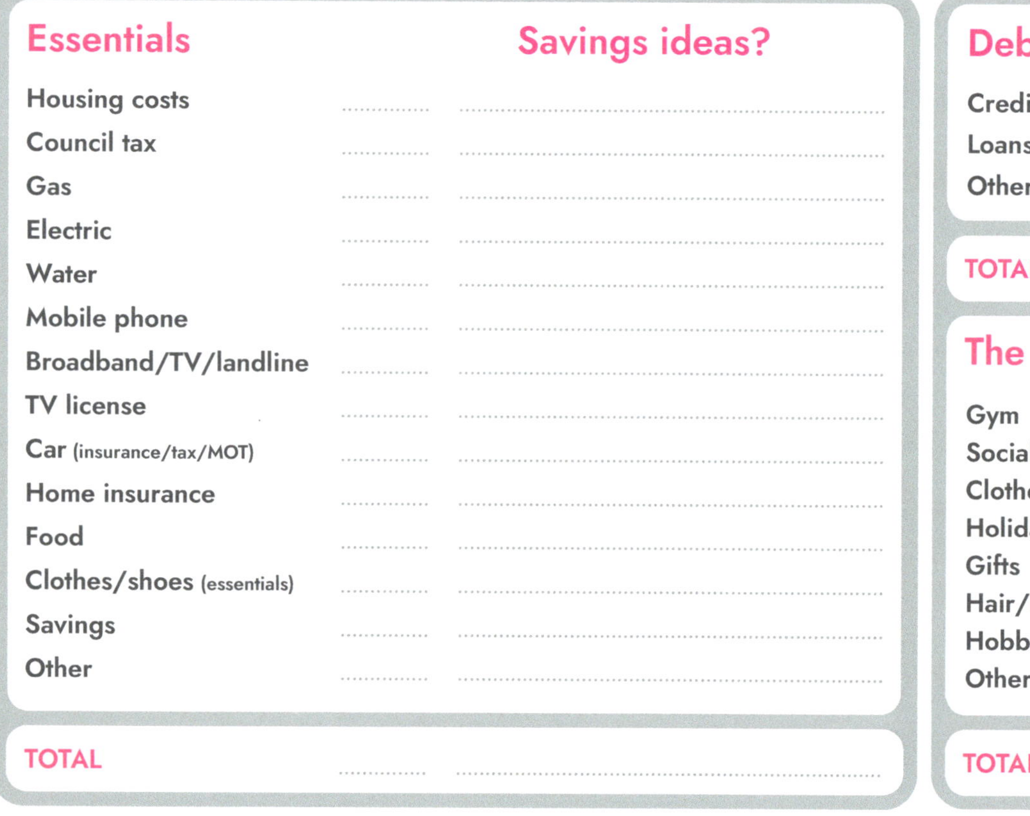

Essentials

Housing costs
Council tax
Gas
Electric
Water
Mobile phone
Broadband/TV/landline
TV license
Car (insurance/tax/MOT)
Home insurance
Food
Clothes/shoes (essentials)
Savings
Other

Savings ideas?

TOTAL

Debts...

Credit cards
Loans
Other

TOTAL

The Fun Stuff

Gym
Socialising
Clothes
Holidays
Gifts
Hair/beauty
Hobbies
Other

TOTAL

Are you getting the best interest rates?

Day to day costs

Lunch/Food
Travelling
Drinks
Extras

Where are we?

Incomings
Outgoings
What's left

Action plan...

Better With A PLAN | BUDGET PLANNER

What's coming in?

Salary	Extras	Bank Balance	Total

What's going out?

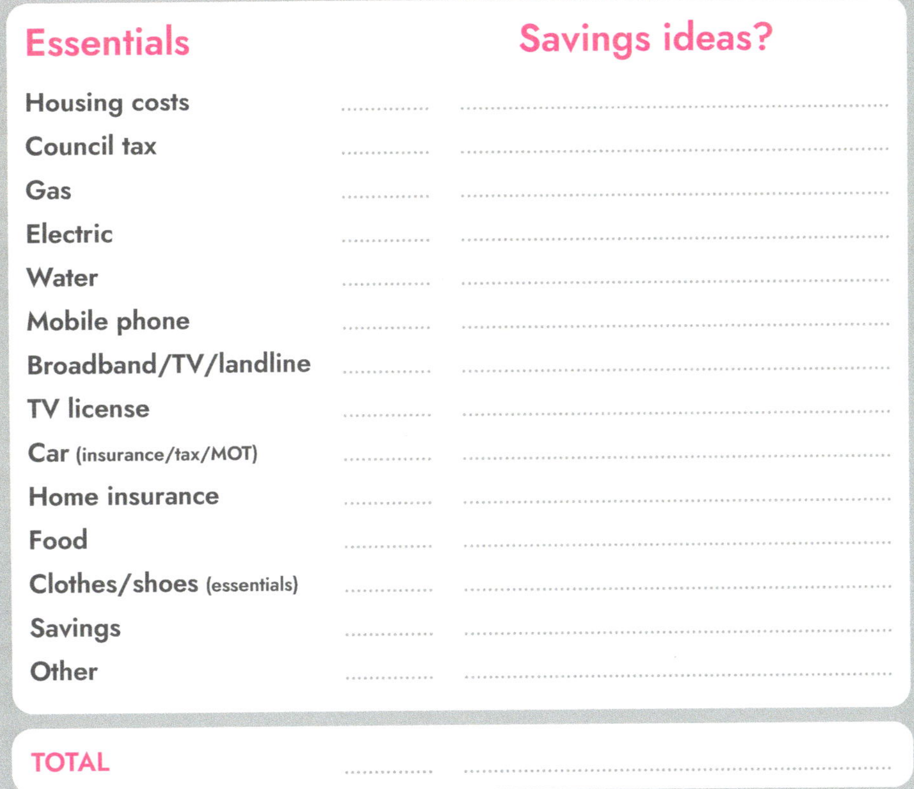

Essentials

	Savings ideas?
Housing costs	
Council tax	
Gas	
Electric	
Water	
Mobile phone	
Broadband/TV/landline	
TV license	
Car (insurance/tax/MOT)	
Home insurance	
Food	
Clothes/shoes (essentials)	
Savings	
Other	

TOTAL

Debts...

Credit cards	
Loans	
Other	

TOTAL

Are you getting the best interest rates?

The Fun Stuff

Gym	
Socialising	
Clothes	
Holidays	
Gifts	
Hair/beauty	
Hobbies	
Other	

TOTAL

Day to day costs

Lunch/Food	
Travelling	
Drinks	
Extras	

Where are we?

Incomings	
Outgoings	
What's left	

Action plan...

Better With A PLAN | BUDGET PLANNER

What's coming in?

Salary	Extras	Bank Balance	Total

What's going out?

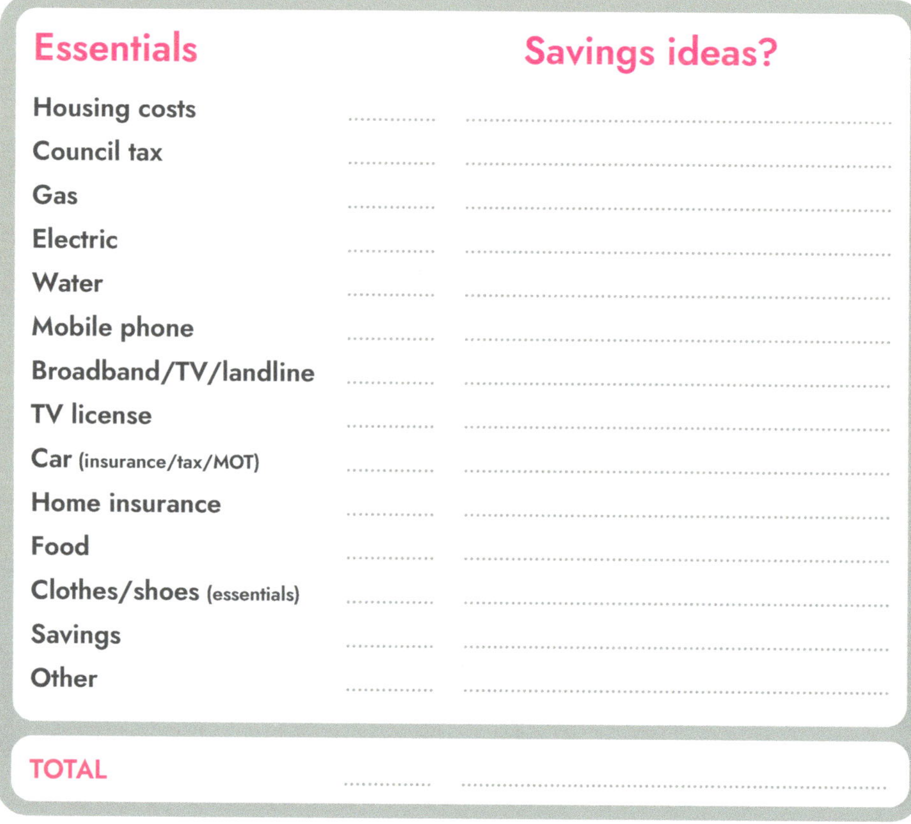

Essentials | Savings ideas?

- Housing costs
- Council tax
- Gas
- Electric
- Water
- Mobile phone
- Broadband/TV/landline
- TV license
- Car (insurance/tax/MOT)
- Home insurance
- Food
- Clothes/shoes (essentials)
- Savings
- Other

TOTAL

Debts...

- Credit cards
- Loans
- Other

TOTAL

The Fun Stuff

- Gym
- Socialising
- Clothes
- Holidays
- Gifts
- Hair/beauty
- Hobbies
- Other

TOTAL

Are you getting the best interest rates?

Day to day costs

- Lunch/Food
- Travelling
- Drinks
- Extras

Where are we?

- Incomings
- Outgoings
- What's left

Action plan...

Better With A PLAN | BUDGET PLANNER

What's coming in?

Salary	Extras	Bank Balance	Total

What's going out?

Essentials

	Savings ideas?
Housing costs	
Council tax	
Gas	
Electric	
Water	
Mobile phone	
Broadband/TV/landline	
TV license	
Car (insurance/tax/MOT)	
Home insurance	
Food	
Clothes/shoes (essentials)	
Savings	
Other	

TOTAL

Day to day costs

Lunch/Food ....
Travelling ....
Drinks ....
Extras ....

Are you getting the best interest rates?

Debts...

Credit cards ....
Loans ....
Other ....

TOTAL ....

The Fun Stuff

Gym ....
Socialising ....
Clothes ....
Holidays ....
Gifts ....
Hair/beauty ....
Hobbies ....
Other ....

TOTAL ....

Where are we?

Incomings ....
Outgoings ....
What's left ....

Action plan...

Better With A PLAN | BUDGET PLANNER

What's coming in?

Salary

Extras

Bank Balance

Total

What's going out?

Essentials

Housing costs

Council tax

Gas

Electric

Water

Mobile phone

Broadband/TV/landline

TV license

Car (insurance/tax/MOT)

Home insurance

Food

Clothes/shoes (essentials)

Savings

Other

TOTAL

Savings ideas?

Debts...

Credit cards

Loans

Other

TOTAL

The Fun Stuff

Gym

Socialising

Clothes

Holidays

Gifts

Hair/beauty

Hobbies

Other

TOTAL

Are you getting the best interest rates?

Day to day costs

Lunch/Food

Travelling

Drinks

Extras

Where are we?

Incomings

Outgoings

What's left

Action plan...

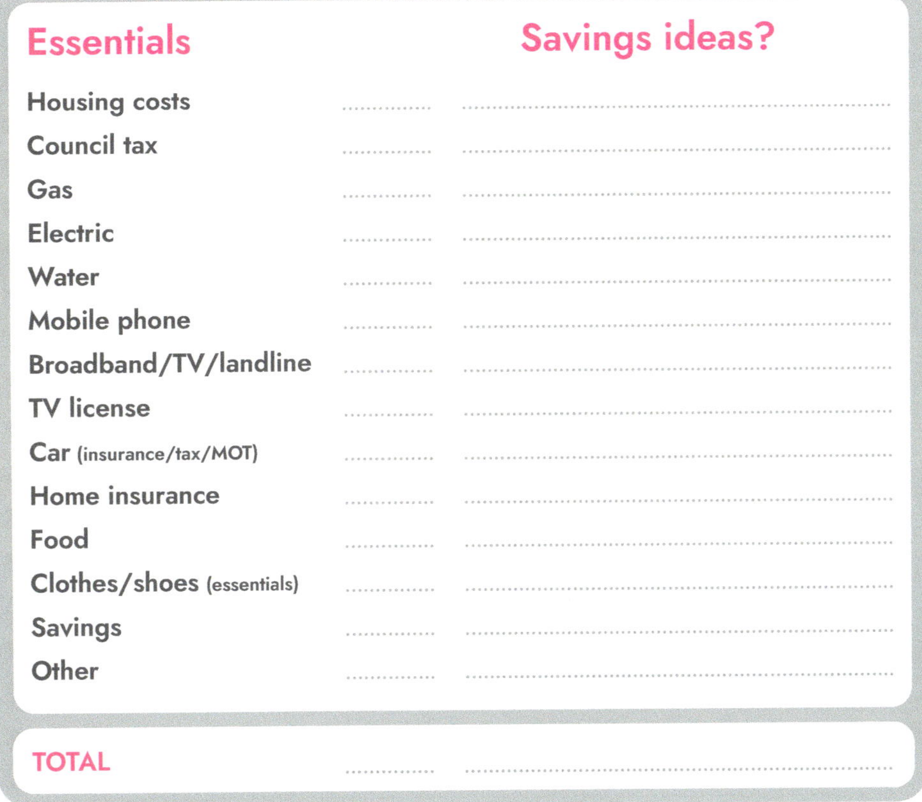

Better With A PLAN | BUDGET PLANNER

What's coming in?

Salary	Extras	Bank Balance	Total

What's going out?

Essentials

Housing costs
Council tax
Gas
Electric
Water
Mobile phone
Broadband/TV/landline
TV license
Car (insurance/tax/MOT)
Home insurance
Food
Clothes/shoes (essentials)
Savings
Other

TOTAL

Savings ideas?

Debts...

Credit cards
Loans
Other

TOTAL

The Fun Stuff

Gym
Socialising
Clothes
Holidays
Gifts
Hair/beauty
Hobbies
Other

TOTAL

Are you getting the best interest rates?

Day to day costs

Lunch/Food
Travelling
Drinks
Extras

Where are we?

Incomings
Outgoings
What's left

Action plan...

BUDGET PLANNER

What's coming in?

Salary | Extras | Bank Balance | Total

What's going out?

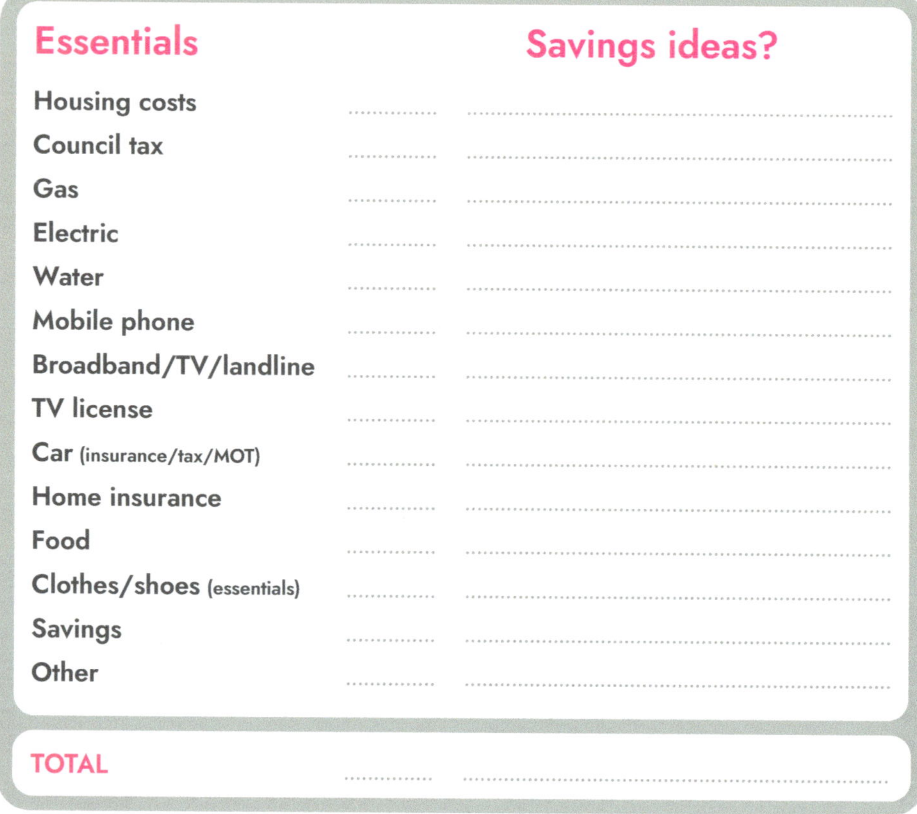

Essentials

Housing costs
Council tax
Gas
Electric
Water
Mobile phone
Broadband/TV/landline
TV license
Car (insurance/tax/MOT)
Home insurance
Food
Clothes/shoes (essentials)
Savings
Other

TOTAL

Savings ideas?

Day to day costs

Lunch/Food
Travelling
Drinks
Extras

Are you getting the best interest rates?

Debts...

Credit cards
Loans
Other

TOTAL

The Fun Stuff

Gym
Socialising
Clothes
Holidays
Gifts
Hair/beauty
Hobbies
Other

TOTAL

Where are we?

Incomings
Outgoings
What's left

Action plan...

Better With A PLAN | BUDGET PLANNER

What's coming in?

Salary	Extras	Bank Balance	Total

What's going out?

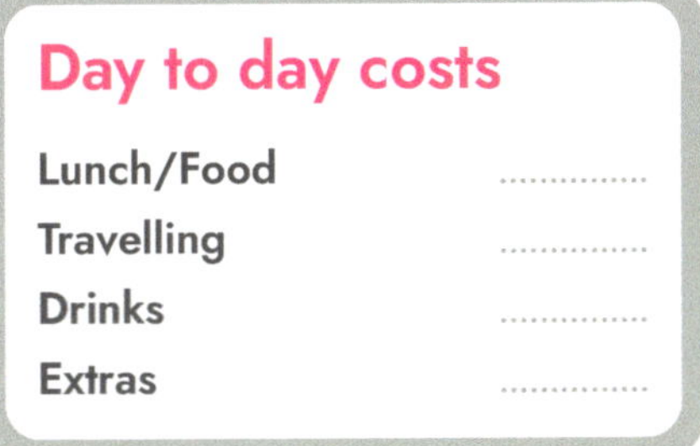

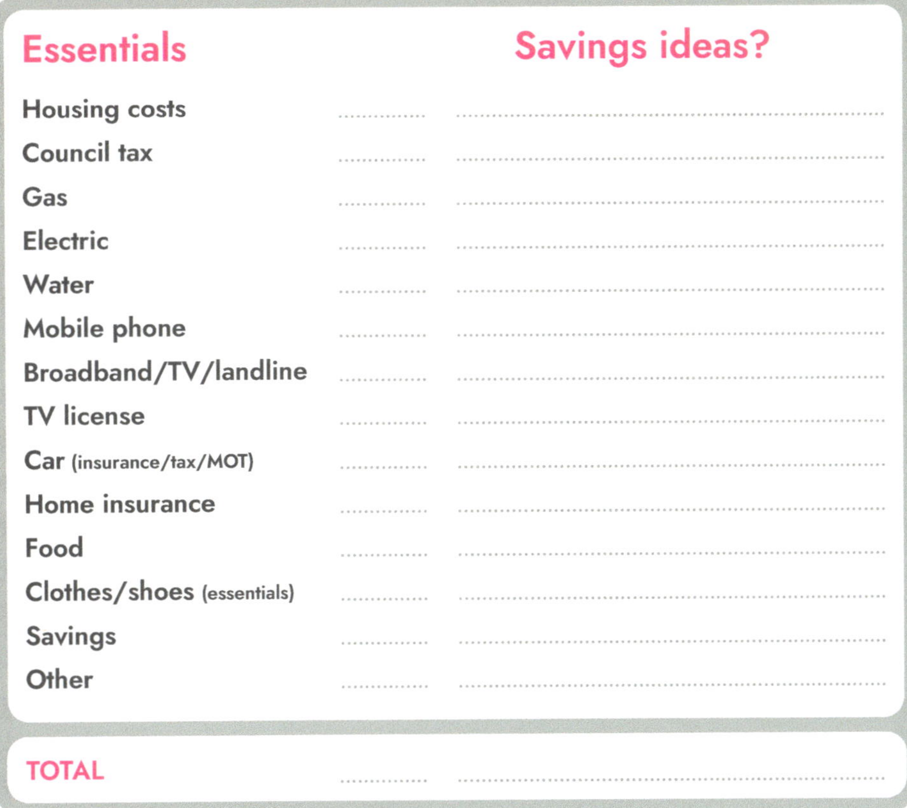

Essentials

Savings ideas?

- Housing costs
- Council tax
- Gas
- Electric
- Water
- Mobile phone
- Broadband/TV/landline
- TV license
- Car (insurance/tax/MOT)
- Home insurance
- Food
- Clothes/shoes (essentials)
- Savings
- Other

TOTAL

Debts...

- Credit cards
- Loans
- Other

TOTAL

The Fun Stuff

- Gym
- Socialising
- Clothes
- Holidays
- Gifts
- Hair/beauty
- Hobbies
- Other

TOTAL

Day to day costs

- Lunch/Food
- Travelling
- Drinks
- Extras

Where are we?

- Incomings
- Outgoings
- What's left

Action plan...

Better With A PLAN | BUDGET PLANNER

What's coming in?

Salary	Extras	Bank Balance	Total

What's going out?

Essentials

Savings ideas?

- Housing costs
- Council tax
- Gas
- Electric
- Water
- Mobile phone
- Broadband/TV/landline
- TV license
- Car (insurance/tax/MOT)
- Home insurance
- Food
- Clothes/shoes (essentials)
- Savings
- Other

TOTAL

Debts...

- Credit cards
- Loans
- Other

TOTAL

The Fun Stuff

- Gym
- Socialising
- Clothes
- Holidays
- Gifts
- Hair/beauty
- Hobbies
- Other

TOTAL

Are you getting the best interest rates?

Day to day costs

- Lunch/Food
- Travelling
- Drinks
- Extras

Where are we?

- Incomings
- Outgoings
- What's left

Action plan...

Better With A PLAN | BUDGET PLANNER

What's coming in?

Salary	Extras	Bank Balance	Total

What's going out?

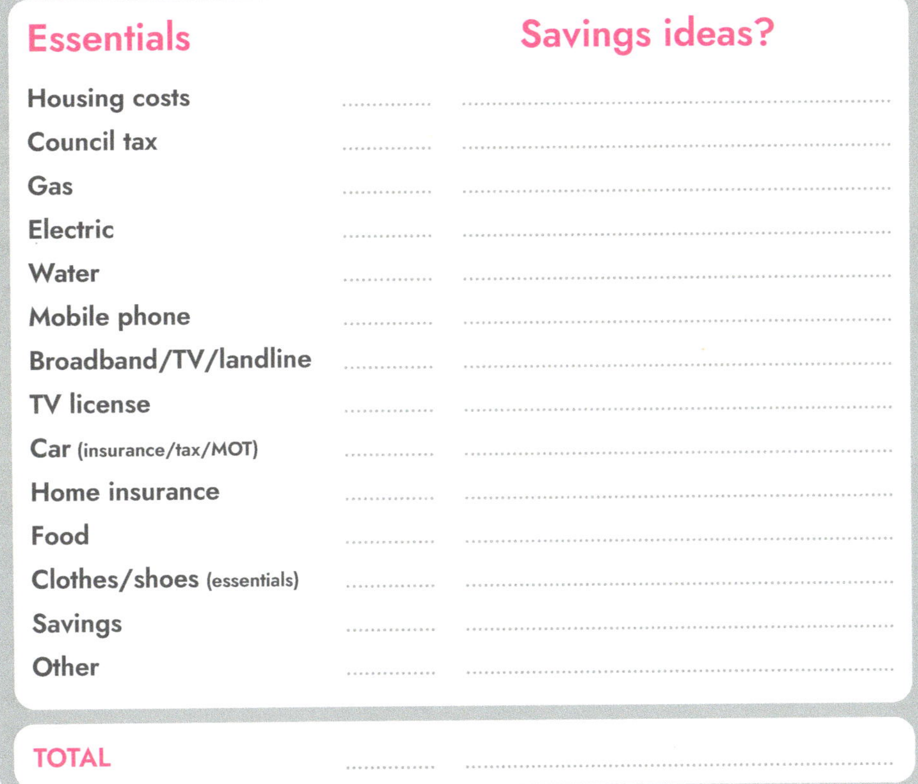

Essentials

	Savings ideas?
Housing costs	
Council tax	
Gas	
Electric	
Water	
Mobile phone	
Broadband/TV/landline	
TV license	
Car (insurance/tax/MOT)	
Home insurance	
Food	
Clothes/shoes (essentials)	
Savings	
Other	

TOTAL

Day to day costs

Lunch/Food	
Travelling	
Drinks	
Extras	

Debts...

Credit cards	
Loans	
Other	

TOTAL

The Fun Stuff

Gym	
Socialising	
Clothes	
Holidays	
Gifts	
Hair/beauty	
Hobbies	
Other	

TOTAL

Where are we?

Incomings	
Outgoings	
What's left	

Action plan...

Better With A PLAN | BUDGET PLANNER

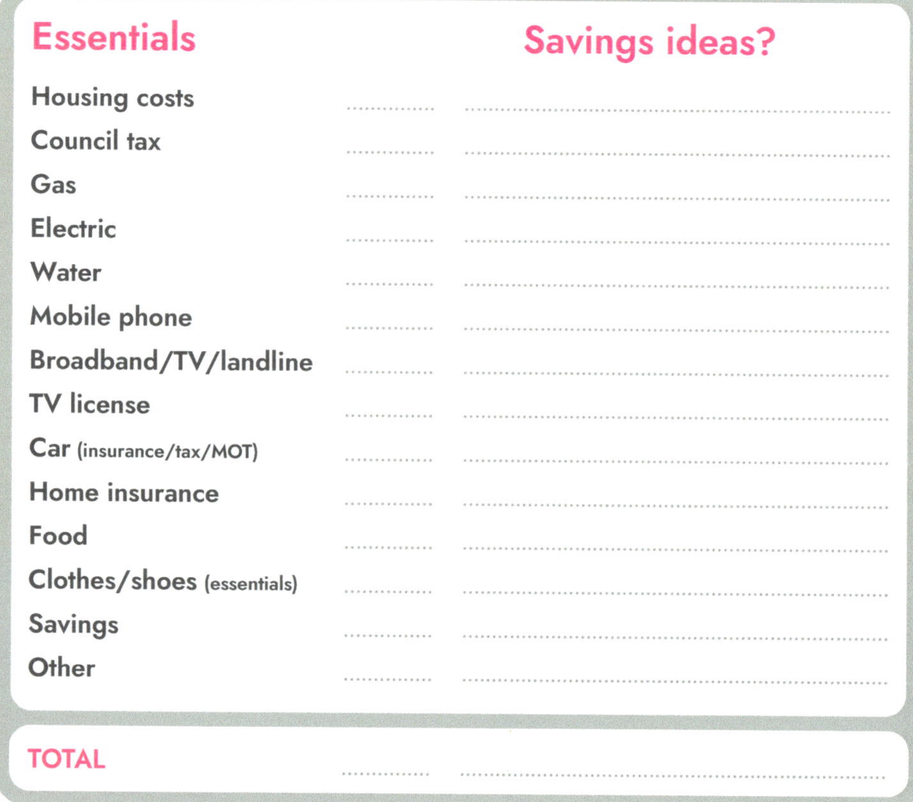

What's coming in?

Salary

Extras

Bank Balance

Total

What's going out?

Essentials

Housing costs

Council tax

Gas

Electric

Water

Mobile phone

Broadband/TV/landline

TV license

Car (insurance/tax/MOT)

Home insurance

Food

Clothes/shoes (essentials)

Savings

Other

Savings ideas?

TOTAL

Debts...

Credit cards

Loans

Other

TOTAL

The Fun Stuff

Gym

Socialising

Clothes

Holidays

Gifts

Hair/beauty

Hobbies

Other

TOTAL

Day to day costs

Lunch/Food

Travelling

Drinks

Extras

Where are we?

Incomings

Outgoings

What's left

Action plan...

Better With A PLAN | BUDGET PLANNER

What's coming in?

Salary | Extras | Bank Balance | Total

What's going out?

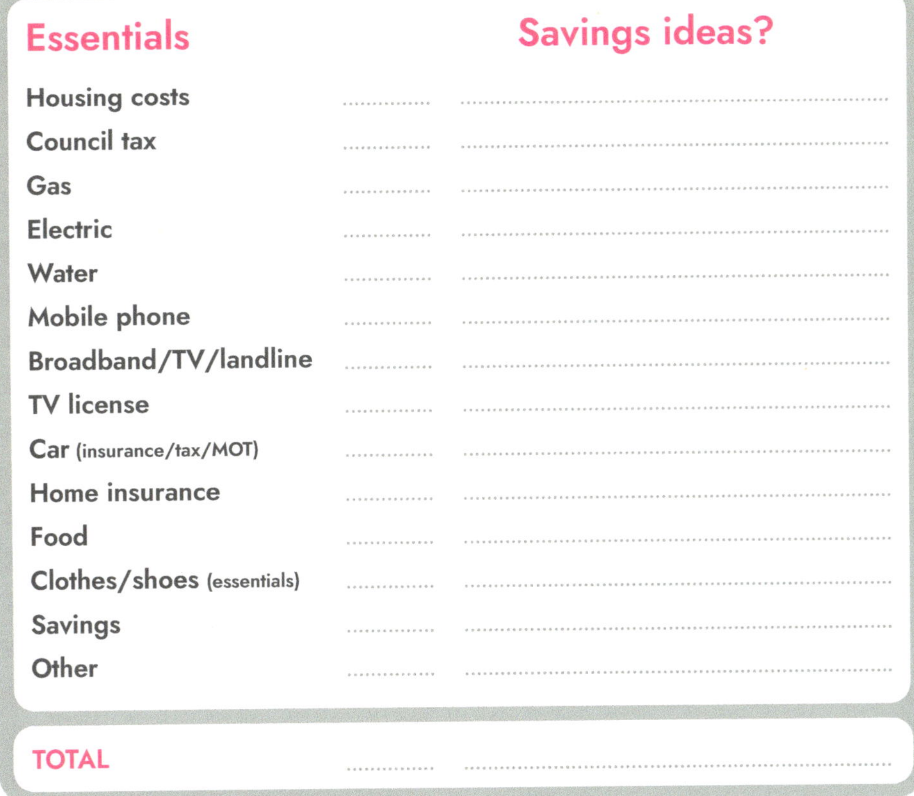

Essentials

Housing costs
Council tax
Gas
Electric
Water
Mobile phone
Broadband/TV/landline
TV license
Car (insurance/tax/MOT)
Home insurance
Food
Clothes/shoes (essentials)
Savings
Other

TOTAL

Savings ideas?

Debts...

Credit cards
Loans
Other

TOTAL

Are you getting the best interest rates?

The Fun Stuff

Gym
Socialising
Clothes
Holidays
Gifts
Hair/beauty
Hobbies
Other

TOTAL

Day to day costs

Lunch/Food
Travelling
Drinks
Extras

Where are we?

Incomings
Outgoings
What's left

Action plan...

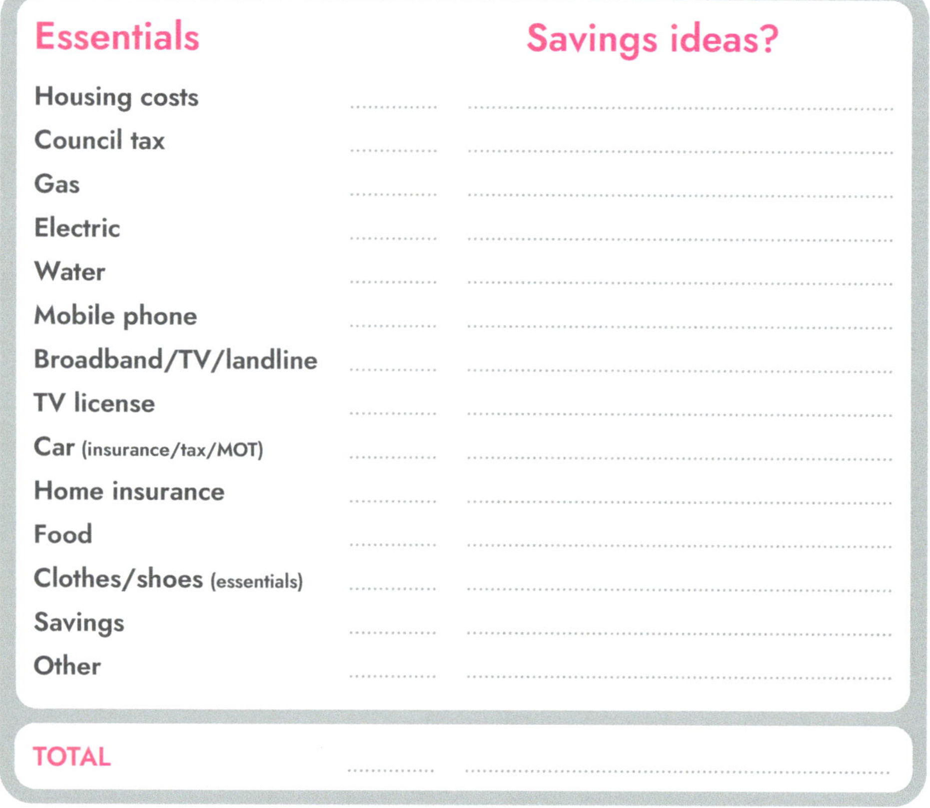

Better With A PLAN | BUDGET PLANNER

What's coming in?

Salary

Extras

Bank Balance

Total

What's going out?

Essentials

Housing costs
Council tax
Gas
Electric
Water
Mobile phone
Broadband/TV/landline
TV license
Car (insurance/tax/MOT)
Home insurance
Food
Clothes/shoes (essentials)
Savings
Other

TOTAL

Savings ideas?

Debts...

Credit cards
Loans
Other

TOTAL

Are you getting the best interest rates?

The Fun Stuff

Gym
Socialising
Clothes
Holidays
Gifts
Hair/beauty
Hobbies
Other

TOTAL

Day to day costs

Lunch/Food
Travelling
Drinks
Extras

Where are we?

Incomings
Outgoings
What's left

Action plan...

Better With A PLAN | BUDGET PLANNER

What's coming in?

| Salary | Extras | Bank Balance | Total |

What's going out?

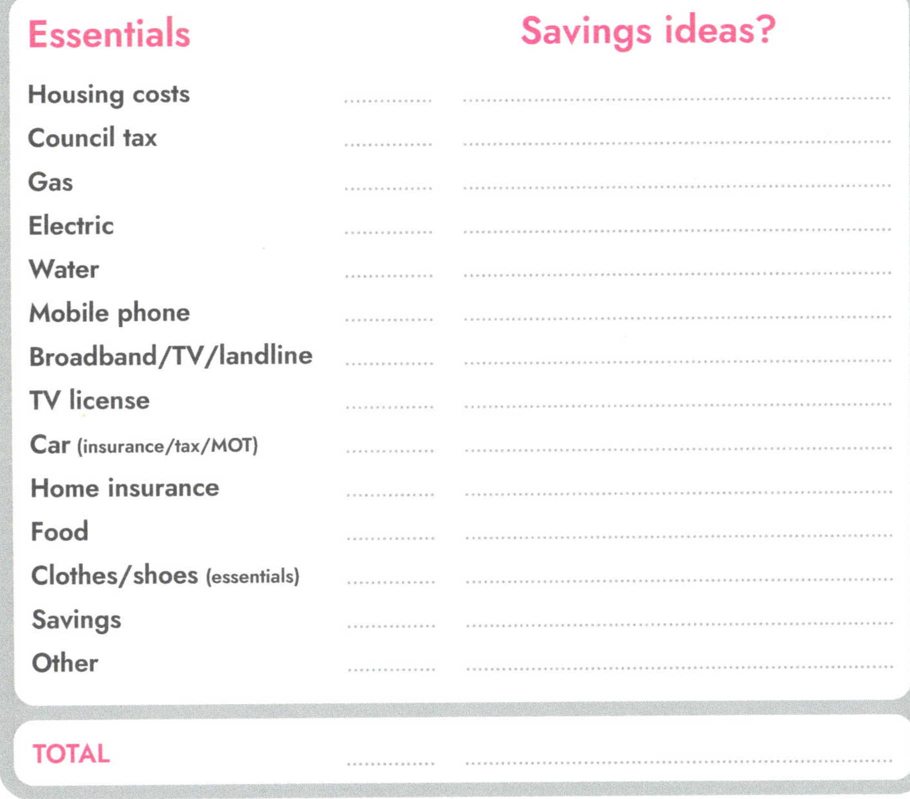

Essentials

Housing costs
Council tax
Gas
Electric
Water
Mobile phone
Broadband/TV/landline
TV license
Car (insurance/tax/MOT)
Home insurance
Food
Clothes/shoes (essentials)
Savings
Other

TOTAL

Savings ideas?

Day to day costs

Lunch/Food
Travelling
Drinks
Extras

Debts...

Credit cards
Loans
Other

TOTAL

Are you getting the best interest rates?

The Fun Stuff

Gym
Socialising
Clothes
Holidays
Gifts
Hair/beauty
Hobbies
Other

TOTAL

Where are we?

Incomings
Outgoings
What's left

Action plan...

86

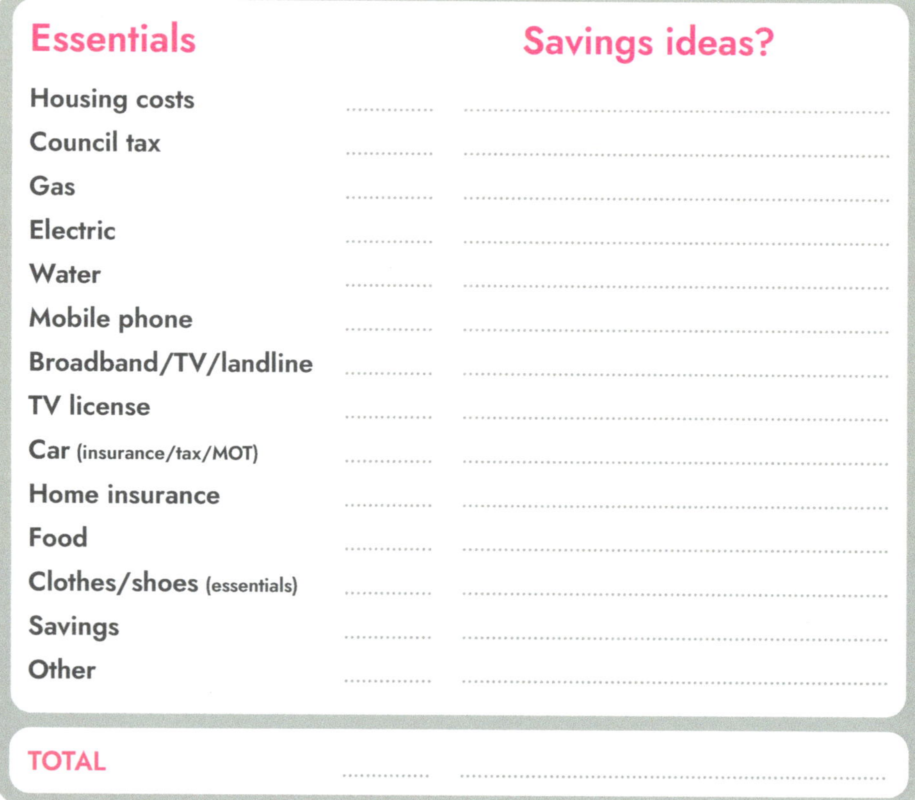

Better With A PLAN | BUDGET PLANNER

What's coming in?

Salary	Extras	Bank Balance	Total

What's going out?

Essentials

Housing costs
Council tax
Gas
Electric
Water
Mobile phone
Broadband/TV/landline
TV license
Car (insurance/tax/MOT)
Home insurance
Food
Clothes/shoes (essentials)
Savings
Other

TOTAL

Savings ideas?

Debts...

Credit cards
Loans
Other

TOTAL

The Fun Stuff

Gym
Socialising
Clothes
Holidays
Gifts
Hair/beauty
Hobbies
Other

TOTAL

Are you getting the best interest rates?

Day to day costs

Lunch/Food
Travelling
Drinks
Extras

Where are we?

Incomings
Outgoings
What's left

Action plan...

Better With A PLAN | BUDGET PLANNER

What's coming in?

Salary	Extras	Bank Balance	Total

What's going out?

Essentials   Savings ideas?

- Housing costs
- Council tax
- Gas
- Electric
- Water
- Mobile phone
- Broadband/TV/landline
- TV license
- Car (insurance/tax/MOT)
- Home insurance
- Food
- Clothes/shoes (essentials)
- Savings
- Other

TOTAL

Debts...

- Credit cards
- Loans
- Other

TOTAL

Are you getting the best interest rates?

The Fun Stuff

- Gym
- Socialising
- Clothes
- Holidays
- Gifts
- Hair/beauty
- Hobbies
- Other

TOTAL

Day to day costs

- Lunch/Food
- Travelling
- Drinks
- Extras

Where are we?

- Incomings
- Outgoings
- What's left

Action plan...

PLAN | BUDGET PLANNER

What's coming in?

Salary

Extras

Bank Balance

Total

What's going out?

Essentials

Housing costs
Council tax
Gas
Electric
Water
Mobile phone
Broadband/TV/landline
TV license
Car (insurance/tax/MOT)
Home insurance
Food
Clothes/shoes (essentials)
Savings
Other

TOTAL

Savings ideas?

Debts...

Credit cards
Loans
Other

TOTAL

Are you getting the best interest rates?

The Fun Stuff

Gym
Socialising
Clothes
Holidays
Gifts
Hair/beauty
Hobbies
Other

TOTAL

Day to day costs

Lunch/Food
Travelling
Drinks
Extras

Where are we?

Incomings
Outgoings
What's left

Action plan...

Better With A PLAN | BUDGET PLANNER

What's coming in?

Salary	Extras	Bank Balance	Total

What's going out?

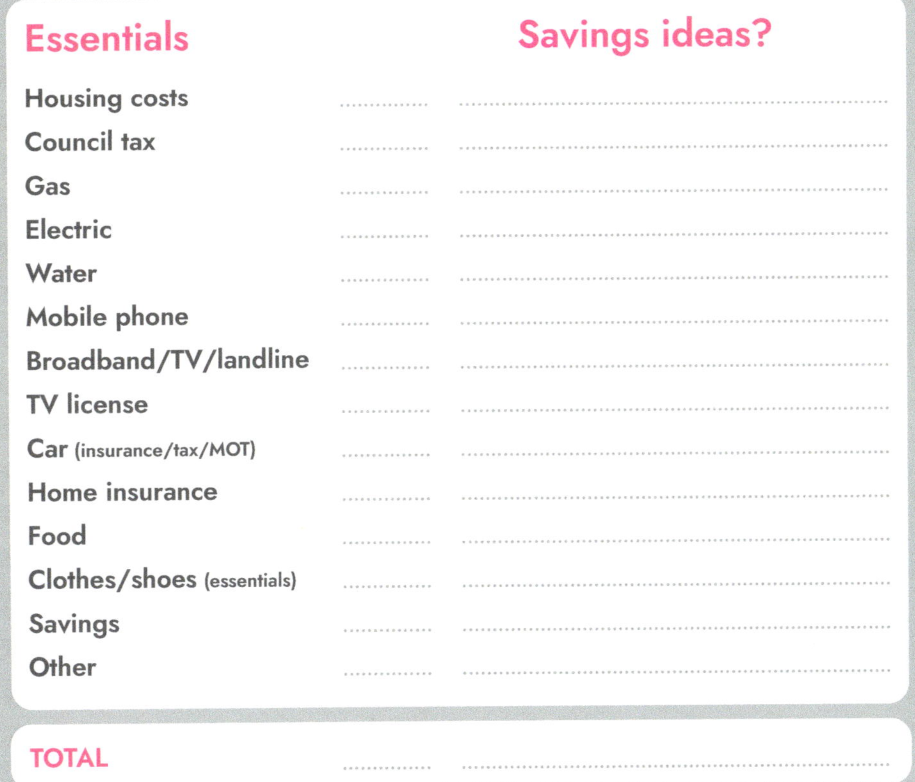

Essentials

Housing costs

Council tax

Gas

Electric

Water

Mobile phone

Broadband/TV/landline

TV license

Car (insurance/tax/MOT)

Home insurance

Food

Clothes/shoes (essentials)

Savings

Other

TOTAL

Savings ideas?

Day to day costs

Lunch/Food

Travelling

Drinks

Extras

Debts...

Credit cards

Loans

Other

TOTAL

Are you getting the best interest rates?

The Fun Stuff

Gym

Socialising

Clothes

Holidays

Gifts

Hair/beauty

Hobbies

Other

TOTAL

Where are we?

Incomings

Outgoings

What's left

Action plan...

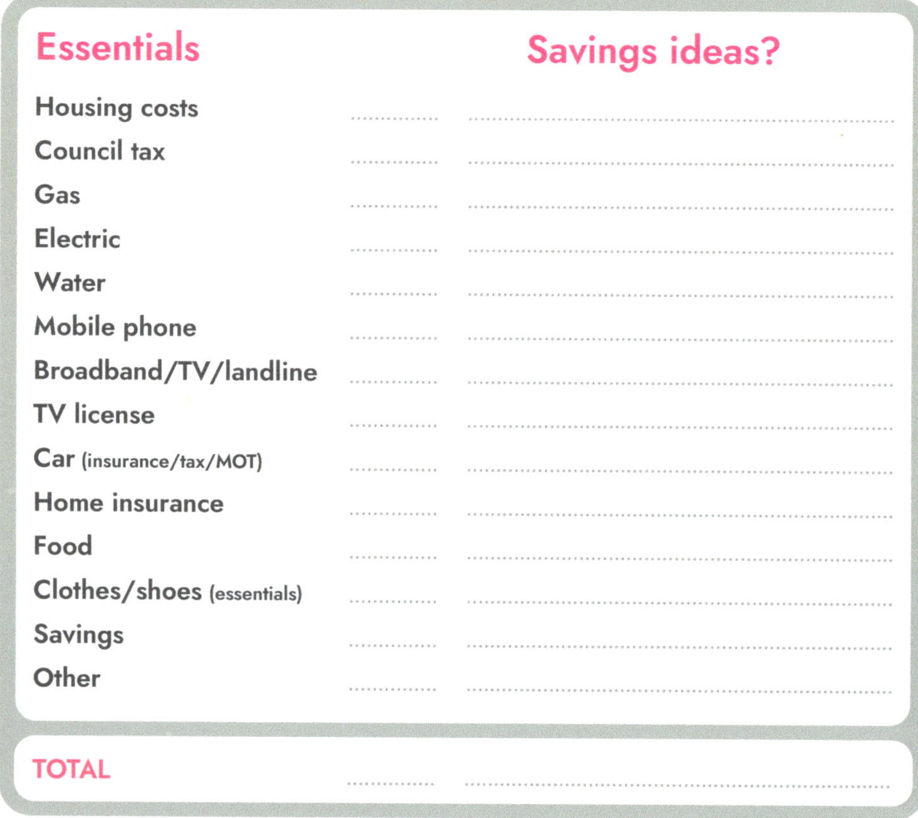

Better With A PLAN | BUDGET PLANNER

What's coming in?

Salary	Extras	Bank Balance	Total

What's going out?

Essentials | Savings ideas?

Housing costs
Council tax
Gas
Electric
Water
Mobile phone
Broadband/TV/landline
TV license
Car (insurance/tax/MOT)
Home insurance
Food
Clothes/shoes (essentials)
Savings
Other

TOTAL

Debts...

Credit cards
Loans
Other

TOTAL

The Fun Stuff

Gym
Socialising
Clothes
Holidays
Gifts
Hair/beauty
Hobbies
Other

TOTAL

Are you getting the best interest rates?

Day to day costs

Lunch/Food
Travelling
Drinks
Extras

Where are we?

Incomings
Outgoings
What's left

Action plan...

Better With A PLAN | BUDGET PLANNER

What's coming in?

Salary

Extras

Bank Balance

Total

What's going out?

Are you getting the best interest rates?

Essentials

Housing costs
Council tax
Gas
Electric
Water
Mobile phone
Broadband/TV/landline
TV license
Car (insurance/tax/MOT)
Home insurance
Food
Clothes/shoes (essentials)
Savings
Other

Savings ideas?

TOTAL

Debts...

Credit cards
Loans
Other

TOTAL

The Fun Stuff

Gym
Socialising
Clothes
Holidays
Gifts
Hair/beauty
Hobbies
Other

TOTAL

Day to day costs

Lunch/Food
Travelling
Drinks
Extras

Where are we?

Incomings
Outgoings
What's left

Action plan...

Better With A PLAN | BUDGET PLANNER

What's coming in?

Salary

Extras

Bank Balance

Total

What's going out?

Essentials

Housing costs
Council tax
Gas
Electric
Water
Mobile phone
Broadband/TV/landline
TV license
Car (insurance/tax/MOT)
Home insurance
Food
Clothes/shoes (essentials)
Savings
Other

TOTAL

Savings ideas?

Debts...

Credit cards
Loans
Other

TOTAL

Are you getting the best interest rates?

The Fun Stuff

Gym
Socialising
Clothes
Holidays
Gifts
Hair/beauty
Hobbies
Other

TOTAL

Day to day costs

Lunch/Food
Travelling
Drinks
Extras

Where are we?

Incomings
Outgoings
What's left

Action plan...

BUDGET PLANNER

Better With A PLAN

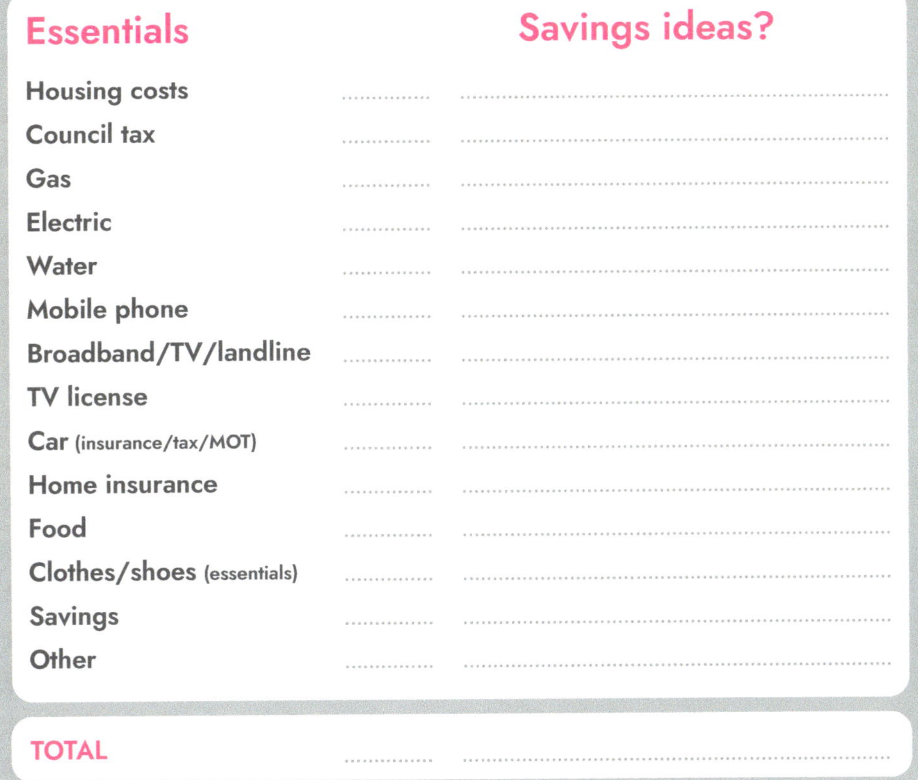

What's coming in?

Salary	Extras	Bank Balance	Total

What's going out?

Essentials

Housing costs
Council tax
Gas
Electric
Water
Mobile phone
Broadband/TV/landline
TV license
Car (insurance/tax/MOT)
Home insurance
Food
Clothes/shoes (essentials)
Savings
Other

Savings ideas?

TOTAL

Debts...

Credit cards
Loans
Other

TOTAL

The Fun Stuff

Gym
Socialising
Clothes
Holidays
Gifts
Hair/beauty
Hobbies
Other

TOTAL

Are you getting the best interest rates?

Day to day costs

Lunch/Food
Travelling
Drinks
Extras

Where are we?

Incomings
Outgoings
What's left

Action plan...

94

Better With A PLAN | BUDGET PLANNER

What's coming in?

Salary

Extras

Bank Balance

Total

What's going out?

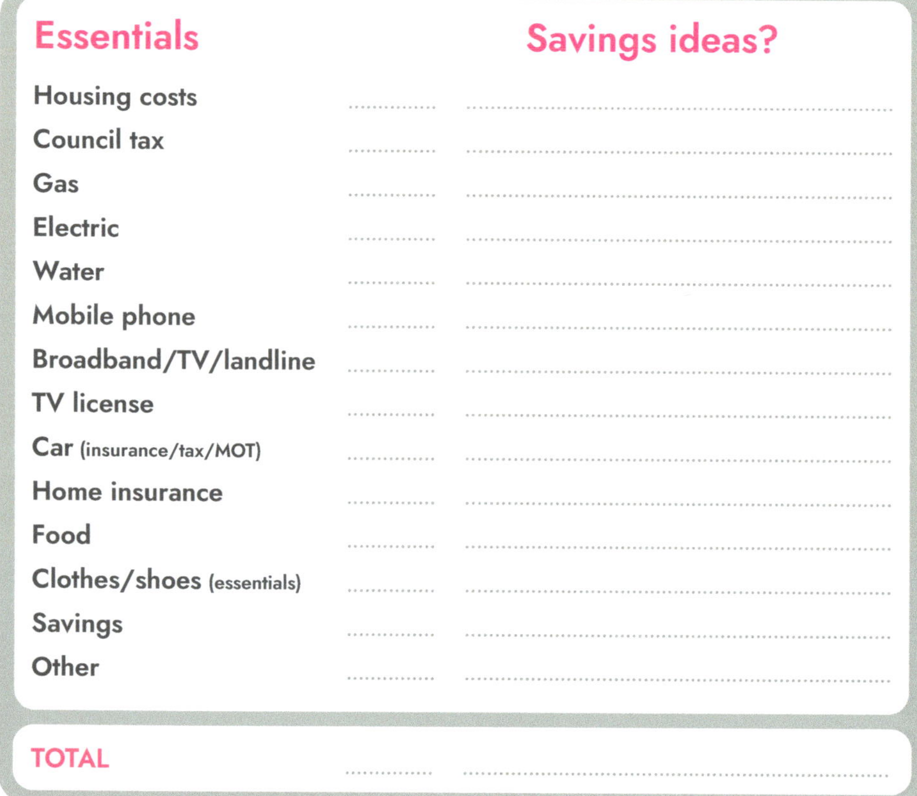

Essentials

Housing costs

Council tax

Gas

Electric

Water

Mobile phone

Broadband/TV/landline

TV license

Car (insurance/tax/MOT)

Home insurance

Food

Clothes/shoes (essentials)

Savings

Other

TOTAL

Savings ideas?

Debts...

Credit cards

Loans

Other

TOTAL

Are you getting the best interest rates?

The Fun Stuff

Gym

Socialising

Clothes

Holidays

Gifts

Hair/beauty

Hobbies

Other

TOTAL

Day to day costs

Lunch/Food

Travelling

Drinks

Extras

Where are we?

Incomings

Outgoings

What's left

Action plan...

Better With A PLAN | BUDGET PLANNER

What's coming in?

| Salary | Extras | Bank Balance | Total |

What's going out?

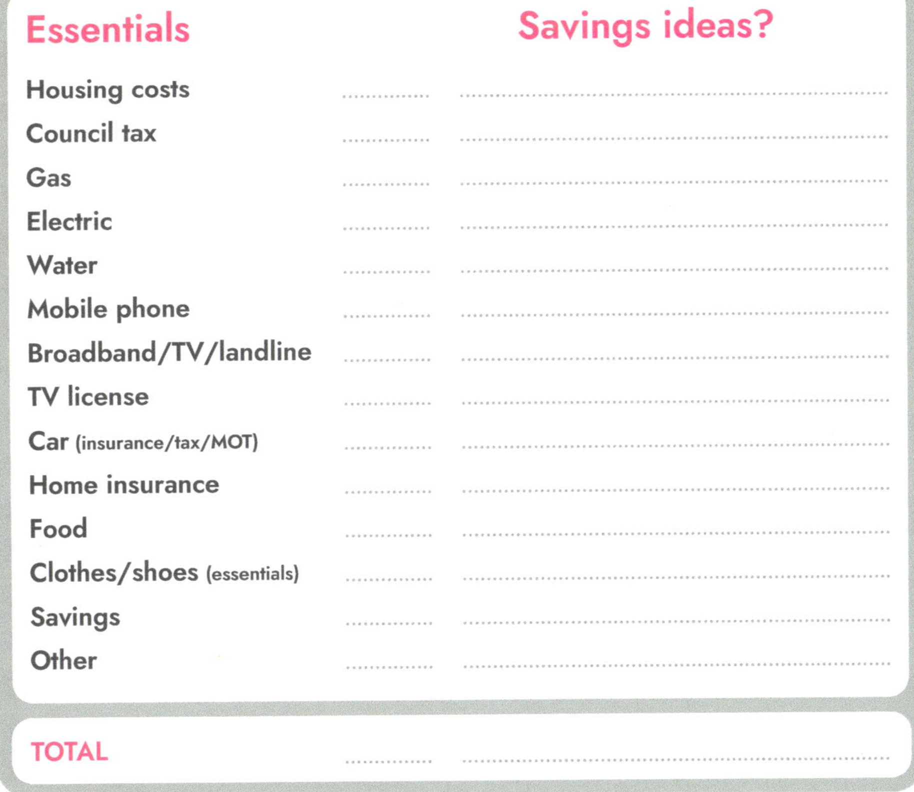

Essentials

Housing costs
Council tax
Gas
Electric
Water
Mobile phone
Broadband/TV/landline
TV license
Car (insurance/tax/MOT)
Home insurance
Food
Clothes/shoes (essentials)
Savings
Other

TOTAL

Savings ideas?

Debts...

Credit cards
Loans
Other

TOTAL

The Fun Stuff

Gym
Socialising
Clothes
Holidays
Gifts
Hair/beauty
Hobbies
Other

TOTAL

Are you getting the best interest rates?

Day to day costs

Lunch/Food
Travelling
Drinks
Extras

Where are we?

Incomings
Outgoings
What's left

Action plan...

Better With A PLAN | BUDGET PLANNER

What's coming in?

Salary

Extras

Bank Balance

Total

What's going out?

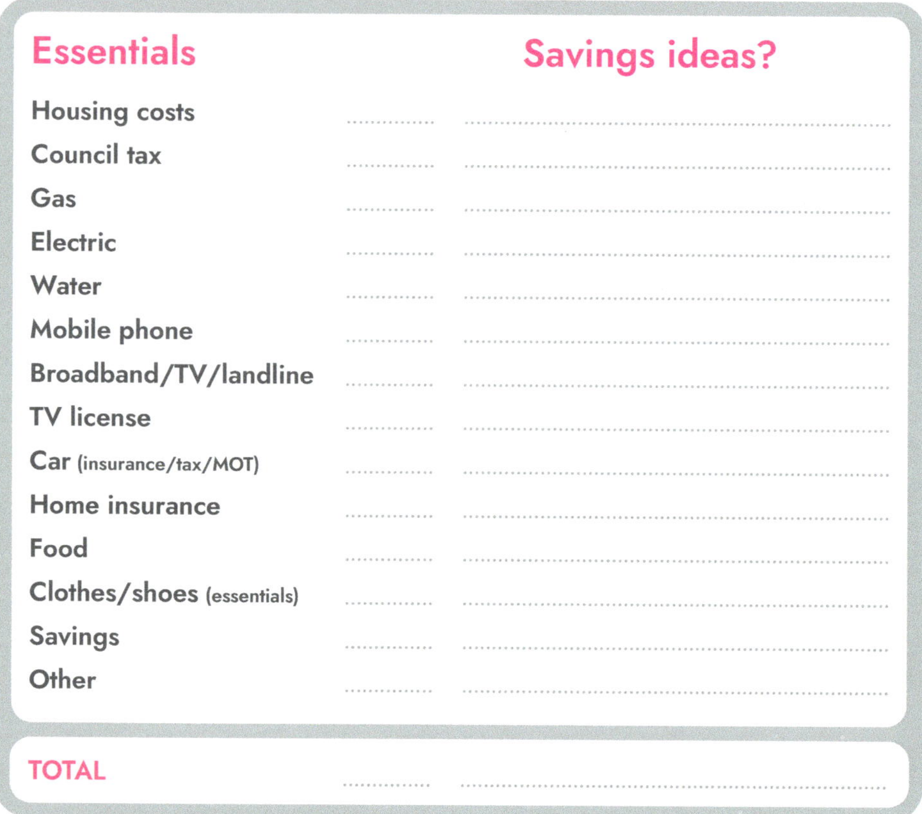

Essentials

Housing costs
Council tax
Gas
Electric
Water
Mobile phone
Broadband/TV/landline
TV license
Car (insurance/tax/MOT)
Home insurance
Food
Clothes/shoes (essentials)
Savings
Other

Savings ideas?

TOTAL

Debts...

Credit cards
Loans
Other

TOTAL

Are you getting the best interest rates?

The Fun Stuff

Gym
Socialising
Clothes
Holidays
Gifts
Hair/beauty
Hobbies
Other

TOTAL

Day to day costs

Lunch/Food
Travelling
Drinks
Extras

Where are we?

Incomings
Outgoings
What's left

Action plan...

What's coming in?

Salary

Extras

Bank Balance

Total

What's going out?

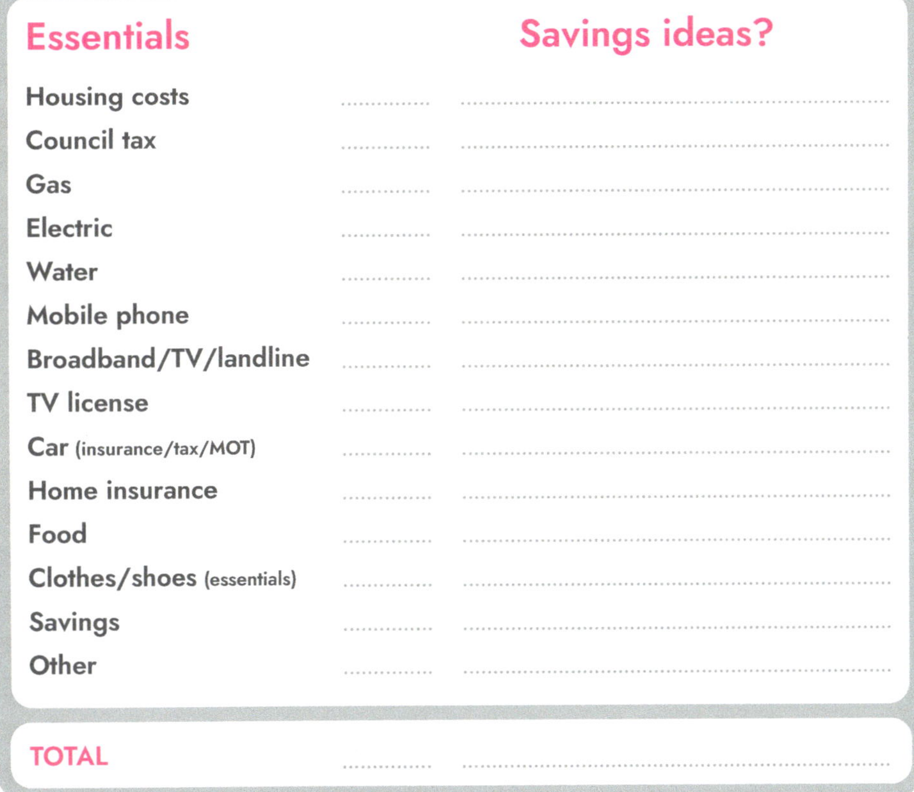

Essentials

Housing costs
Council tax
Gas
Electric
Water
Mobile phone
Broadband/TV/landline
TV license
Car (insurance/tax/MOT)
Home insurance
Food
Clothes/shoes (essentials)
Savings
Other

TOTAL

Savings ideas?

Day to day costs

Lunch/Food
Travelling
Drinks
Extras

Debts...

Are you getting the best interest rates?

Credit cards
Loans
Other

TOTAL

The Fun Stuff

Gym
Socialising
Clothes
Holidays
Gifts
Hair/beauty
Hobbies
Other

TOTAL

Where are we?

Incomings
Outgoings
What's left

Action plan...

Better With A PLAN | BUDGET PLANNER

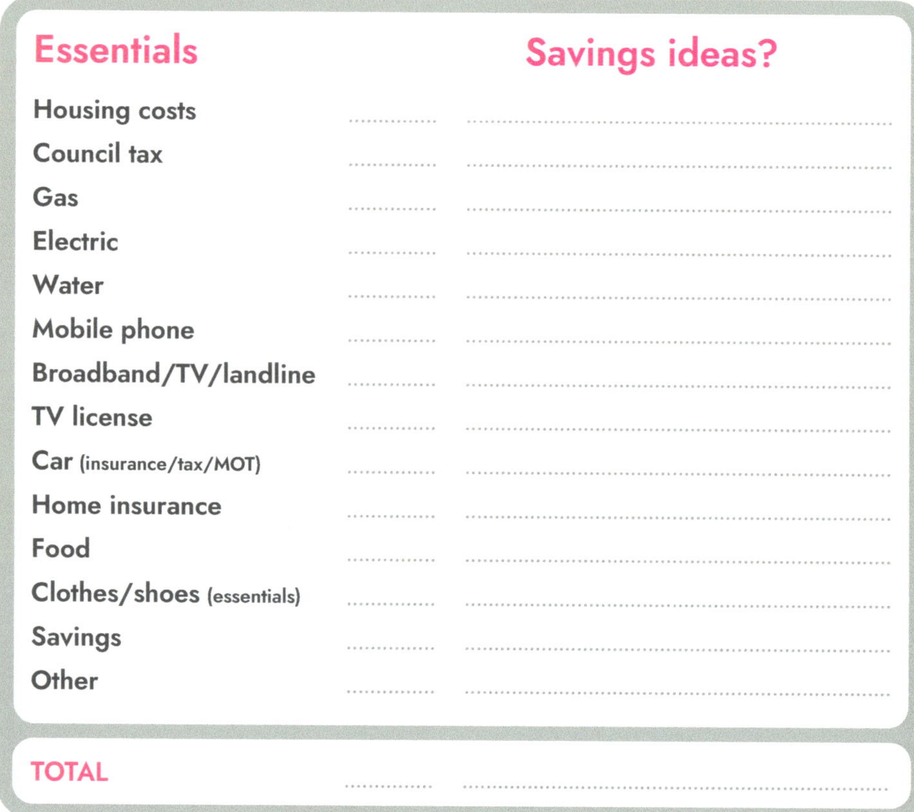

What's coming in?

Salary

Extras

Bank Balance

Total

What's going out?

Essentials

Savings ideas?

Housing costs
Council tax
Gas
Electric
Water
Mobile phone
Broadband/TV/landline
TV license
Car (insurance/tax/MOT)
Home insurance
Food
Clothes/shoes (essentials)
Savings
Other

TOTAL

Debts...

Credit cards
Loans
Other

TOTAL

Are you getting the best interest rates?

The Fun Stuff

Gym
Socialising
Clothes
Holidays
Gifts
Hair/beauty
Hobbies
Other

TOTAL

Day to day costs

Lunch/Food
Travelling
Drinks
Extras

Where are we?

Incomings
Outgoings
What's left

Action plan...

Better With A PLAN | BUDGET PLANNER

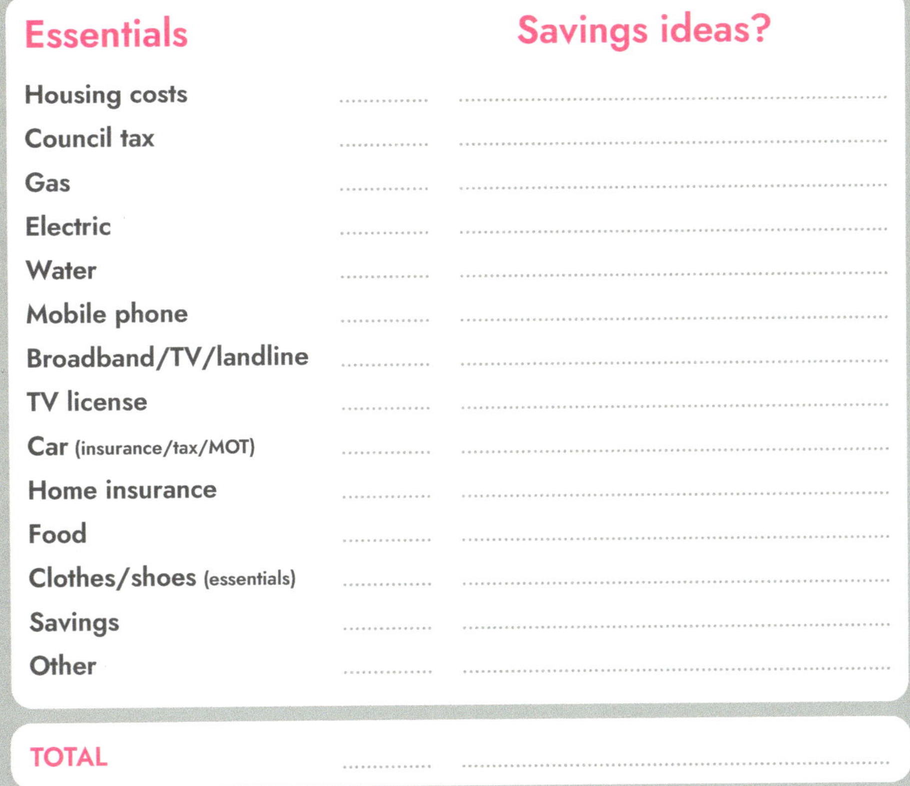

What's coming in?

Salary

Extras

Bank Balance

Total

What's going out?

Essentials

Housing costs

Council tax

Gas

Electric

Water

Mobile phone

Broadband/TV/landline

TV license

Car (insurance/tax/MOT)

Home insurance

Food

Clothes/shoes (essentials)

Savings

Other

TOTAL

Savings ideas?

Debts...

Credit cards

Loans

Other

TOTAL

Are you getting the best interest rates?

The Fun Stuff

Gym

Socialising

Clothes

Holidays

Gifts

Hair/beauty

Hobbies

Other

TOTAL

Day to day costs

Lunch/Food

Travelling

Drinks

Extras

Where are we?

Incomings

Outgoings

What's left

Action plan...

Better With A PLAN | BUDGET PLANNER

What's coming in?

Salary

Extras

Bank Balance

Total

Day to day costs

Lunch/Food
Travelling
Drinks
Extras

What's going out?

Are you getting the best interest rates?

Essentials

Housing costs
Council tax
Gas
Electric
Water
Mobile phone
Broadband/TV/landline
TV license
Car (insurance/tax/MOT)
Home insurance
Food
Clothes/shoes (essentials)
Savings
Other

Savings ideas?

TOTAL

Debts...

Credit cards
Loans
Other

TOTAL

The Fun Stuff

Gym
Socialising
Clothes
Holidays
Gifts
Hair/beauty
Hobbies
Other

TOTAL

Where are we?

Incomings
Outgoings
What's left

Action plan...

BUDGET PLANNER

What's coming in?

Salary

Extras

Bank Balance

Total

What's going out?

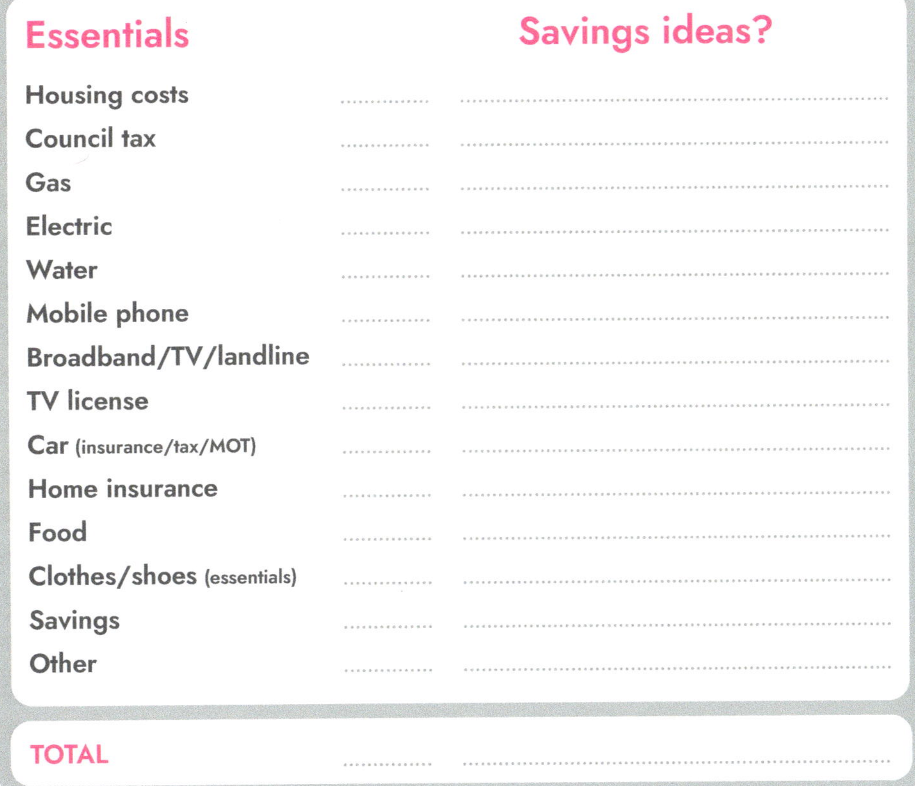

Essentials

Savings ideas?

Housing costs
Council tax
Gas
Electric
Water
Mobile phone
Broadband/TV/landline
TV license
Car (insurance/tax/MOT)
Home insurance
Food
Clothes/shoes (essentials)
Savings
Other

TOTAL

Debts...

Credit cards
Loans
Other

TOTAL

The Fun Stuff

Gym
Socialising
Clothes
Holidays
Gifts
Hair/beauty
Hobbies
Other

TOTAL

Day to day costs

Lunch/Food
Travelling
Drinks
Extras

Where are we?

Incomings
Outgoings
What's left

Action plan...

Better With A PLAN | BUDGET PLANNER

What's coming in?

Salary | Extras | Bank Balance | Total

What's going out?

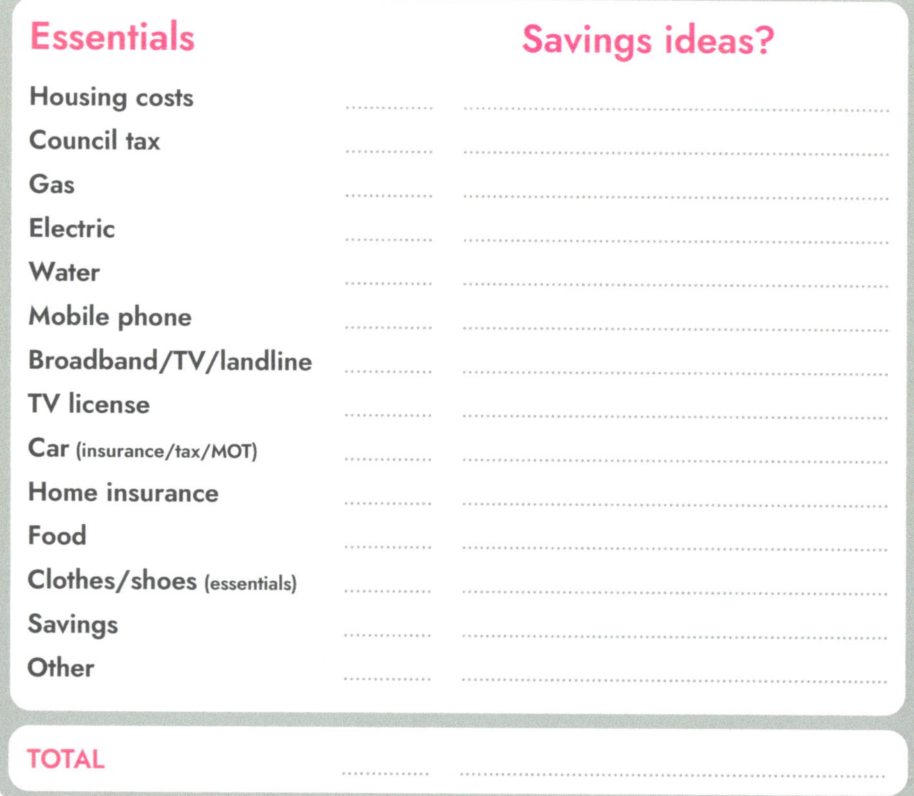

Essentials

Housing costs
Council tax
Gas
Electric
Water
Mobile phone
Broadband/TV/landline
TV license
Car (insurance/tax/MOT)
Home insurance
Food
Clothes/shoes (essentials)
Savings
Other

Savings ideas?

TOTAL

Debts...

Credit cards
Loans
Other

TOTAL

The Fun Stuff

Gym
Socialising
Clothes
Holidays
Gifts
Hair/beauty
Hobbies
Other

TOTAL

Are you getting the best interest rates?

Day to day costs

Lunch/Food
Travelling
Drinks
Extras

Where are we?

Incomings
Outgoings
What's left

Action plan...

Better With A PLAN | BUDGET PLANNER

What's coming in?

| Salary | Extras | Bank Balance | Total |

What's going out?

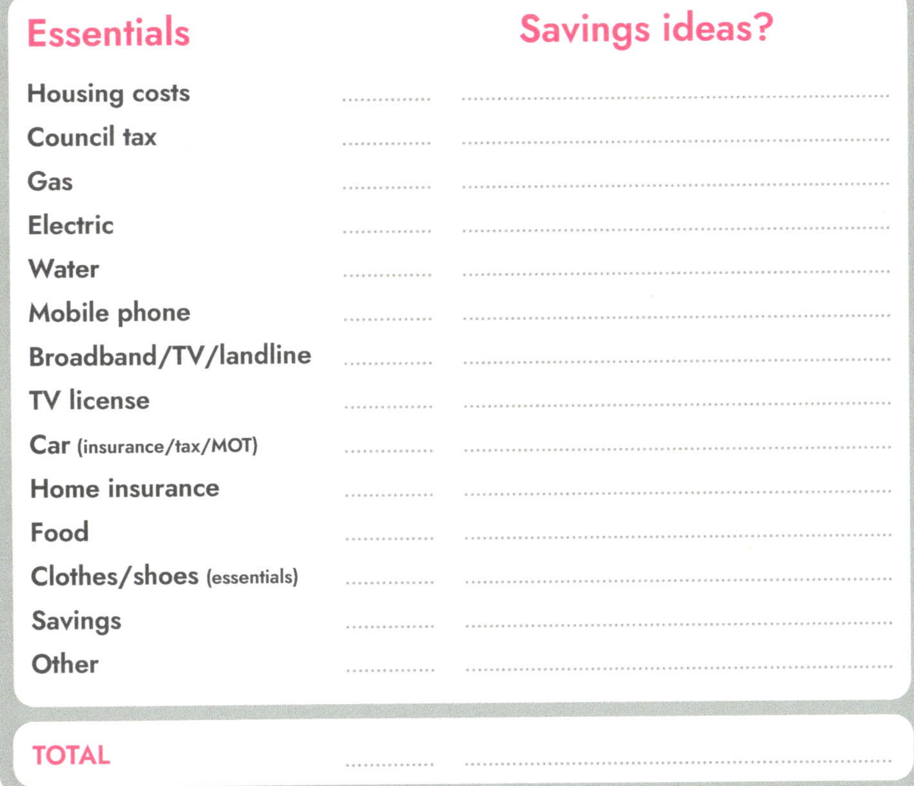

Essentials

Housing costs
Council tax
Gas
Electric
Water
Mobile phone
Broadband/TV/landline
TV license
Car (insurance/tax/MOT)
Home insurance
Food
Clothes/shoes (essentials)
Savings
Other

TOTAL

Savings ideas?

Debts...

Credit cards
Loans
Other

TOTAL

Are you getting the best interest rates?

The Fun Stuff

Gym
Socialising
Clothes
Holidays
Gifts
Hair/beauty
Hobbies
Other

TOTAL

Day to day costs

Lunch/Food
Travelling
Drinks
Extras

Where are we?

Incomings
Outgoings
What's left

Action plan...

Better With A PLAN | BUDGET PLANNER

What's coming in?

Salary

Extras

Bank Balance

Total

What's going out?

Essentials

Housing costs
Council tax
Gas
Electric
Water
Mobile phone
Broadband/TV/landline
TV license
Car (insurance/tax/MOT)
Home insurance
Food
Clothes/shoes (essentials)
Savings
Other

TOTAL

Savings ideas?

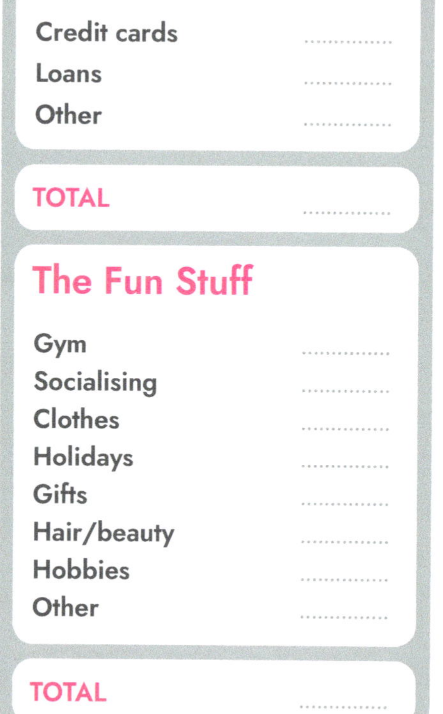

Debts...

Credit cards
Loans
Other

TOTAL

The Fun Stuff

Gym
Socialising
Clothes
Holidays
Gifts
Hair/beauty
Hobbies
Other

TOTAL

Day to day costs

Lunch/Food
Travelling
Drinks
Extras

Where are we?

Incomings
Outgoings
What's left

Action plan...

Better With A **PLAN** | BUDGET PLANNER

What's coming in?

Salary	Extras	Bank Balance	Total

What's going out?

Essentials

Savings ideas?

Housing costs
Council tax
Gas
Electric
Water
Mobile phone
Broadband/TV/landline
TV license
Car (insurance/tax/MOT)
Home insurance
Food
Clothes/shoes (essentials)
Savings
Other

TOTAL

Debts...

Credit cards
Loans
Other

TOTAL

The Fun Stuff

Gym
Socialising
Clothes
Holidays
Gifts
Hair/beauty
Hobbies
Other

TOTAL

Are you getting the best interest rates?

Day to day costs

Lunch/Food
Travelling
Drinks
Extras

Where are we?

Incomings
Outgoings
What's left

Action plan...

Better With A PLAN | BUDGET PLANNER

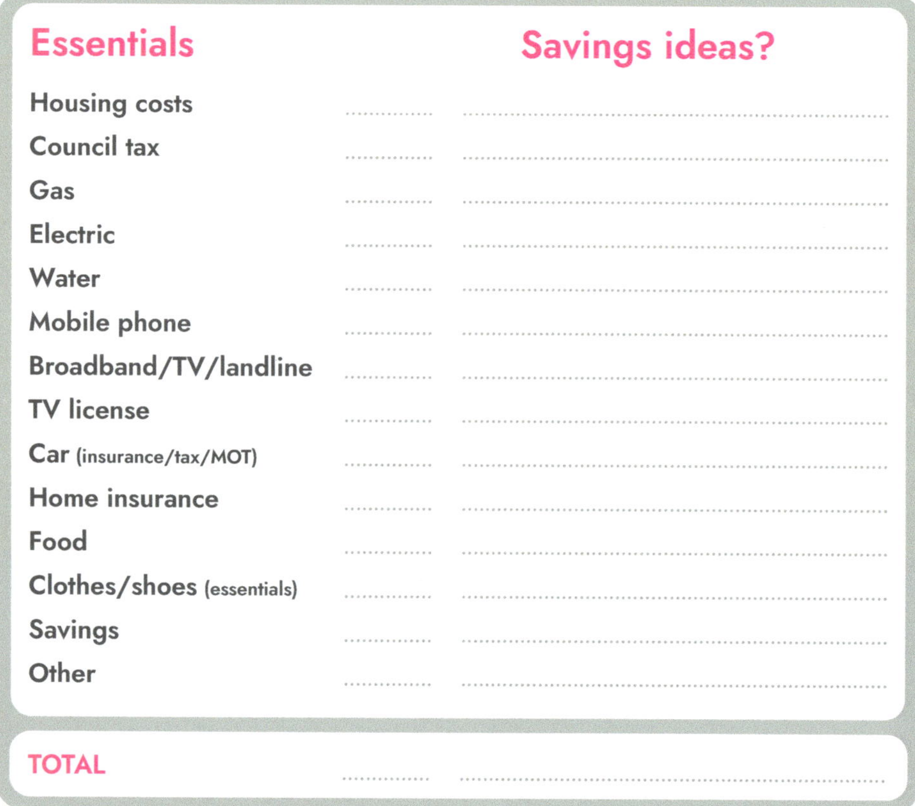

What's coming in?

Salary	Extras	Bank Balance	Total

What's going out?

Essentials | Savings ideas?

- Housing costs
- Council tax
- Gas
- Electric
- Water
- Mobile phone
- Broadband/TV/landline
- TV license
- Car (insurance/tax/MOT)
- Home insurance
- Food
- Clothes/shoes (essentials)
- Savings
- Other

TOTAL

Debts...

- Credit cards
- Loans
- Other

TOTAL

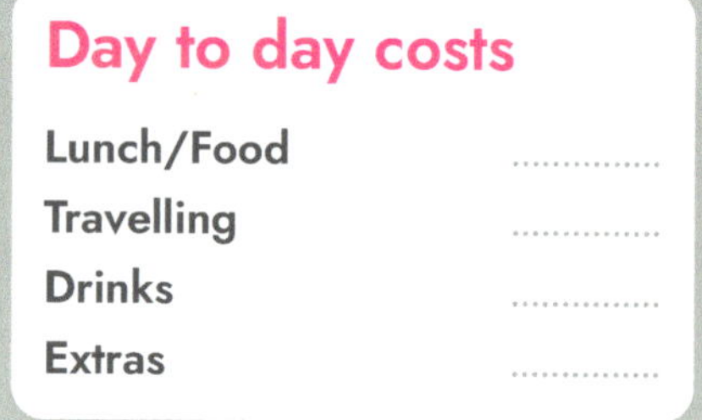

The Fun Stuff

- Gym
- Socialising
- Clothes
- Holidays
- Gifts
- Hair/beauty
- Hobbies
- Other

TOTAL

Day to day costs

- Lunch/Food
- Travelling
- Drinks
- Extras

Where are we?

- Incomings
- Outgoings
- What's left

Action plan...

BUDGET PLANNER

What's coming in?

Salary | Extras | Bank Balance | Total

What's going out?

Day to day costs

Lunch/Food ....
Travelling ....
Drinks ....
Extras ....

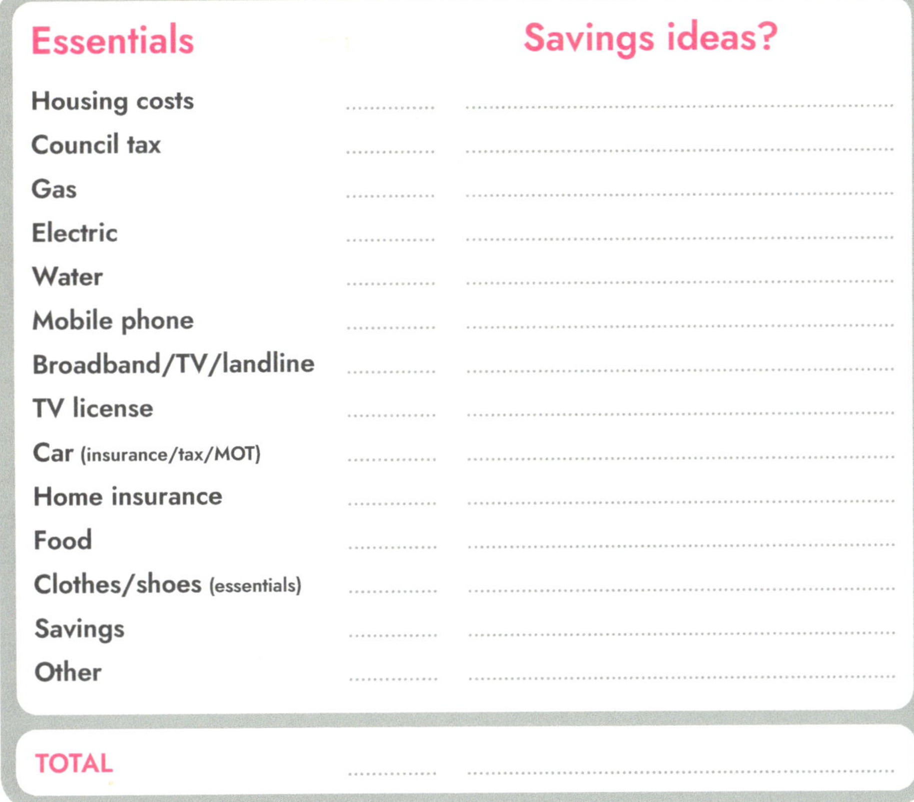

Essentials

Housing costs
Council tax
Gas
Electric
Water
Mobile phone
Broadband/TV/landline
TV license
Car (insurance/tax/MOT)
Home insurance
Food
Clothes/shoes (essentials)
Savings
Other

TOTAL

Savings ideas?

Debts...

Credit cards ....
Loans ....
Other ....

TOTAL ....

Are you getting the best interest rates?

The Fun Stuff

Gym
Socialising
Clothes
Holidays
Gifts
Hair/beauty
Hobbies
Other

TOTAL ....

Where are we?

Incomings ....
Outgoings ....
What's left ....

Action plan...

Better With A PLAN | BUDGET PLANNER

What's coming in?

Salary	Extras	Bank Balance	Total

What's going out?

Essentials

	Savings ideas?
Housing costs	
Council tax	
Gas	
Electric	
Water	
Mobile phone	
Broadband/TV/landline	
TV license	
Car (insurance/tax/MOT)	
Home insurance	
Food	
Clothes/shoes (essentials)	
Savings	
Other	

TOTAL

Debts...

Credit cards
Loans
Other

TOTAL

Are you getting the best interest rates?

The Fun Stuff

Gym
Socialising
Clothes
Holidays
Gifts
Hair/beauty
Hobbies
Other

TOTAL

Day to day costs

Lunch/Food
Travelling
Drinks
Extras

Where are we?

Incomings
Outgoings
What's left

Action plan...

Better With A PLAN | BUDGET PLANNER

What's coming in?

Salary

Extras

Bank Balance

Total

Day to day costs

Lunch/Food ....
Travelling ....
Drinks ....
Extras ....

What's going out?

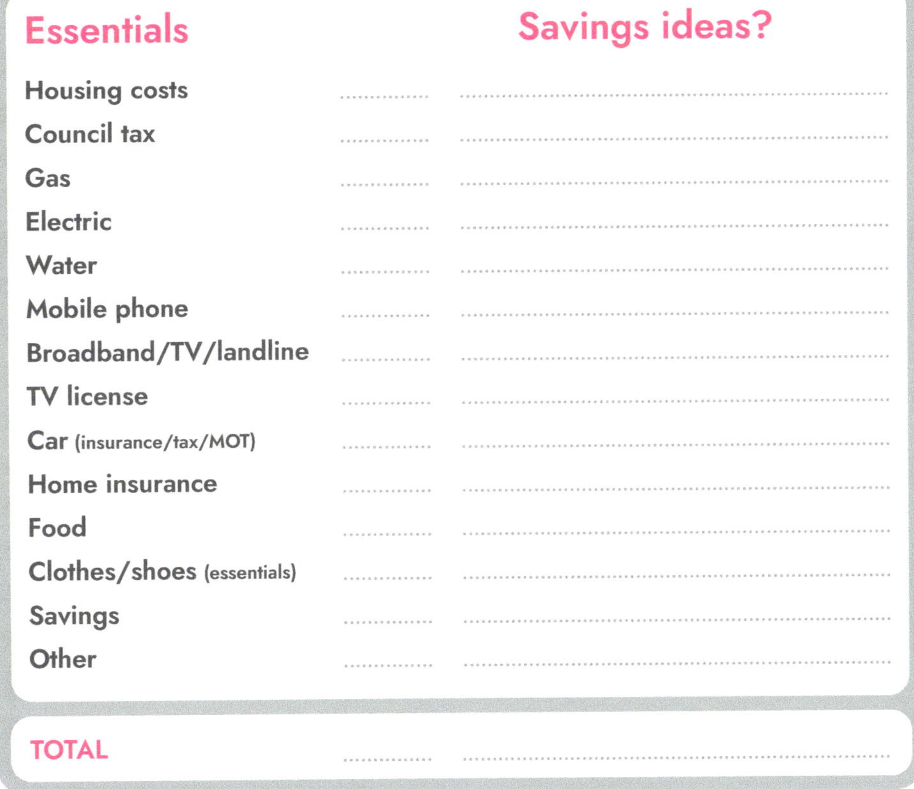

Are you getting the best interest rates?

Essentials

Housing costs ....
Council tax ....
Gas ....
Electric ....
Water ....
Mobile phone ....
Broadband/TV/landline ....
TV license ....
Car (insurance/tax/MOT) ....
Home insurance ....
Food ....
Clothes/shoes (essentials) ....
Savings ....
Other ....

Savings ideas?

TOTAL ....

Debts...

Credit cards ....
Loans ....
Other ....

TOTAL ....

The Fun Stuff

Gym ....
Socialising ....
Clothes ....
Holidays ....
Gifts ....
Hair/beauty ....
Hobbies ....
Other ....

TOTAL ....

Where are we?

Incomings ....
Outgoings ....
What's left ....

Action plan...

Better With A PLAN | BUDGET PLANNER

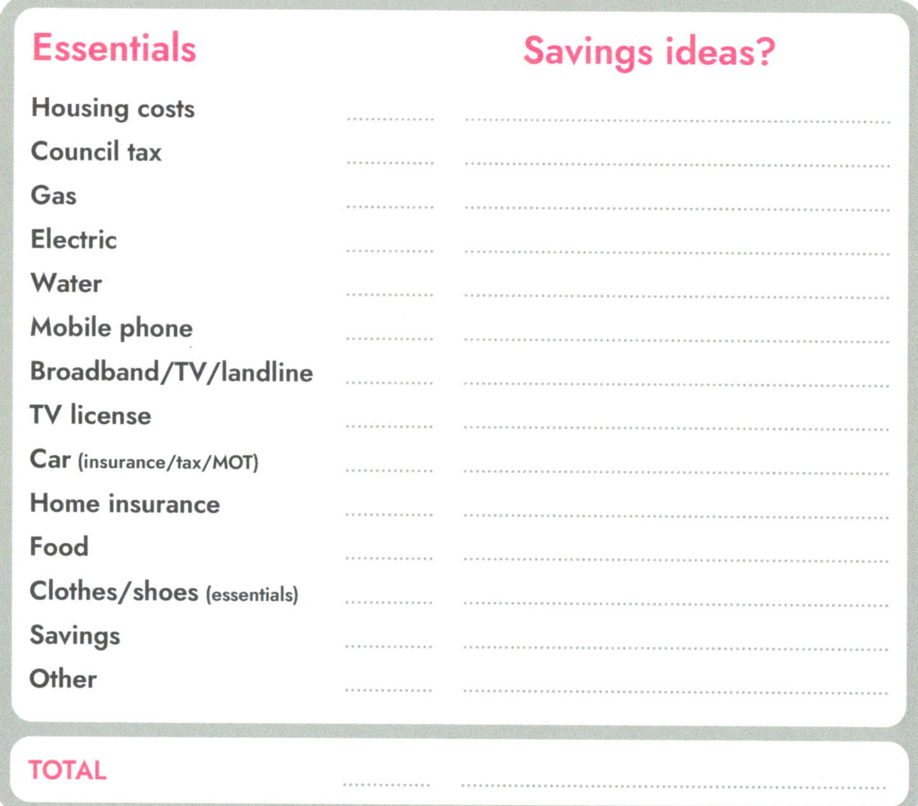

What's coming in?

Salary

Extras

Bank Balance

Total

What's going out?

Essentials

Housing costs
Council tax
Gas
Electric
Water
Mobile phone
Broadband/TV/landline
TV license
Car (insurance/tax/MOT)
Home insurance
Food
Clothes/shoes (essentials)
Savings
Other

TOTAL

Savings ideas?

Debts...

Credit cards
Loans
Other

TOTAL

Are you getting the best interest rates?

The Fun Stuff

Gym
Socialising
Clothes
Holidays
Gifts
Hair/beauty
Hobbies
Other

TOTAL

Day to day costs

Lunch/Food
Travelling
Drinks
Extras

Where are we?

Incomings
Outgoings
What's left

Action plan...

Better With A PLAN | BUDGET PLANNER

What's coming in?

| Salary | Extras | Bank Balance | Total |

What's going out?

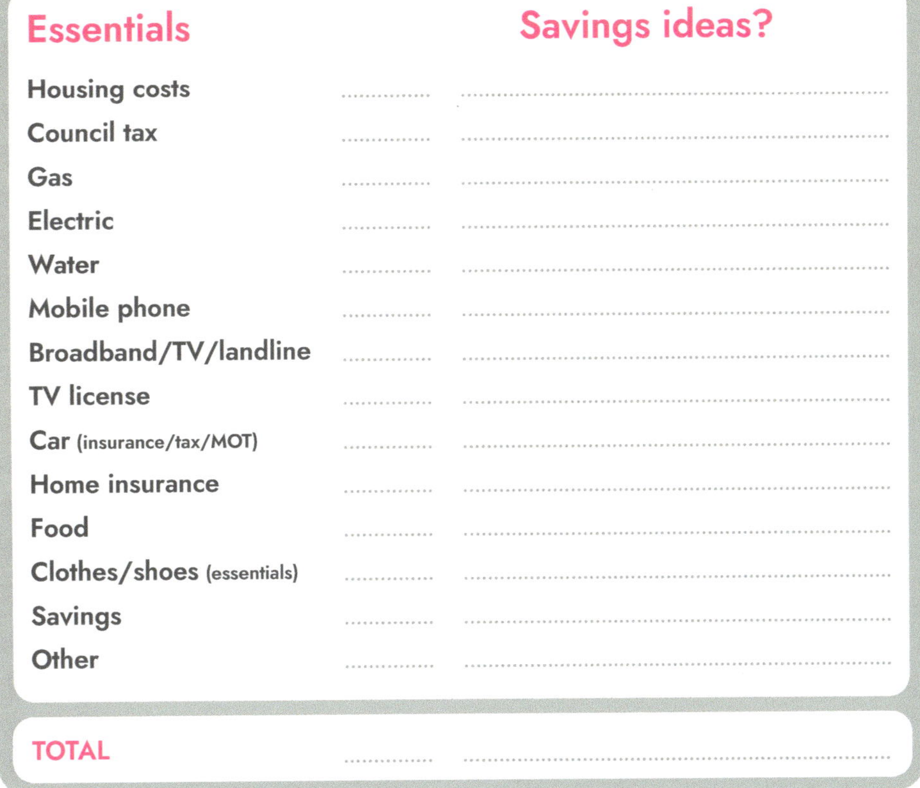

Essentials

Housing costs
Council tax
Gas
Electric
Water
Mobile phone
Broadband/TV/landline
TV license
Car (insurance/tax/MOT)
Home insurance
Food
Clothes/shoes (essentials)
Savings
Other

Savings ideas?

TOTAL

Debts...

Credit cards
Loans
Other

TOTAL

Are you getting the best interest rates?

The Fun Stuff

Gym
Socialising
Clothes
Holidays
Gifts
Hair/beauty
Hobbies
Other

TOTAL

Day to day costs

Lunch/Food
Travelling
Drinks
Extras

Where are we?

Incomings
Outgoings
What's left

Action plan...

Better With A **PLAN** | BUDGET PLANNER

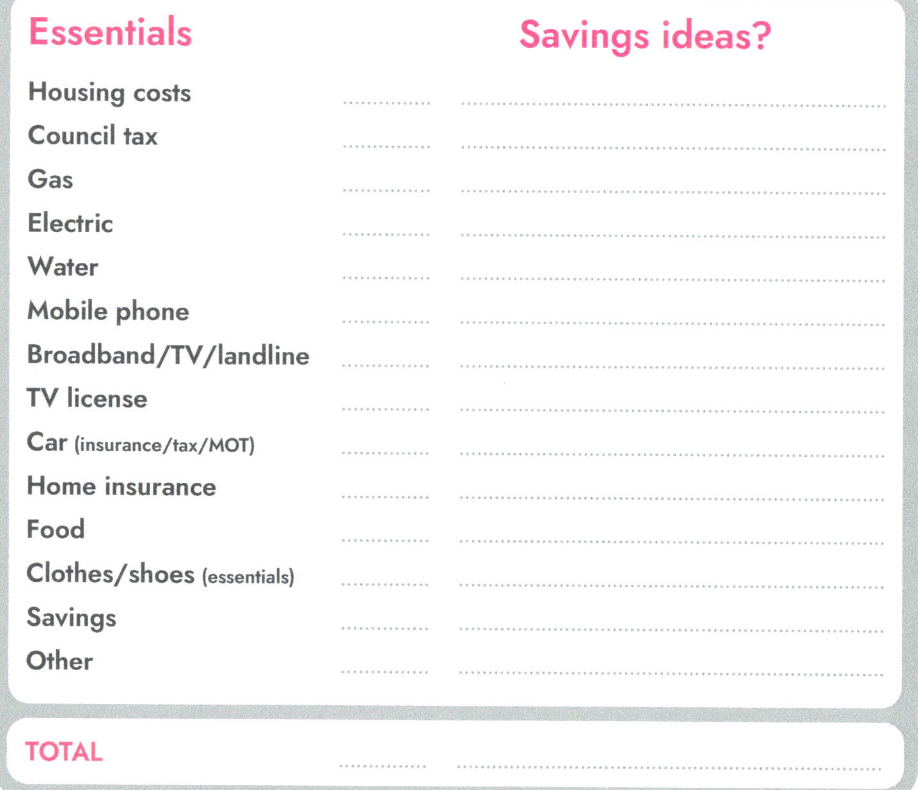

What's coming in?

Salary	Extras	Bank Balance	Total

What's going out?

Essentials

Housing costs

Council tax

Gas

Electric

Water

Mobile phone

Broadband/TV/landline

TV license

Car (insurance/tax/MOT)

Home insurance

Food

Clothes/shoes (essentials)

Savings

Other

TOTAL

Savings ideas?

Day to day costs

Lunch/Food

Travelling

Drinks

Extras

Debts...

Credit cards

Loans

Other

TOTAL

Are you getting the best interest rates?

The Fun Stuff

Gym

Socialising

Clothes

Holidays

Gifts

Hair/beauty

Hobbies

Other

TOTAL

Where are we?

Incomings

Outgoings

What's left

Action plan...

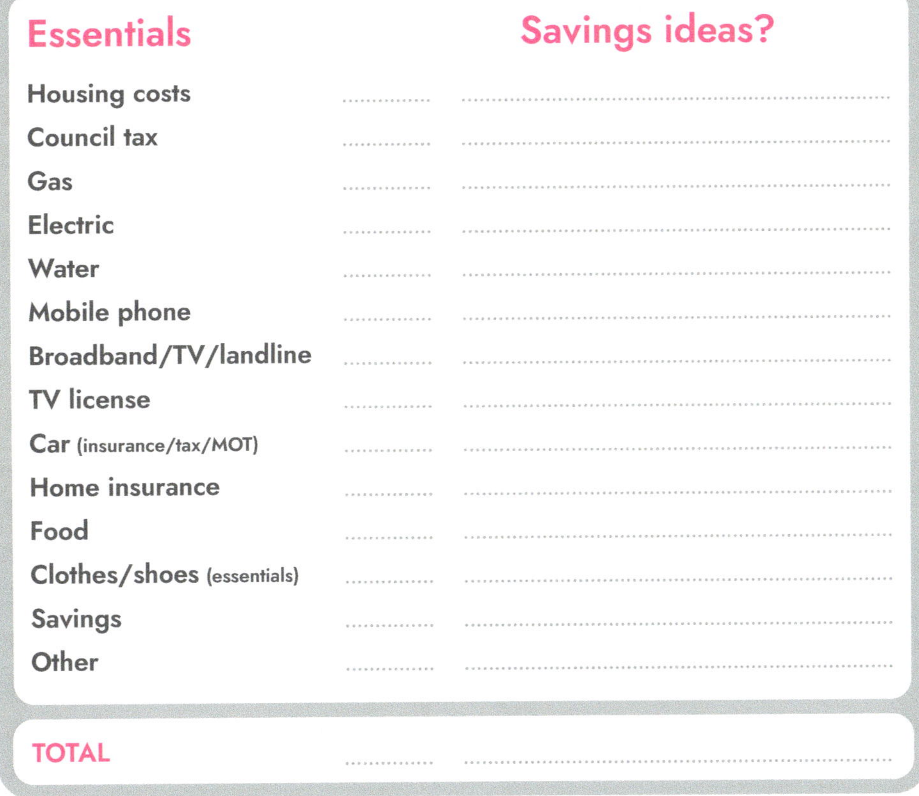

Better With A PLAN | BUDGET PLANNER

What's coming in?

Salary

Extras

Bank Balance

Total

What's going out?

Essentials

Savings ideas?

Housing costs

Council tax

Gas

Electric

Water

Mobile phone

Broadband/TV/landline

TV license

Car (insurance/tax/MOT)

Home insurance

Food

Clothes/shoes (essentials)

Savings

Other

TOTAL

Debts...

Are you getting the best interest rates?

Credit cards

Loans

Other

TOTAL

The Fun Stuff

Gym

Socialising

Clothes

Holidays

Gifts

Hair/beauty

Hobbies

Other

TOTAL

Day to day costs

Lunch/Food

Travelling

Drinks

Extras

Where are we?

Incomings

Outgoings

What's left

Action plan...

What's coming in?

Salary   **Extras**   **Bank Balance**   **Total**

What's going out?

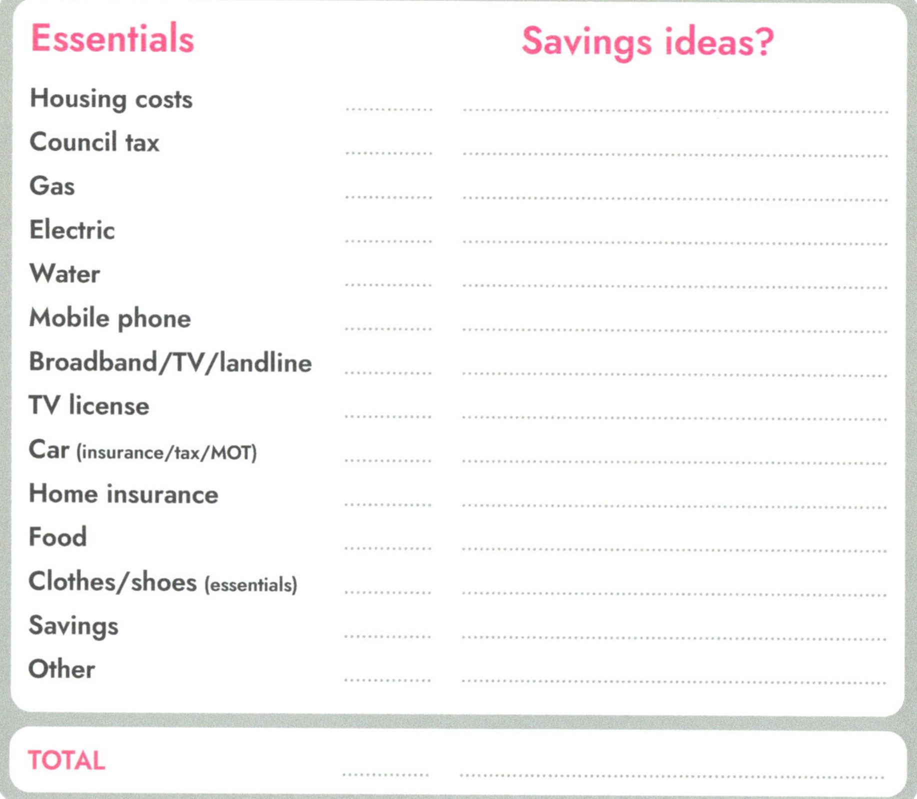

Essentials

Housing costs
Council tax
Gas
Electric
Water
Mobile phone
Broadband/TV/landline
TV license
Car (insurance/tax/MOT)
Home insurance
Food
Clothes/shoes (essentials)
Savings
Other

Savings ideas?

TOTAL

Debts...

Credit cards
Loans
Other

TOTAL

The Fun Stuff

Gym
Socialising
Clothes
Holidays
Gifts
Hair/beauty
Hobbies
Other

TOTAL

Are you getting the best interest rates?

Day to day costs

Lunch/Food
Travelling
Drinks
Extras

Where are we?

Incomings
Outgoings
What's left

Action plan...

Better With A
PLAN

BUDGET PLANNER

What's coming in?

Salary

Extras

Bank Balance

Total

What's going out?

Are you getting the best interest rates?

Essentials

Housing costs
Council tax
Gas
Electric
Water
Mobile phone
Broadband/TV/landline
TV license
Car (insurance/tax/MOT)
Home insurance
Food
Clothes/shoes (essentials)
Savings
Other

Savings ideas?

TOTAL

Debts...

Credit cards
Loans
Other

TOTAL

The Fun Stuff

Gym
Socialising
Clothes
Holidays
Gifts
Hair/beauty
Hobbies
Other

TOTAL

Day to day costs

Lunch/Food
Travelling
Drinks
Extras

Where are we?

Incomings
Outgoings
What's left

Action plan...

Better With A PLAN | BUDGET PLANNER

What's coming in?

Salary

Extras

Bank Balance

Total

What's going out?

Essentials

Housing costs
Council tax
Gas
Electric
Water
Mobile phone
Broadband/TV/landline
TV license
Car (insurance/tax/MOT)
Home insurance
Food
Clothes/shoes (essentials)
Savings
Other

TOTAL

Savings ideas?

Debts...

Credit cards
Loans
Other

TOTAL

Are you getting the best interest rates?

The Fun Stuff

Gym
Socialising
Clothes
Holidays
Gifts
Hair/beauty
Hobbies
Other

TOTAL

Day to day costs

Lunch/Food
Travelling
Drinks
Extras

Where are we?

Incomings
Outgoings
What's left

Action plan...

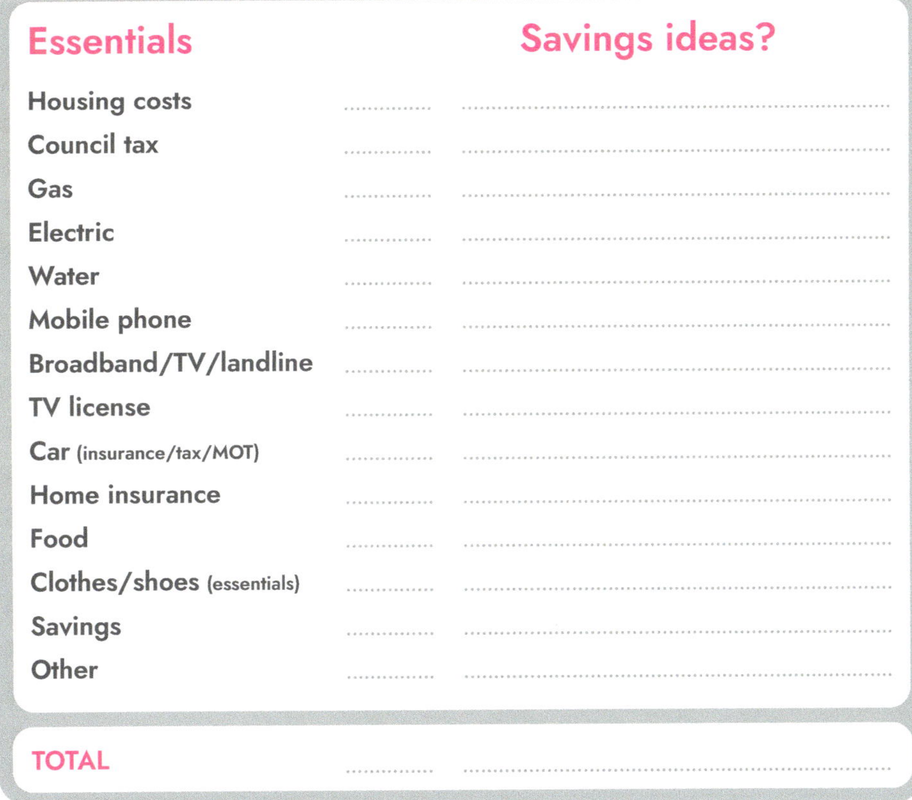

Better With A PLAN | BUDGET PLANNER

What's coming in?

Salary	Extras	Bank Balance	Total

What's going out?

Day to day costs

Lunch/Food ....
Travelling ....
Drinks ....
Extras ....

Essentials

Savings ideas?

Housing costs ....
Council tax ....
Gas ....
Electric ....
Water ....
Mobile phone ....
Broadband/TV/landline ....
TV license ....
Car (insurance/tax/MOT) ....
Home insurance ....
Food ....
Clothes/shoes (essentials) ....
Savings ....
Other ....

TOTAL ....

Debts...

Are you getting the best interest rates?

Credit cards ....
Loans ....
Other ....

TOTAL ....

The Fun Stuff

Gym ....
Socialising ....
Clothes ....
Holidays ....
Gifts ....
Hair/beauty ....
Hobbies ....
Other ....

TOTAL ....

Where are we?

Incomings ....
Outgoings ....
What's left ....

Action plan...

Better With A PLAN | BUDGET PLANNER

What's coming in?

Salary   Extras   Bank Balance   Total

What's going out?

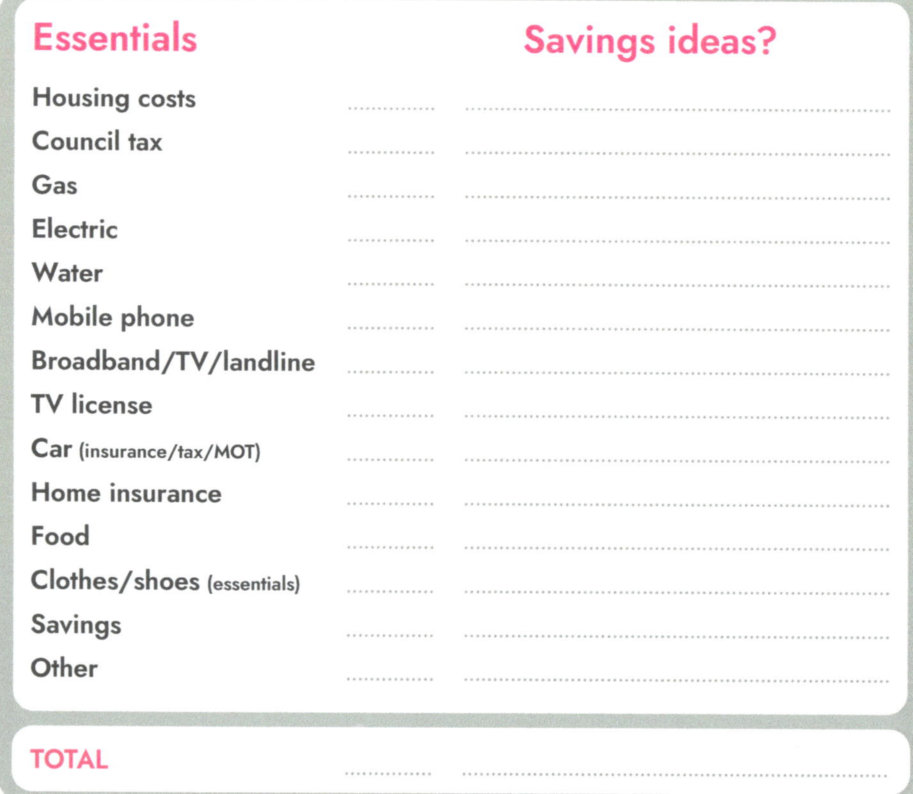

Essentials

Housing costs
Council tax
Gas
Electric
Water
Mobile phone
Broadband/TV/landline
TV license
Car (insurance/tax/MOT)
Home insurance
Food
Clothes/shoes (essentials)
Savings
Other

TOTAL

Savings ideas?

Debts...

Credit cards
Loans
Other

TOTAL

The Fun Stuff

Gym
Socialising
Clothes
Holidays
Gifts
Hair/beauty
Hobbies
Other

TOTAL

Are you getting the best interest rates?

Day to day costs

Lunch/Food
Travelling
Drinks
Extras

Where are we?

Incomings
Outgoings
What's left

Action plan...

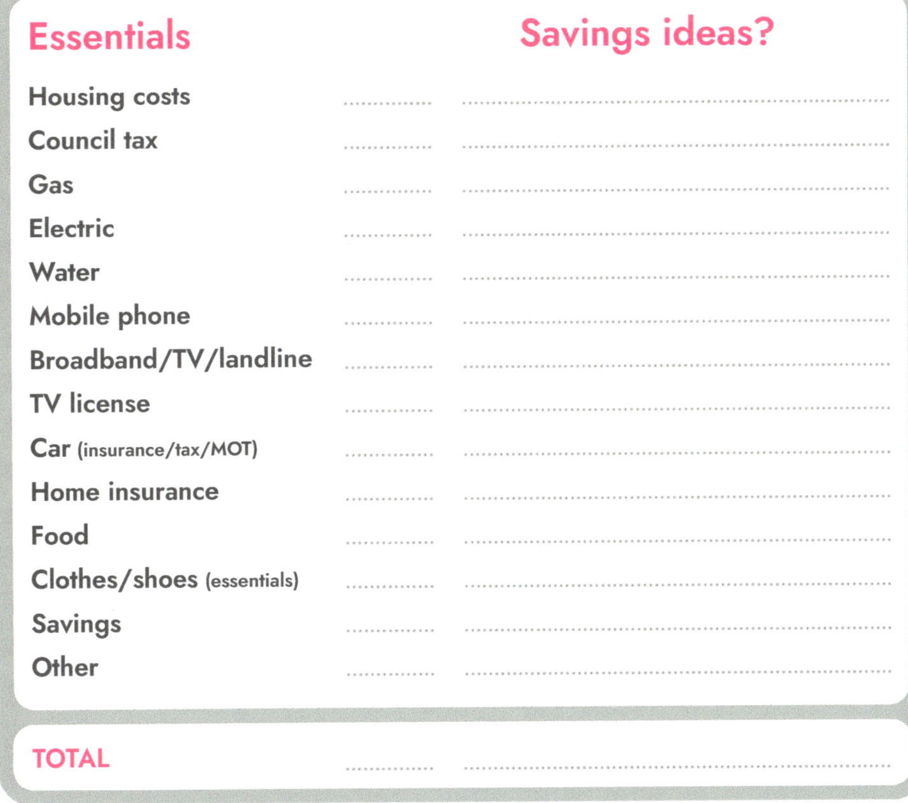

Better With A PLAN | BUDGET PLANNER

What's coming in?

| Salary | Extras | Bank Balance | Total |

What's going out?

Essentials   Savings ideas?

Housing costs
Council tax
Gas
Electric
Water
Mobile phone
Broadband/TV/landline
TV license
Car (insurance/tax/MOT)
Home insurance
Food
Clothes/shoes (essentials)
Savings
Other

TOTAL

Debts...

Credit cards
Loans
Other

TOTAL

Are you getting the best interest rates?

The Fun Stuff

Gym
Socialising
Clothes
Holidays
Gifts
Hair/beauty
Hobbies
Other

TOTAL

Day to day costs

Lunch/Food
Travelling
Drinks
Extras

Where are we?

Incomings
Outgoings
What's left

Action plan...

Better With A PLAN | BUDGET PLANNER

What's coming in?

Salary	Extras	Bank Balance	Total

What's going out?

Essentials

Savings ideas?

- Housing costs
- Council tax
- Gas
- Electric
- Water
- Mobile phone
- Broadband/TV/landline
- TV license
- Car (insurance/tax/MOT)
- Home insurance
- Food
- Clothes/shoes (essentials)
- Savings
- Other

TOTAL

Debts...

- Credit cards
- Loans
- Other

TOTAL

Are you getting the best interest rates?

The Fun Stuff

- Gym
- Socialising
- Clothes
- Holidays
- Gifts
- Hair/beauty
- Hobbies
- Other

TOTAL

Day to day costs

- Lunch/Food
- Travelling
- Drinks
- Extras

Where are we?

- Incomings
- Outgoings
- What's left

Action plan...

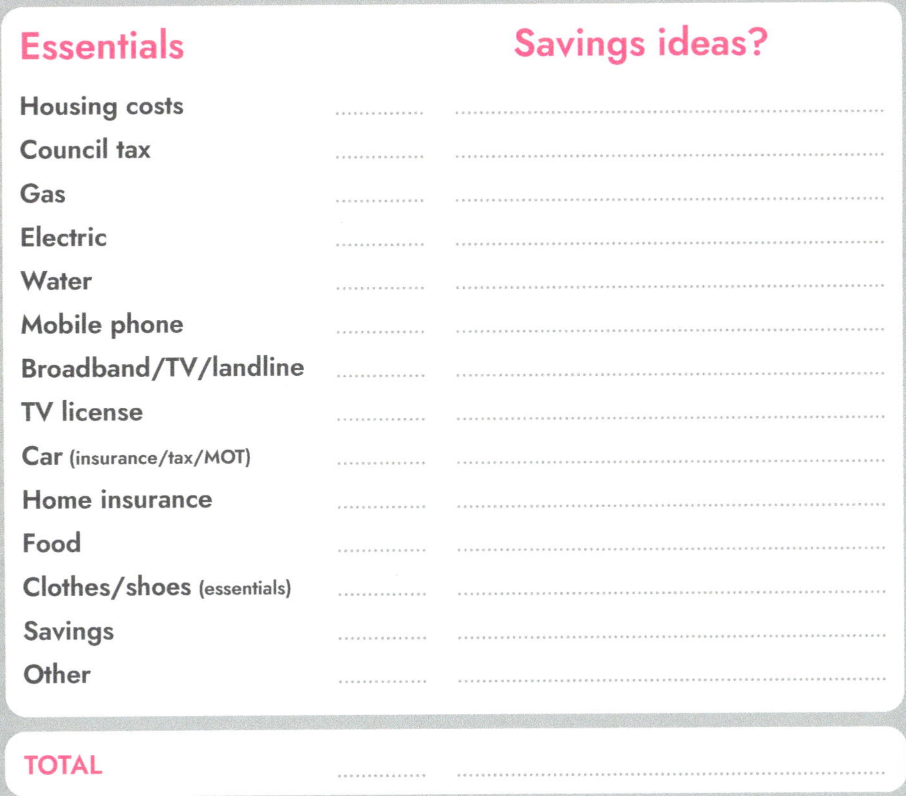

BUDGET PLANNER

What's coming in?

Salary

Extras

Bank Balance

Total

What's going out?

Essentials

Housing costs
Council tax
Gas
Electric
Water
Mobile phone
Broadband/TV/landline
TV license
Car (insurance/tax/MOT)
Home insurance
Food
Clothes/shoes (essentials)
Savings
Other

TOTAL

Savings ideas?

Debts...

Credit cards
Loans
Other

TOTAL

The Fun Stuff

Gym
Socialising
Clothes
Holidays
Gifts
Hair/beauty
Hobbies
Other

TOTAL

Are you getting the best interest rates?

Day to day costs

Lunch/Food
Travelling
Drinks
Extras

Where are we?

Incomings
Outgoings
What's left

Action plan...

BUDGET PLANNER

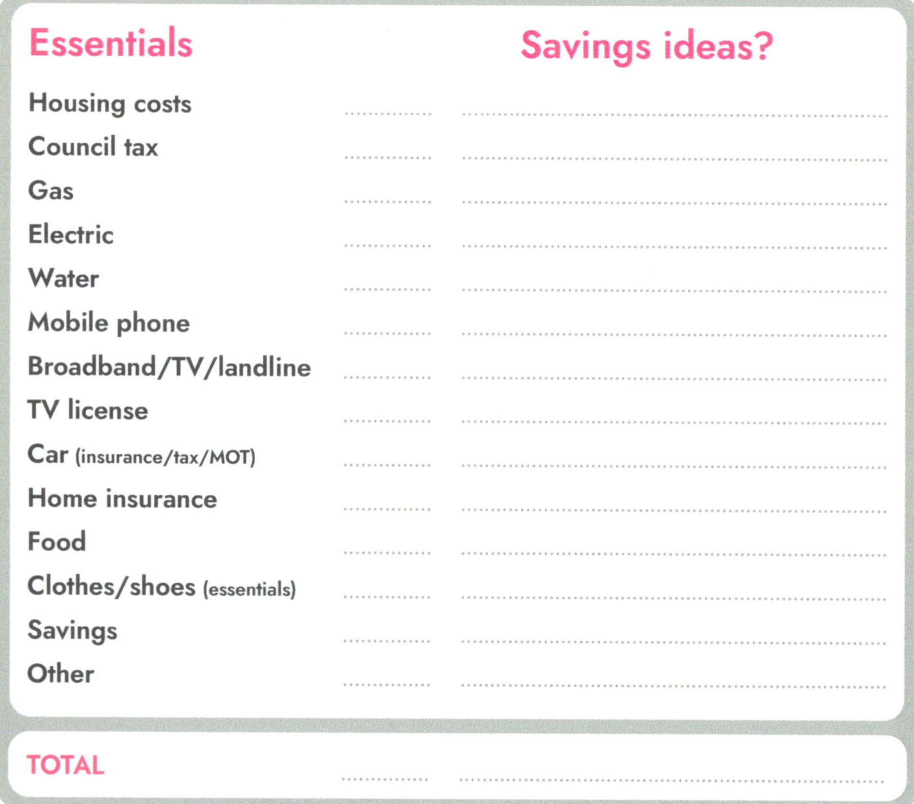

What's coming in?

Salary   Extras   Bank Balance   Total

What's going out?

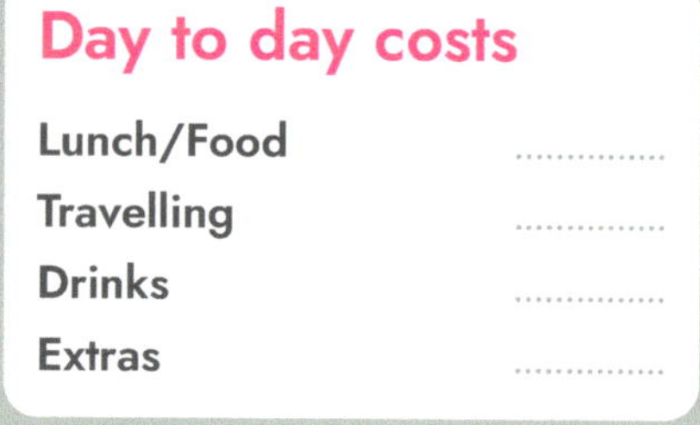

Essentials   Savings ideas?

Housing costs
Council tax
Gas
Electric
Water
Mobile phone
Broadband/TV/landline
TV license
Car (insurance/tax/MOT)
Home insurance
Food
Clothes/shoes (essentials)
Savings
Other

TOTAL

Debts...

Credit cards
Loans
Other

TOTAL

The Fun Stuff

Gym
Socialising
Clothes
Holidays
Gifts
Hair/beauty
Hobbies
Other

TOTAL

Day to day costs

Lunch/Food
Travelling
Drinks
Extras

Where are we?

Incomings
Outgoings
What's left

Action plan...

BUDGET PLANNER

What's coming in?

Salary

Extras

Bank Balance

Total

What's going out?

Essentials

Housing costs
Council tax
Gas
Electric
Water
Mobile phone
Broadband/TV/landline
TV license
Car (insurance/tax/MOT)
Home insurance
Food
Clothes/shoes (essentials)
Savings
Other

TOTAL

Savings ideas?

Debts...

Credit cards
Loans
Other

TOTAL

The Fun Stuff

Gym
Socialising
Clothes
Holidays
Gifts
Hair/beauty
Hobbies
Other

TOTAL

Are you getting the best interest rates?

Day to day costs

Lunch/Food
Travelling
Drinks
Extras

Where are we?

Incomings
Outgoings
What's left

Action plan...

PLAN | BUDGET PLANNER

What's coming in?

Salary **Extras** **Bank Balance** **Total**

What's going out?

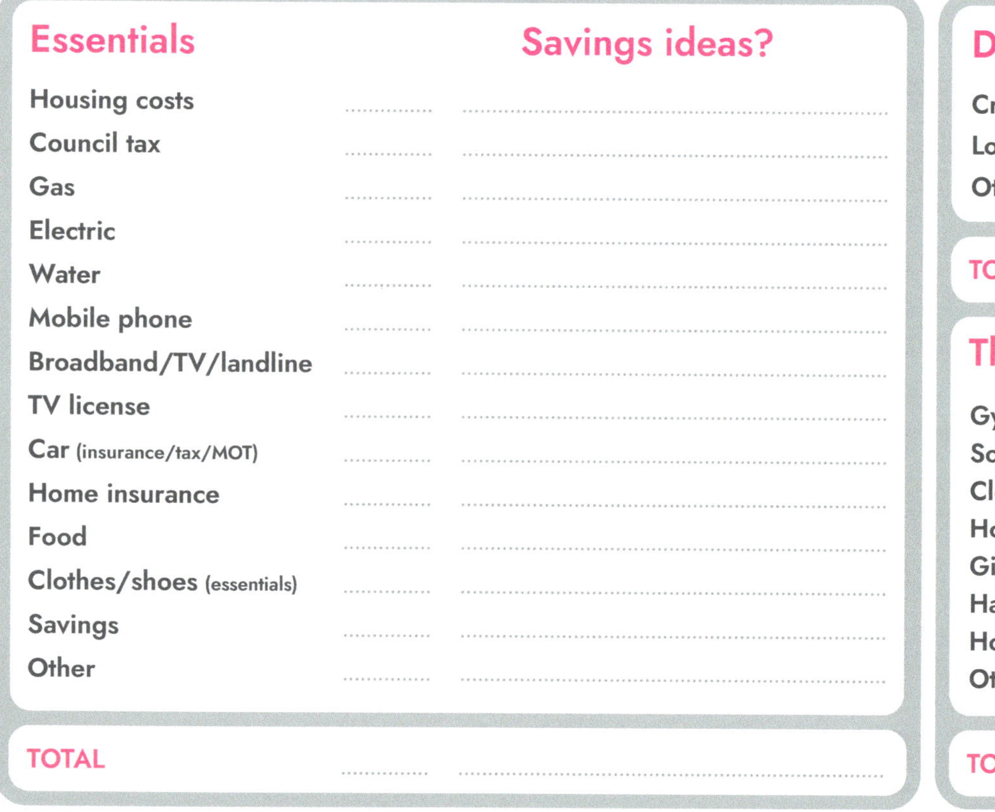

Essentials

Housing costs
Council tax
Gas
Electric
Water
Mobile phone
Broadband/TV/landline
TV license
Car (insurance/tax/MOT)
Home insurance
Food
Clothes/shoes (essentials)
Savings
Other

Savings ideas?

TOTAL

Day to day costs

Lunch/Food
Travelling
Drinks
Extras

Are you getting the best interest rates?

Debts...

Credit cards
Loans
Other

TOTAL

The Fun Stuff

Gym
Socialising
Clothes
Holidays
Gifts
Hair/beauty
Hobbies
Other

TOTAL

Where are we?

Incomings
Outgoings
What's left

Action plan...

Better With A PLAN | BUDGET PLANNER

What's coming in?

Salary | Extras | Bank Balance | Total

What's going out?

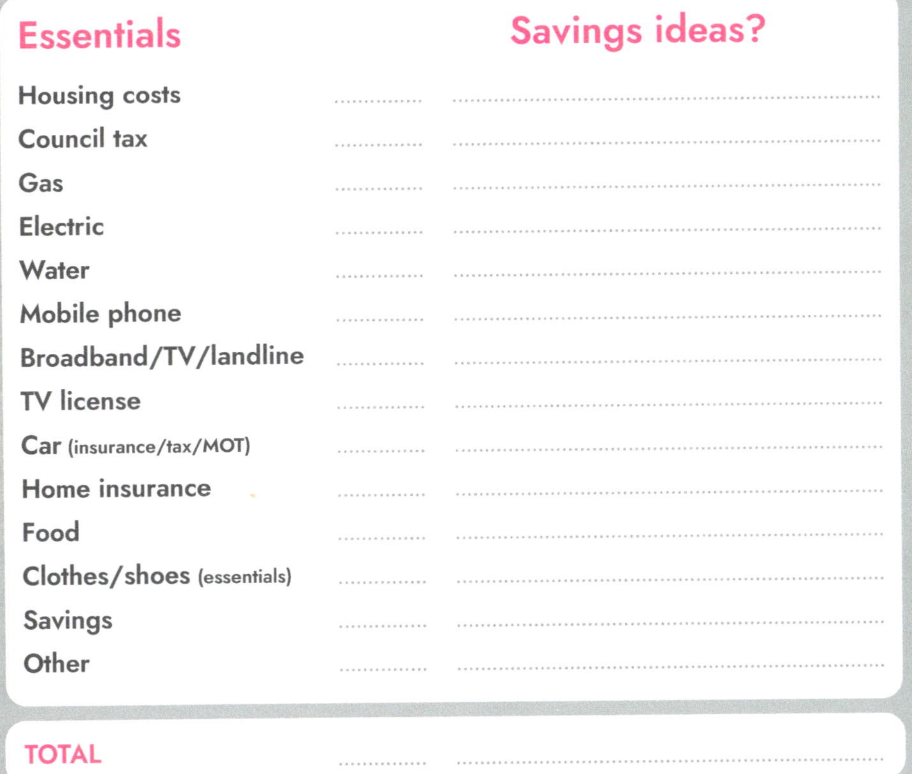

Essentials

Savings ideas?

Housing costs
Council tax
Gas
Electric
Water
Mobile phone
Broadband/TV/landline
TV license
Car (insurance/tax/MOT)
Home insurance
Food
Clothes/shoes (essentials)
Savings
Other

TOTAL

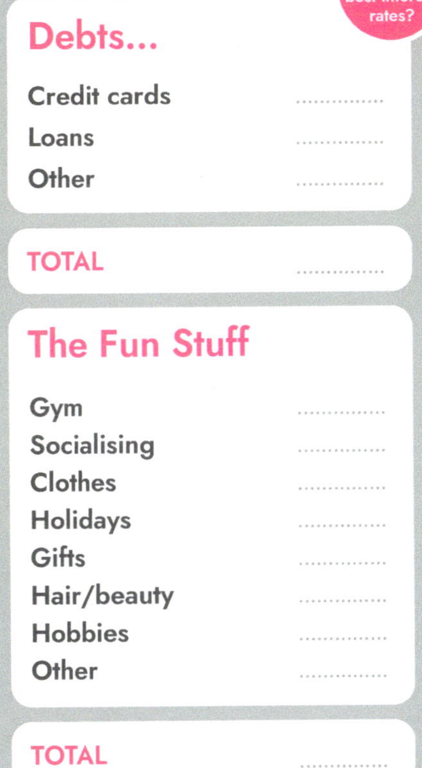

Debts...

Credit cards
Loans
Other

TOTAL

The Fun Stuff

Gym
Socialising
Clothes
Holidays
Gifts
Hair/beauty
Hobbies
Other

TOTAL

Day to day costs

Lunch/Food
Travelling
Drinks
Extras

Where are we?

Incomings
Outgoings
What's left

Action plan...

BUDGET PLANNER

What's coming in?

Salary

Extras

Bank Balance

Total

What's going out?

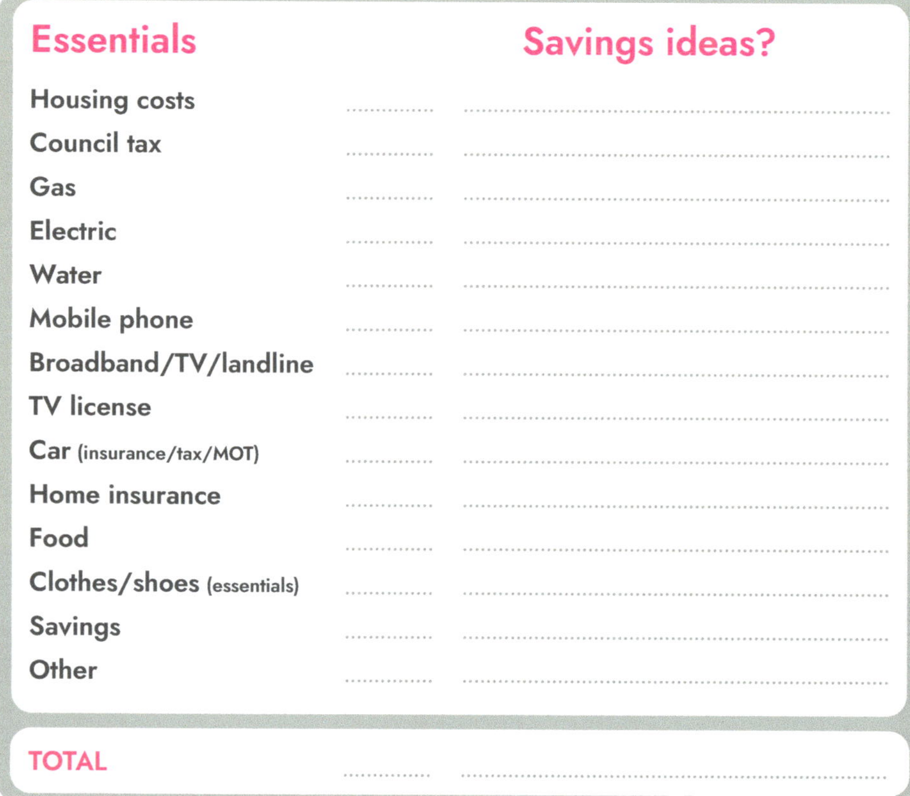

Essentials

Housing costs
Council tax
Gas
Electric
Water
Mobile phone
Broadband/TV/landline
TV license
Car (insurance/tax/MOT)
Home insurance
Food
Clothes/shoes (essentials)
Savings
Other

Savings ideas?

TOTAL

Debts...

Credit cards
Loans
Other

TOTAL

The Fun Stuff

Gym
Socialising
Clothes
Holidays
Gifts
Hair/beauty
Hobbies
Other

TOTAL

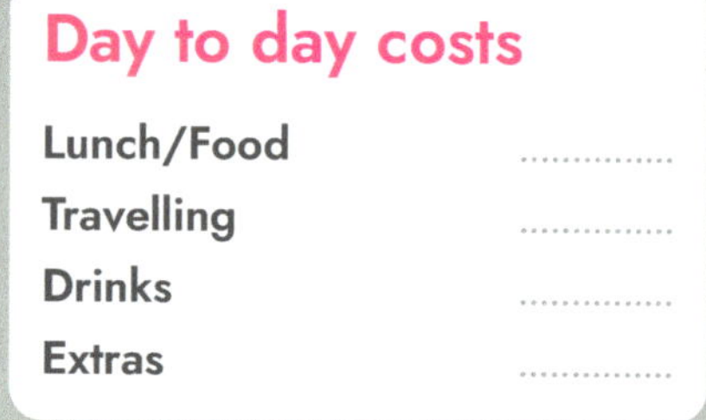

Day to day costs

Lunch/Food
Travelling
Drinks
Extras

Where are we?

Incomings
Outgoings
What's left

Action plan...

BUDGET PLANNER

What's coming in?

Salary | Extras | Bank Balance | Total

What's going out?

Day to day costs

Lunch/Food ....
Travelling ....
Drinks ....
Extras ....

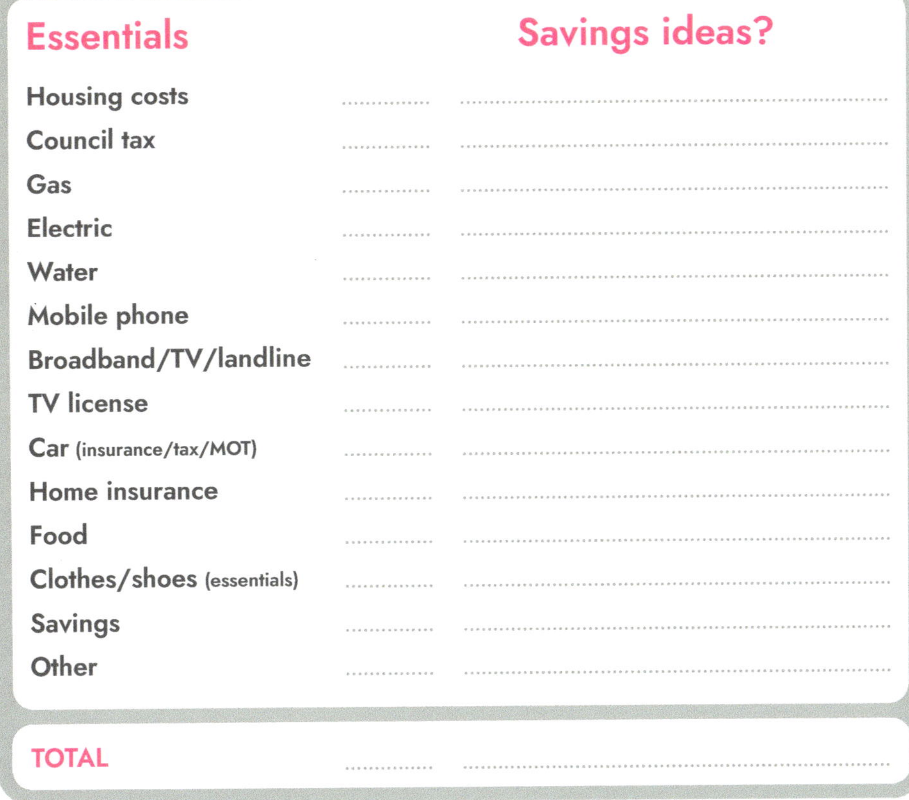

Are you getting the best interest rates?

Essentials

Savings ideas?

Housing costs ....
Council tax ....
Gas ....
Electric ....
Water ....
Mobile phone ....
Broadband/TV/landline ....
TV license ....
Car (insurance/tax/MOT) ....
Home insurance ....
Food ....
Clothes/shoes (essentials) ....
Savings ....
Other ....

TOTAL

Debts...

Credit cards ....
Loans ....
Other ....

TOTAL

The Fun Stuff

Gym ....
Socialising ....
Clothes ....
Holidays ....
Gifts ....
Hair/beauty ....
Hobbies ....
Other ....

TOTAL

Where are we?

Incomings ....
Outgoings ....
What's left ....

Action plan...

Better With A PLAN | BUDGET PLANNER

What's coming in?

Salary	Extras	Bank Balance	Total

What's going out?

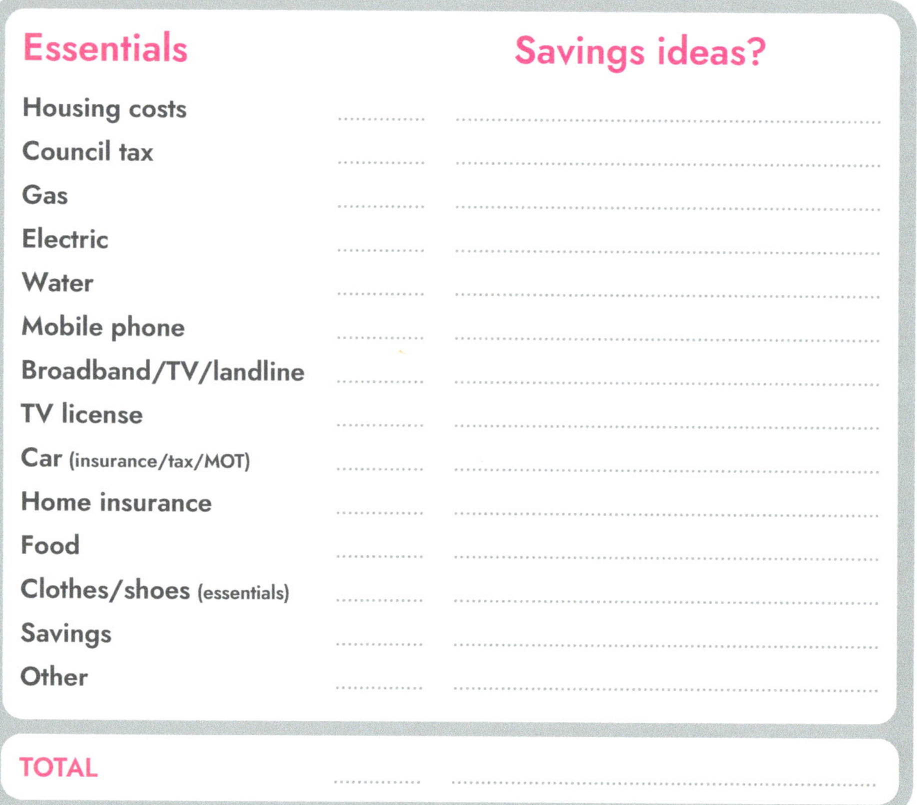

Essentials | Savings ideas?

Housing costs
Council tax
Gas
Electric
Water
Mobile phone
Broadband/TV/landline
TV license
Car (insurance/tax/MOT)
Home insurance
Food
Clothes/shoes (essentials)
Savings
Other

TOTAL

Debts...

Credit cards
Loans
Other

TOTAL

The Fun Stuff

Gym
Socialising
Clothes
Holidays
Gifts
Hair/beauty
Hobbies
Other

TOTAL

Day to day costs

Lunch/Food
Travelling
Drinks
Extras

Where are we?

Incomings
Outgoings
What's left

Action plan...

129

What's coming in?

Salary

Extras

Bank Balance

Total

What's going out?

Essentials

Housing costs

Council tax

Gas

Electric

Water

Mobile phone

Broadband/TV/landline

TV license

Car (insurance/tax/MOT)

Home insurance

Food

Clothes/shoes (essentials)

Savings

Other

Savings ideas?

TOTAL

Debts...

Credit cards

Loans

Other

TOTAL

The Fun Stuff

Gym

Socialising

Clothes

Holidays

Gifts

Hair/beauty

Hobbies

Other

TOTAL

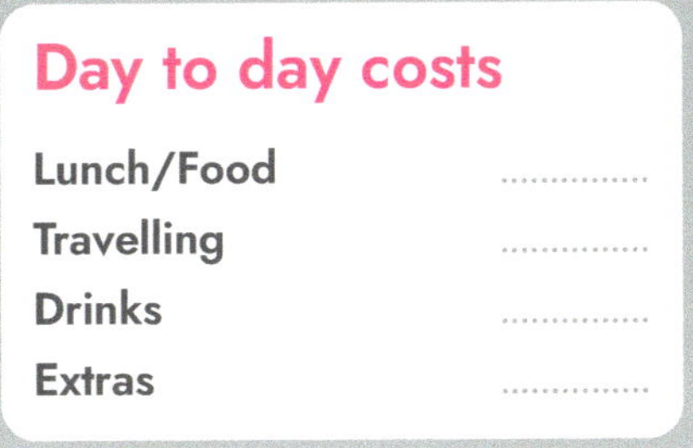

Day to day costs

Lunch/Food

Travelling

Drinks

Extras

Where are we?

Incomings

Outgoings

What's left

Action plan...

Better With A PLAN | BUDGET PLANNER

What's coming in?

| Salary | Extras | Bank Balance | Total |

What's going out?

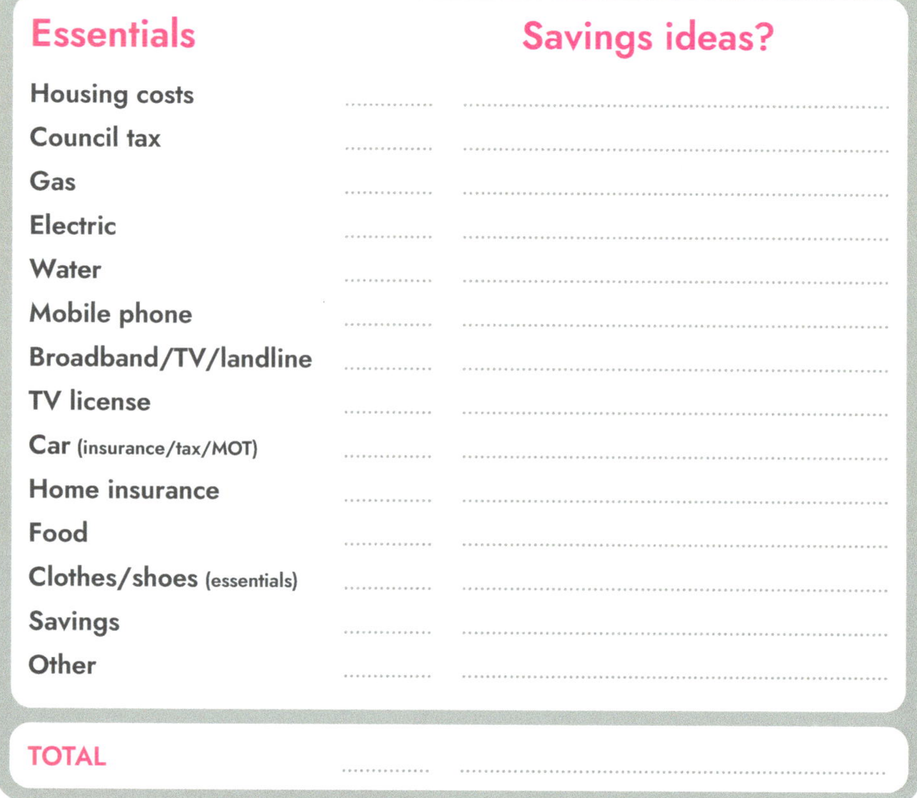

Essentials

Savings ideas?

Housing costs
Council tax
Gas
Electric
Water
Mobile phone
Broadband/TV/landline
TV license
Car (insurance/tax/MOT)
Home insurance
Food
Clothes/shoes (essentials)
Savings
Other

TOTAL

Debts...

Credit cards
Loans
Other

TOTAL

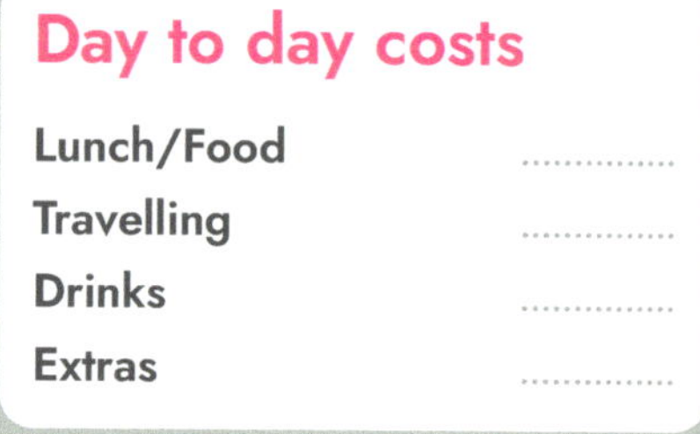

The Fun Stuff

Gym
Socialising
Clothes
Holidays
Gifts
Hair/beauty
Hobbies
Other

TOTAL

Day to day costs

Lunch/Food
Travelling
Drinks
Extras

Where are we?

Incomings
Outgoings
What's left

Action plan...

BUDGET PLANNER

What's coming in?

Salary | Extras | Bank Balance | Total

What's going out?

Are you getting the best interest rates?

Day to day costs

Lunch/Food ....
Travelling ....
Drinks ....
Extras ....

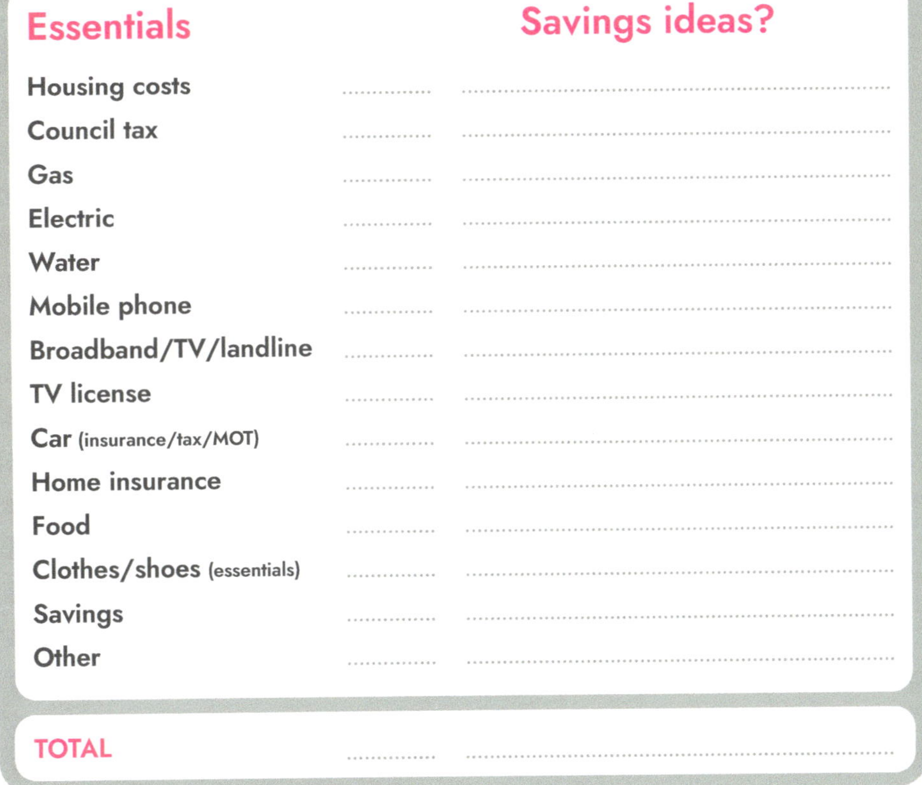

Essentials | Savings ideas?

Housing costs
Council tax
Gas
Electric
Water
Mobile phone
Broadband/TV/landline
TV license
Car (insurance/tax/MOT)
Home insurance
Food
Clothes/shoes (essentials)
Savings
Other

TOTAL

Debts...

Credit cards ....
Loans ....
Other ....

TOTAL ....

The Fun Stuff

Gym ....
Socialising ....
Clothes ....
Holidays ....
Gifts ....
Hair/beauty ....
Hobbies ....
Other ....

TOTAL ....

Where are we?

Incomings ....
Outgoings ....
What's left ....

Action plan...

Better With A PLAN | BUDGET PLANNER

What's coming in?

Salary | Extras | Bank Balance | Total

What's going out?

Day to day costs

Lunch/Food
Travelling
Drinks
Extras

Essentials

Housing costs
Council tax
Gas
Electric
Water
Mobile phone
Broadband/TV/landline
TV license
Car (insurance/tax/MOT)
Home insurance
Food
Clothes/shoes (essentials)
Savings
Other

TOTAL

Savings ideas?

Debts...

Are you getting the best interest rates?

Credit cards
Loans
Other

TOTAL

The Fun Stuff

Gym
Socialising
Clothes
Holidays
Gifts
Hair/beauty
Hobbies
Other

TOTAL

Where are we?

Incomings
Outgoings
What's left

Action plan...

Better With A
PLAN | BUDGET PLANNER

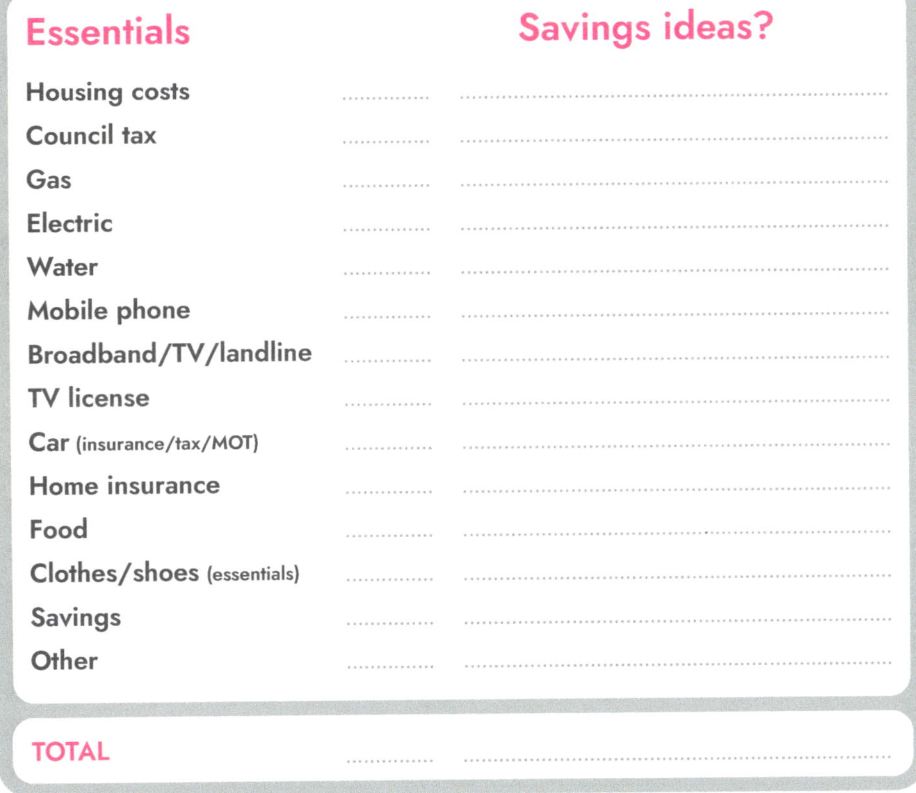

What's coming in?

Salary   Extras   Bank Balance   Total

What's going out?

Are you getting the best interest rates?

Essentials   Savings ideas?

Housing costs
Council tax
Gas
Electric
Water
Mobile phone
Broadband/TV/landline
TV license
Car (insurance/tax/MOT)
Home insurance
Food
Clothes/shoes (essentials)
Savings
Other

TOTAL

Day to day costs

Lunch/Food
Travelling
Drinks
Extras

Debts...

Credit cards
Loans
Other

TOTAL

The Fun Stuff

Gym
Socialising
Clothes
Holidays
Gifts
Hair/beauty
Hobbies
Other

TOTAL

Where are we?

Incomings
Outgoings
What's left

Action plan...

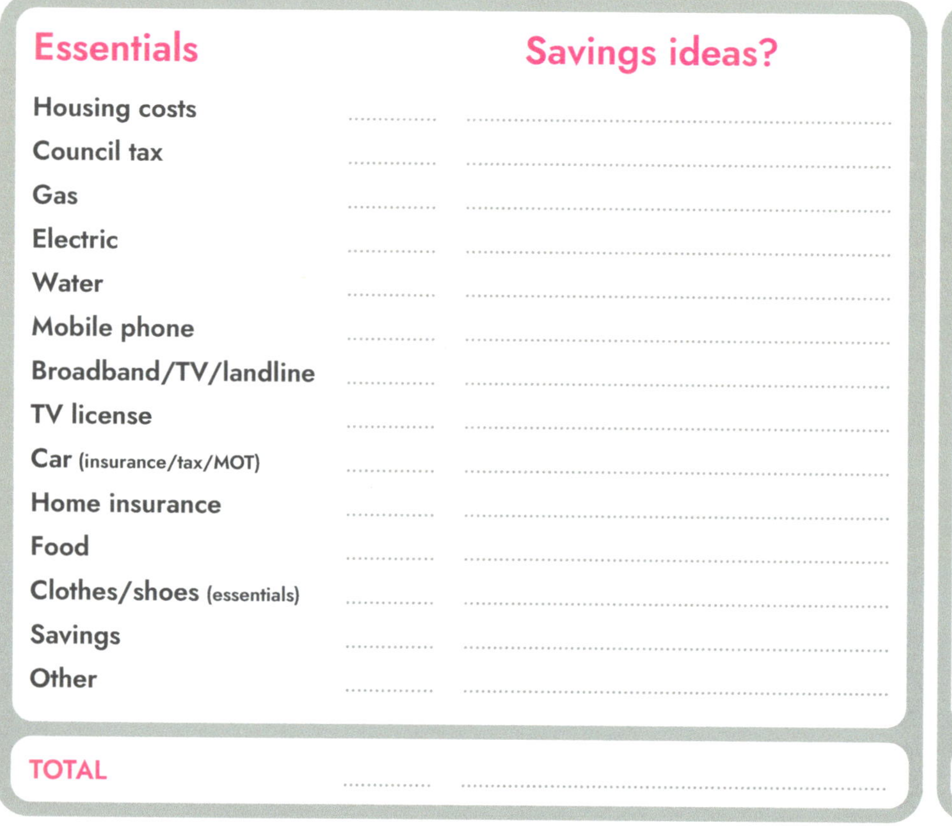

Better With A PLAN | BUDGET PLANNER

What's coming in?

Salary

Extras

Bank Balance

Total

What's going out?

Essentials

Housing costs
Council tax
Gas
Electric
Water
Mobile phone
Broadband/TV/landline
TV license
Car (insurance/tax/MOT)
Home insurance
Food
Clothes/shoes (essentials)
Savings
Other

TOTAL

Savings ideas?

Debts...

Credit cards
Loans
Other

TOTAL

Are you getting the best interest rates?

The Fun Stuff

Gym
Socialising
Clothes
Holidays
Gifts
Hair/beauty
Hobbies
Other

TOTAL

Day to day costs

Lunch/Food
Travelling
Drinks
Extras

Where are we?

Incomings
Outgoings
What's left

Action plan...

Better With A PLAN | BUDGET PLANNER

What's coming in?

Salary

Extras

Bank Balance

Total

What's going out?

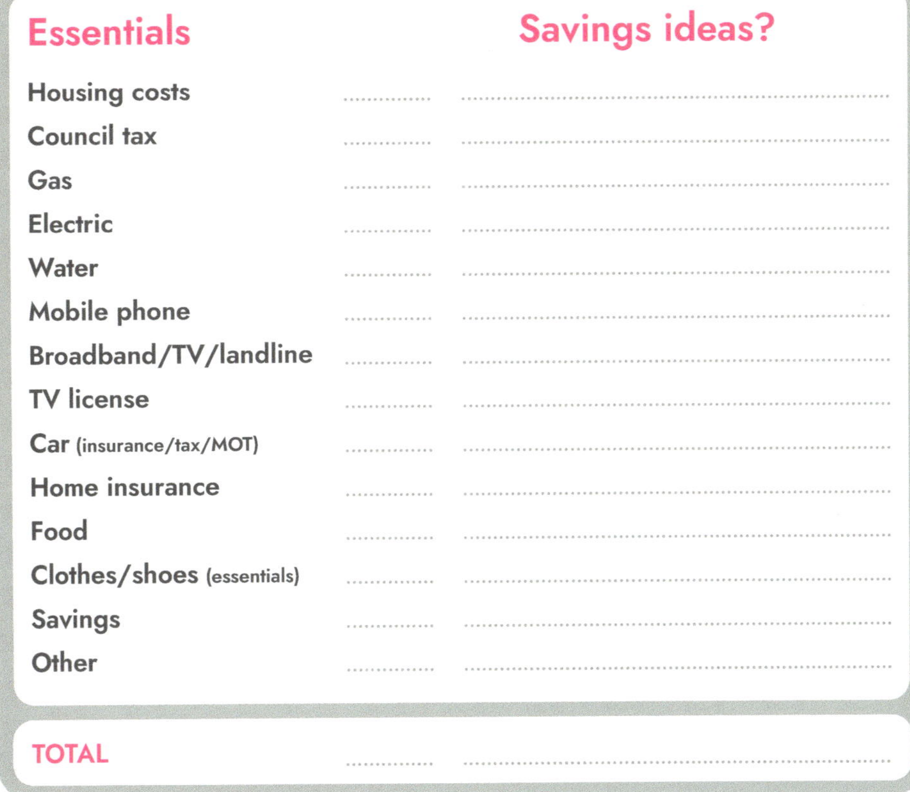

Essentials

Savings ideas?

Housing costs

Council tax

Gas

Electric

Water

Mobile phone

Broadband/TV/landline

TV license

Car (insurance/tax/MOT)

Home insurance

Food

Clothes/shoes (essentials)

Savings

Other

TOTAL

Day to day costs

Lunch/Food

Travelling

Drinks

Extras

Are you getting the best interest rates?

Debts...

Credit cards

Loans

Other

TOTAL

The Fun Stuff

Gym

Socialising

Clothes

Holidays

Gifts

Hair/beauty

Hobbies

Other

TOTAL

Where are we?

Incomings

Outgoings

What's left

Action plan...

Better With A PLAN | BUDGET PLANNER

What's coming in?

Salary	Extras	Bank Balance	Total

What's going out?

Essentials / Savings ideas?

- Housing costs
- Council tax
- Gas
- Electric
- Water
- Mobile phone
- Broadband/TV/landline
- TV license
- Car (insurance/tax/MOT)
- Home insurance
- Food
- Clothes/shoes (essentials)
- Savings
- Other

TOTAL

Debts...

- Credit cards
- Loans
- Other

TOTAL

Are you getting the best interest rates?

The Fun Stuff

- Gym
- Socialising
- Clothes
- Holidays
- Gifts
- Hair/beauty
- Hobbies
- Other

TOTAL

Day to day costs

- Lunch/Food
- Travelling
- Drinks
- Extras

Where are we?

- Incomings
- Outgoings
- What's left

Action plan...

Better With A PLAN | BUDGET PLANNER

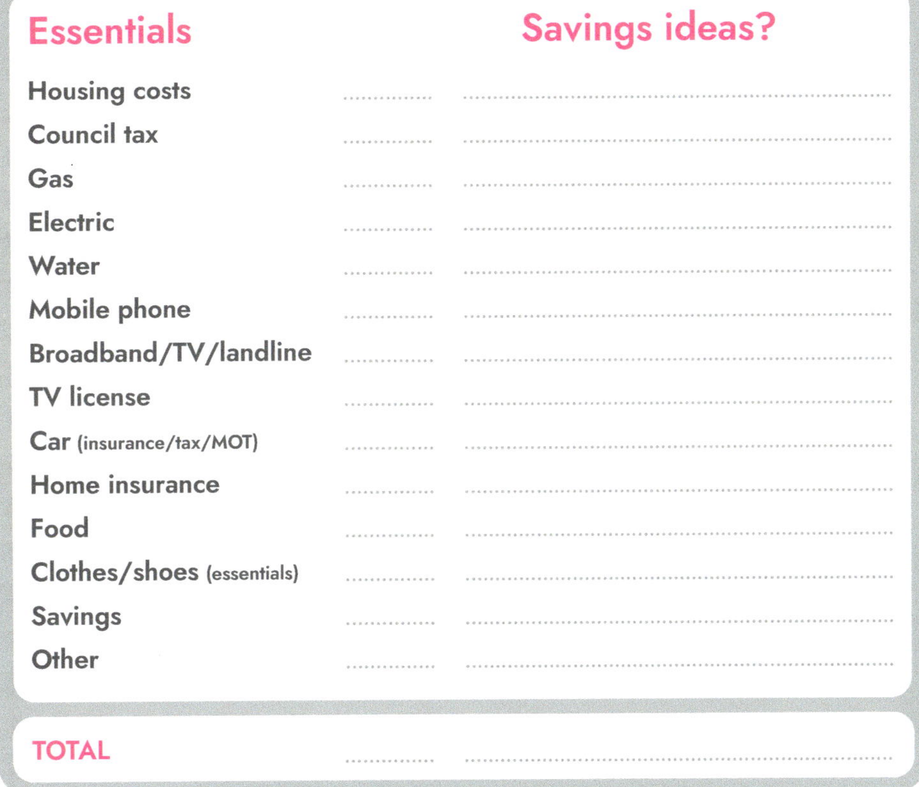

What's coming in?

Salary	Extras	Bank Balance	Total

What's going out?

Essentials

Housing costs
Council tax
Gas
Electric
Water
Mobile phone
Broadband/TV/landline
TV license
Car (insurance/tax/MOT)
Home insurance
Food
Clothes/shoes (essentials)
Savings
Other

TOTAL

Savings ideas?

Debts...

Credit cards
Loans
Other

TOTAL

The Fun Stuff

Gym
Socialising
Clothes
Holidays
Gifts
Hair/beauty
Hobbies
Other

TOTAL

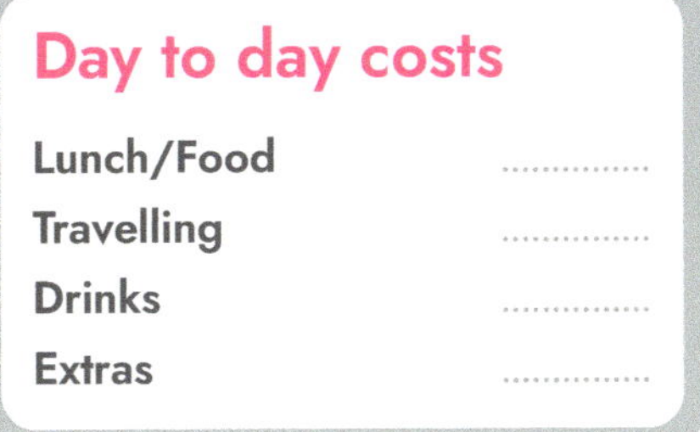

Day to day costs

Lunch/Food
Travelling
Drinks
Extras

Where are we?

Incomings
Outgoings
What's left

Action plan...

Better With A PLAN | BUDGET PLANNER

What's coming in?

Salary   **Extras**   **Bank Balance**   **Total**

What's going out?

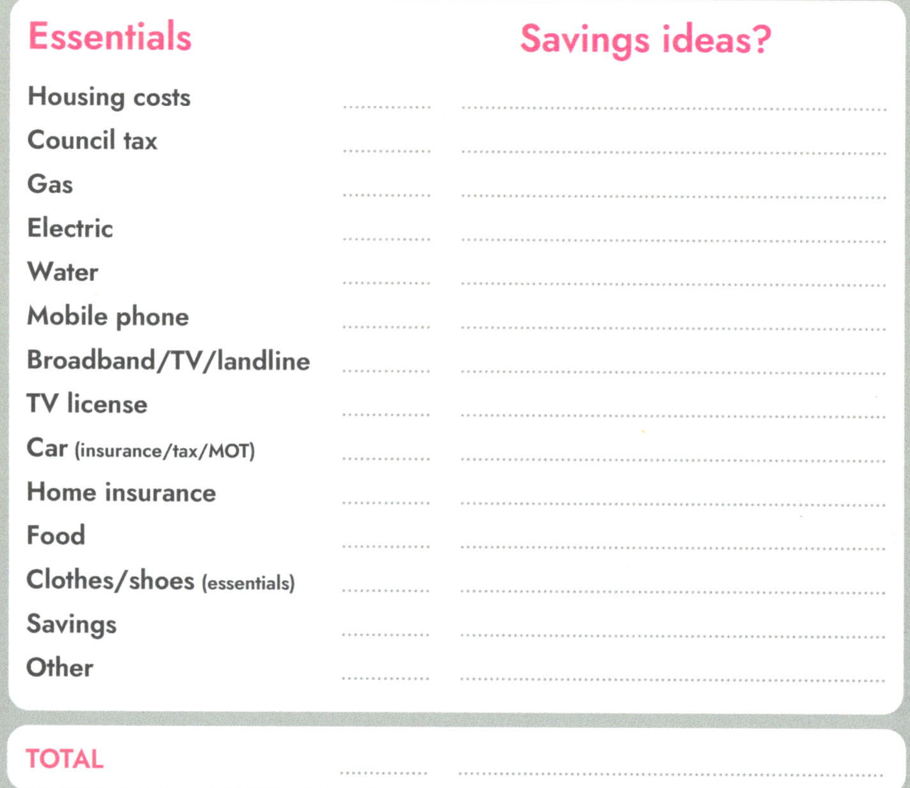

Essentials

Housing costs

Council tax

Gas

Electric

Water

Mobile phone

Broadband/TV/landline

TV license

Car (insurance/tax/MOT)

Home insurance

Food

Clothes/shoes (essentials)

Savings

Other

TOTAL

Savings ideas?

Debts...

Credit cards

Loans

Other

TOTAL

The Fun Stuff

Gym

Socialising

Clothes

Holidays

Gifts

Hair/beauty

Hobbies

Other

TOTAL

Are you getting the best interest rates?

Day to day costs

Lunch/Food

Travelling

Drinks

Extras

Where are we?

Incomings

Outgoings

What's left

Action plan...

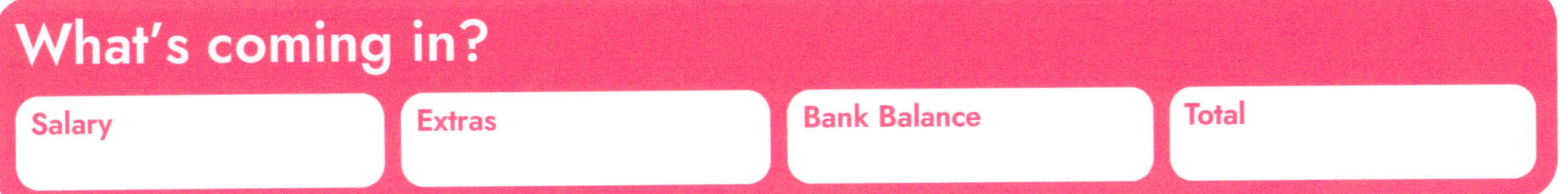

What's coming in?

Salary

Extras

Bank Balance

Total

What's going out?

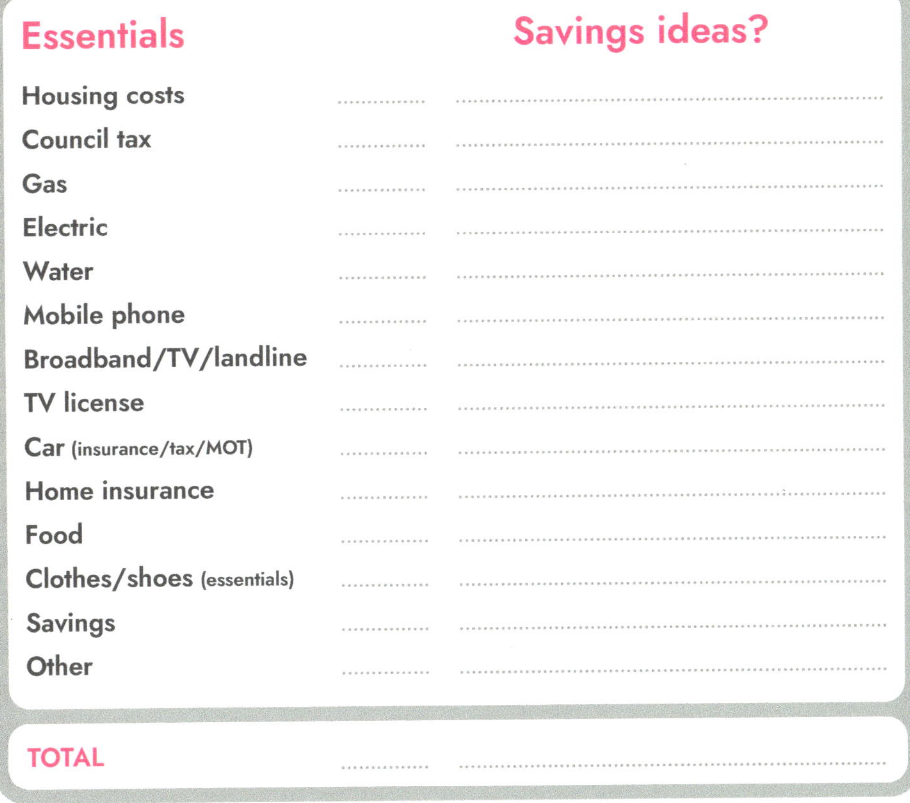

Essentials

Housing costs

Council tax

Gas

Electric

Water

Mobile phone

Broadband/TV/landline

TV license

Car (insurance/tax/MOT)

Home insurance

Food

Clothes/shoes (essentials)

Savings

Other

TOTAL

Savings ideas?

Debts...

Credit cards

Loans

Other

TOTAL

The Fun Stuff

Gym

Socialising

Clothes

Holidays

Gifts

Hair/beauty

Hobbies

Other

TOTAL

Are you getting the best interest rates?

Day to day costs

Lunch/Food

Travelling

Drinks

Extras

Where are we?

Incomings

Outgoings

What's left

Action plan...

Better With A PLAN | BUDGET PLANNER

What's coming in?

Salary

Extras

Bank Balance

Total

What's going out?

Essentials

Housing costs
Council tax
Gas
Electric
Water
Mobile phone
Broadband/TV/landline
TV license
Car (insurance/tax/MOT)
Home insurance
Food
Clothes/shoes (essentials)
Savings
Other

TOTAL

Savings ideas?

Debts...

Credit cards
Loans
Other

TOTAL

Are you getting the best interest rates?

The Fun Stuff

Gym
Socialising
Clothes
Holidays
Gifts
Hair/beauty
Hobbies
Other

TOTAL

Day to day costs

Lunch/Food
Travelling
Drinks
Extras

Where are we?

Incomings
Outgoings
What's left

Action plan...

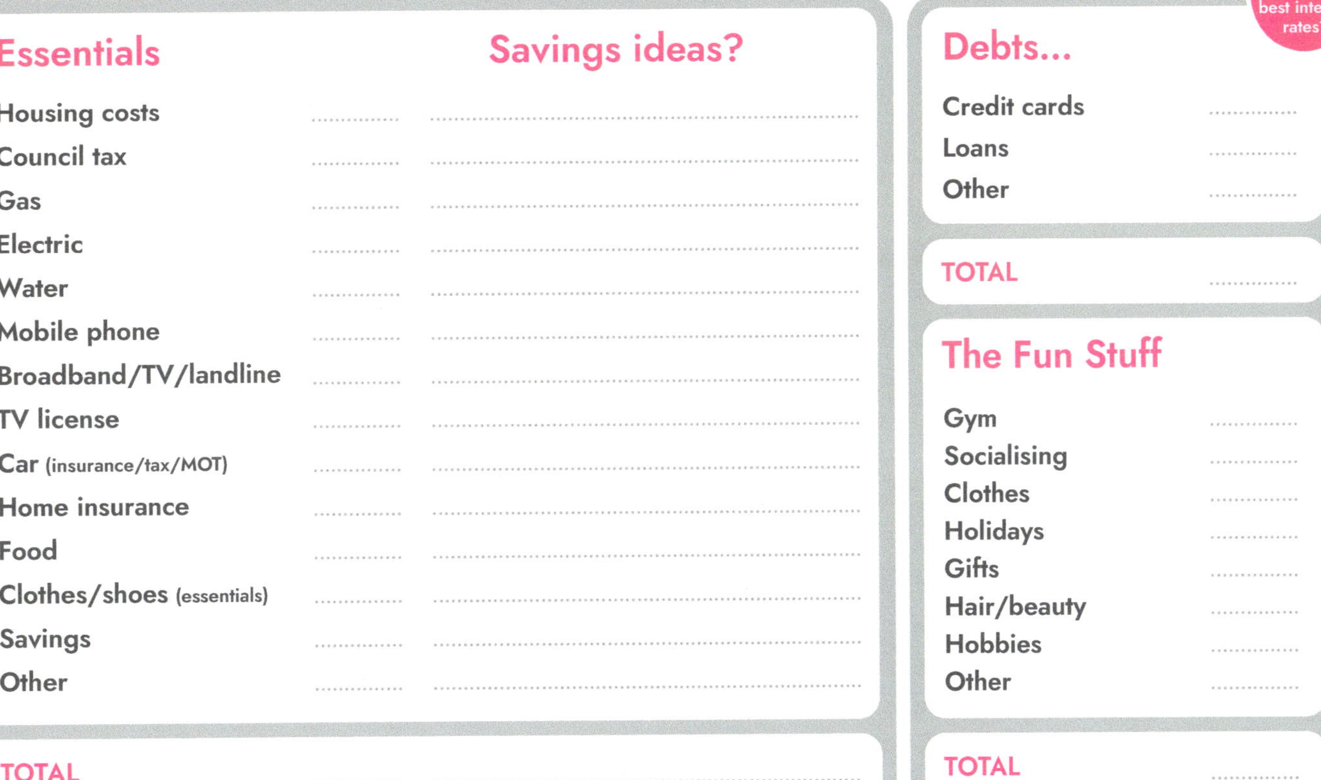

Better With A PLAN | BUDGET PLANNER

What's coming in?

Salary

Extras

Bank Balance

Total

What's going out?

Essentials

Housing costs

Council tax

Gas

Electric

Water

Mobile phone

Broadband/TV/landline

TV license

Car (insurance/tax/MOT)

Home insurance

Food

Clothes/shoes (essentials)

Savings

Other

TOTAL

Savings ideas?

Debts...

Credit cards

Loans

Other

TOTAL

The Fun Stuff

Gym

Socialising

Clothes

Holidays

Gifts

Hair/beauty

Hobbies

Other

TOTAL

Are you getting the best interest rates?

Day to day costs

Lunch/Food

Travelling

Drinks

Extras

Where are we?

Incomings

Outgoings

What's left

Action plan...

Better With A PLAN | BUDGET PLANNER

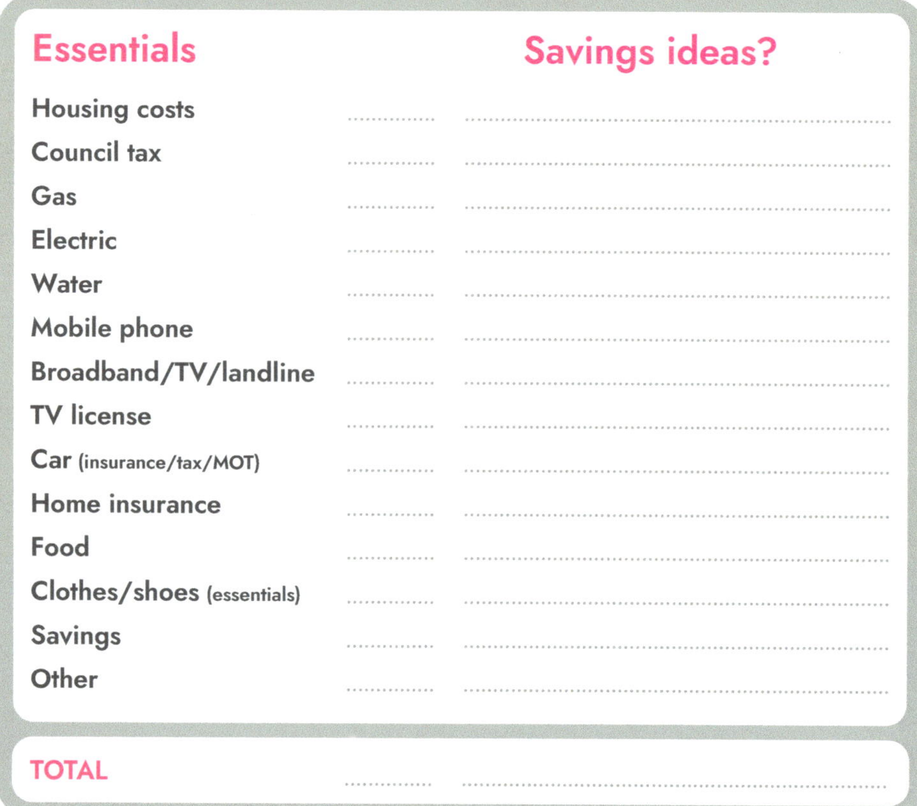

What's coming in?

| Salary | Extras | Bank Balance | Total |

What's going out?

Essentials   Savings ideas?

Housing costs
Council tax
Gas
Electric
Water
Mobile phone
Broadband/TV/landline
TV license
Car (insurance/tax/MOT)
Home insurance
Food
Clothes/shoes (essentials)
Savings
Other

TOTAL

Debts...

Credit cards
Loans
Other

TOTAL

The Fun Stuff

Gym
Socialising
Clothes
Holidays
Gifts
Hair/beauty
Hobbies
Other

TOTAL

Are you getting the best interest rates?

Day to day costs

Lunch/Food
Travelling
Drinks
Extras

Where are we?

Incomings
Outgoings
What's left

Action plan...

143

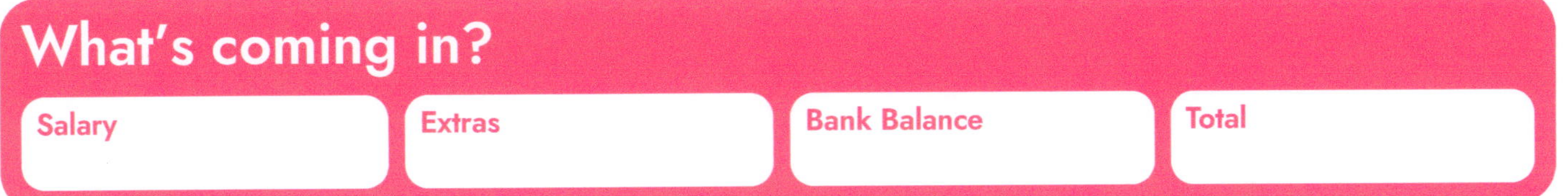

What's coming in?

Salary

Extras

Bank Balance

Total

Day to day costs

Lunch/Food ....
Travelling ....
Drinks ....
Extras ....

What's going out?

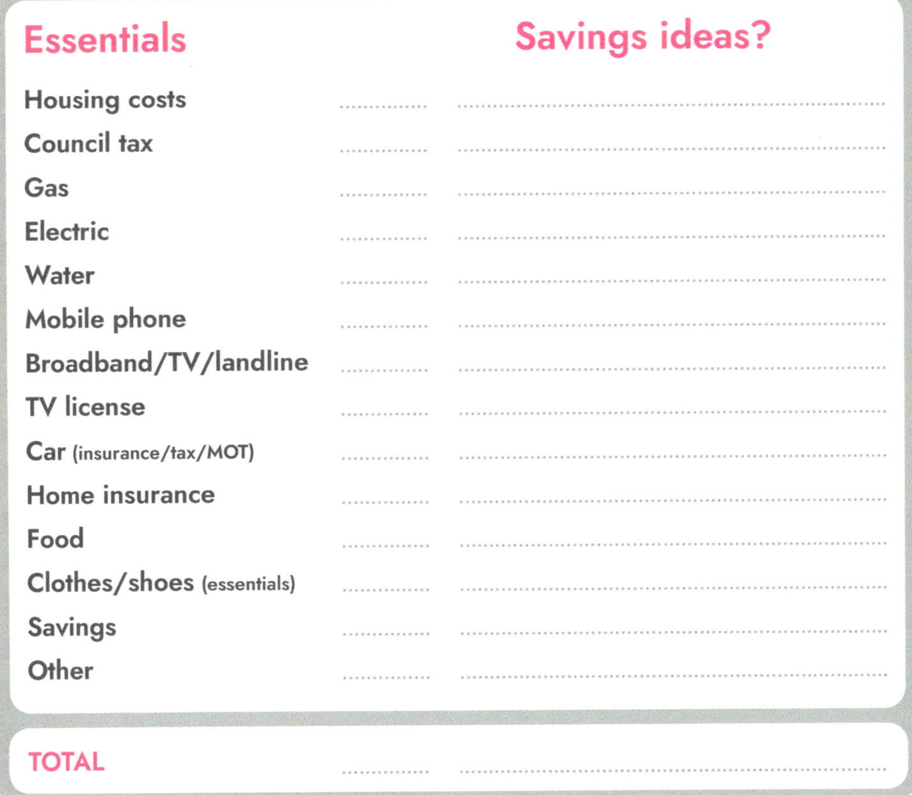

Essentials

Housing costs ....
Council tax ....
Gas ....
Electric ....
Water ....
Mobile phone ....
Broadband/TV/landline ....
TV license ....
Car (insurance/tax/MOT) ....
Home insurance ....
Food ....
Clothes/shoes (essentials) ....
Savings ....
Other ....

TOTAL ....

Savings ideas?

Debts...

Credit cards ....
Loans ....
Other ....

TOTAL ....

The Fun Stuff

Gym ....
Socialising ....
Clothes ....
Holidays ....
Gifts ....
Hair/beauty ....
Hobbies ....
Other ....

TOTAL ....

Where are we?

Incomings ....
Outgoings ....
What's left ....

Action plan...

Better With A PLAN | BUDGET PLANNER

What's coming in?

Salary

Extras

Bank Balance

Total

What's going out?

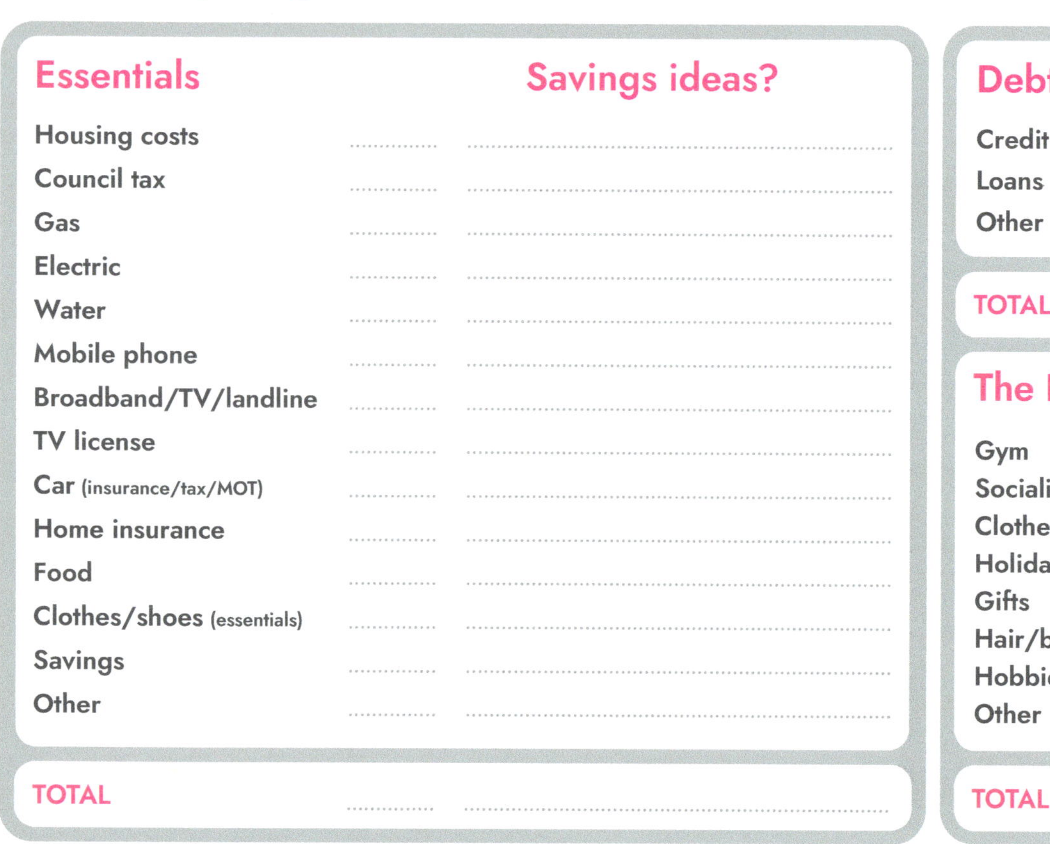

Essentials

Housing costs
Council tax
Gas
Electric
Water
Mobile phone
Broadband/TV/landline
TV license
Car (insurance/tax/MOT)
Home insurance
Food
Clothes/shoes (essentials)
Savings
Other

TOTAL

Savings ideas?

Debts...

Credit cards
Loans
Other

TOTAL

Are you getting the best interest rates?

The Fun Stuff

Gym
Socialising
Clothes
Holidays
Gifts
Hair/beauty
Hobbies
Other

TOTAL

Day to day costs

Lunch/Food
Travelling
Drinks
Extras

Where are we?

Incomings
Outgoings
What's left

Action plan...

Better With A PLAN | BUDGET PLANNER

What's coming in?

Salary

Extras

Bank Balance

Total

What's going out?

Essentials

Housing costs

Council tax

Gas

Electric

Water

Mobile phone

Broadband/TV/landline

TV license

Car (insurance/tax/MOT)

Home insurance

Food

Clothes/shoes (essentials)

Savings

Other

Savings ideas?

TOTAL

Debts...

Credit cards

Loans

Other

TOTAL

The Fun Stuff

Gym

Socialising

Clothes

Holidays

Gifts

Hair/beauty

Hobbies

Other

TOTAL

Day to day costs

Lunch/Food

Travelling

Drinks

Extras

Where are we?

Incomings

Outgoings

What's left

Action plan...

Better With A PLAN | BUDGET PLANNER

What's coming in?

Salary   Extras   Bank Balance   Total

What's going out?

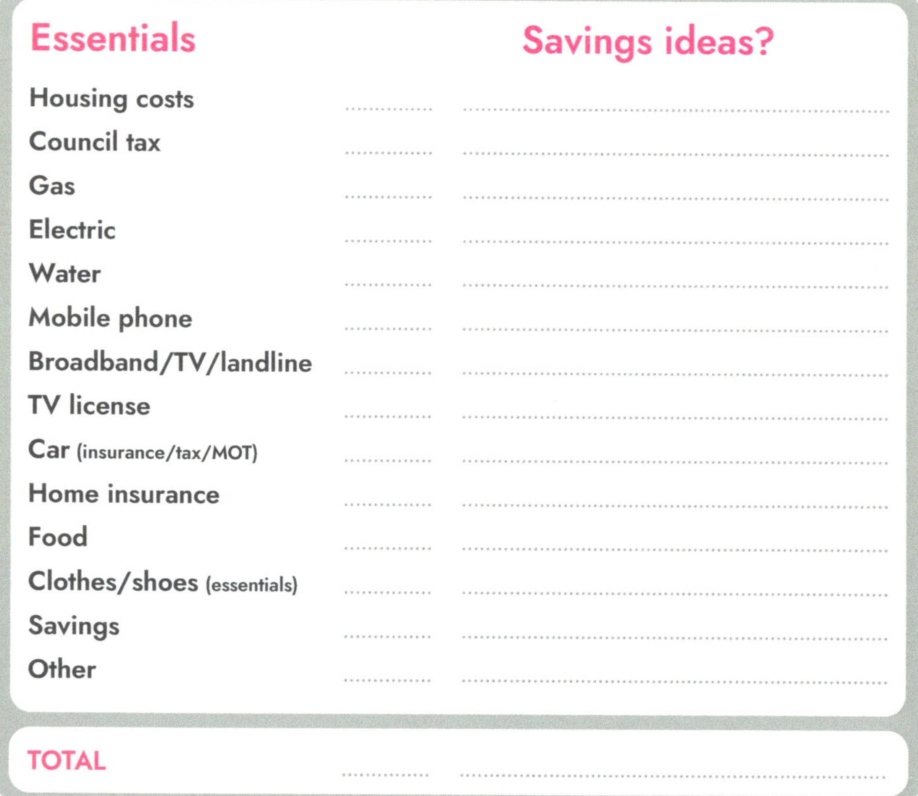

Essentials

Savings ideas?

Housing costs
Council tax
Gas
Electric
Water
Mobile phone
Broadband/TV/landline
TV license
Car (insurance/tax/MOT)
Home insurance
Food
Clothes/shoes (essentials)
Savings
Other

TOTAL

Debts...

Are you getting the best interest rates?

Credit cards
Loans
Other

TOTAL

The Fun Stuff

Gym
Socialising
Clothes
Holidays
Gifts
Hair/beauty
Hobbies
Other

TOTAL

Day to day costs

Lunch/Food
Travelling
Drinks
Extras

Where are we?

Incomings
Outgoings
What's left

Action plan...

Better With A PLAN | BUDGET PLANNER

What's coming in?

Salary | **Extras** | **Bank Balance** | **Total**

What's going out?

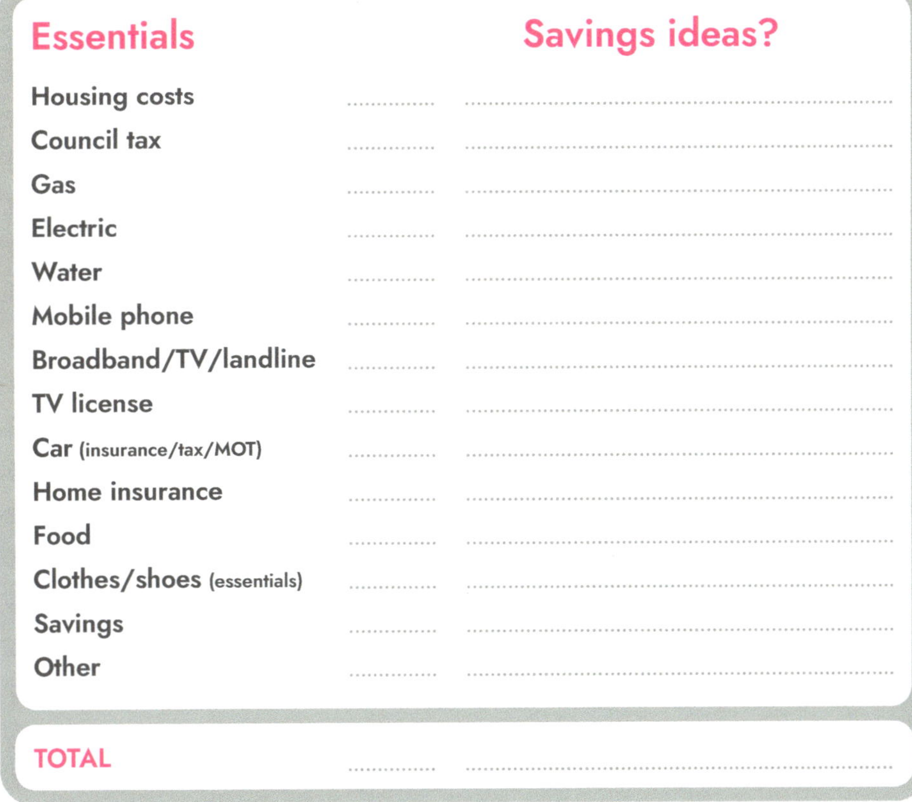

Essentials

Savings ideas?

Housing costs
Council tax
Gas
Electric
Water
Mobile phone
Broadband/TV/landline
TV license
Car (insurance/tax/MOT)
Home insurance
Food
Clothes/shoes (essentials)
Savings
Other

TOTAL

Debts...

Credit cards
Loans
Other

TOTAL

The Fun Stuff

Gym
Socialising
Clothes
Holidays
Gifts
Hair/beauty
Hobbies
Other

TOTAL

Are you getting the best interest rates?

Day to day costs

Lunch/Food
Travelling
Drinks
Extras

Where are we?

Incomings
Outgoings
What's left

Action plan...

Better With A PLAN | BUDGET PLANNER

What's coming in?

Salary	Extras	Bank Balance	Total

What's going out?

Essentials

Housing costs
Council tax
Gas
Electric
Water
Mobile phone
Broadband/TV/landline
TV license
Car (insurance/tax/MOT)
Home insurance
Food
Clothes/shoes (essentials)
Savings
Other

TOTAL

Savings ideas?

Debts...

Credit cards
Loans
Other

TOTAL

Are you getting the best interest rates?

The Fun Stuff

Gym
Socialising
Clothes
Holidays
Gifts
Hair/beauty
Hobbies
Other

TOTAL

Day to day costs

Lunch/Food
Travelling
Drinks
Extras

Where are we?

Incomings
Outgoings
What's left

Action plan...

Better With A PLAN | BUDGET PLANNER

What's coming in?

Salary	Extras	Bank Balance	Total

What's going out?

Essentials — Savings ideas?

Essentials	Savings ideas?
Housing costs	
Council tax	
Gas	
Electric	
Water	
Mobile phone	
Broadband/TV/landline	
TV license	
Car (insurance/tax/MOT)	
Home insurance	
Food	
Clothes/shoes (essentials)	
Savings	
Other	

TOTAL

Debts...

Credit cards	
Loans	
Other	

TOTAL

Are you getting the best interest rates?

The Fun Stuff

Gym	
Socialising	
Clothes	
Holidays	
Gifts	
Hair/beauty	
Hobbies	
Other	

TOTAL

Day to day costs

Lunch/Food	
Travelling	
Drinks	
Extras	

Where are we?

Incomings	
Outgoings	
What's left	

Action plan...

Better With A PLAN | BUDGET PLANNER

What's coming in?

Salary **Extras** **Bank Balance** **Total**

What's going out?

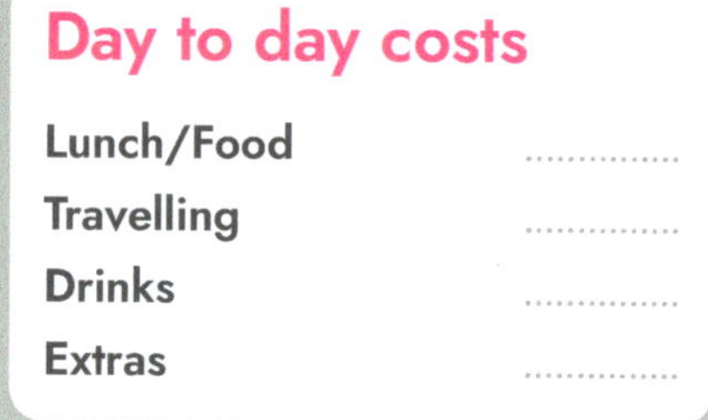

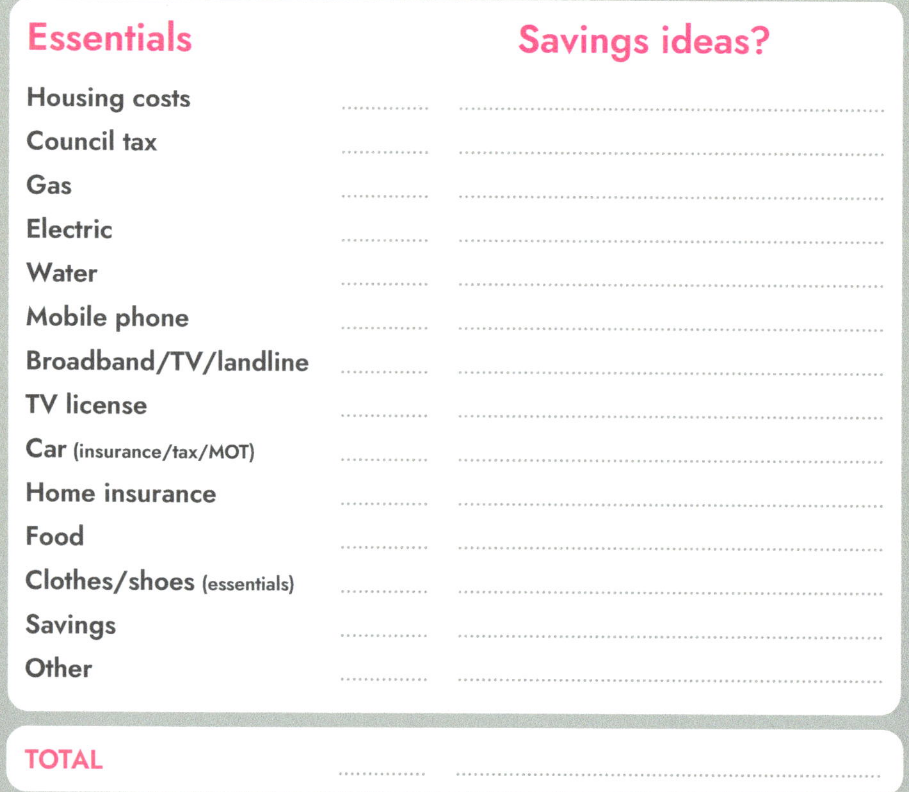

Essentials

Housing costs

Council tax

Gas

Electric

Water

Mobile phone

Broadband/TV/landline

TV license

Car (insurance/tax/MOT)

Home insurance

Food

Clothes/shoes (essentials)

Savings

Other

Savings ideas?

TOTAL

Debts...

Credit cards

Loans

Other

TOTAL

The Fun Stuff

Gym

Socialising

Clothes

Holidays

Gifts

Hair/beauty

Hobbies

Other

TOTAL

Day to day costs

Lunch/Food

Travelling

Drinks

Extras

Where are we?

Incomings

Outgoings

What's left

Action plan...

Better With A
PLAN | BUDGET PLANNER

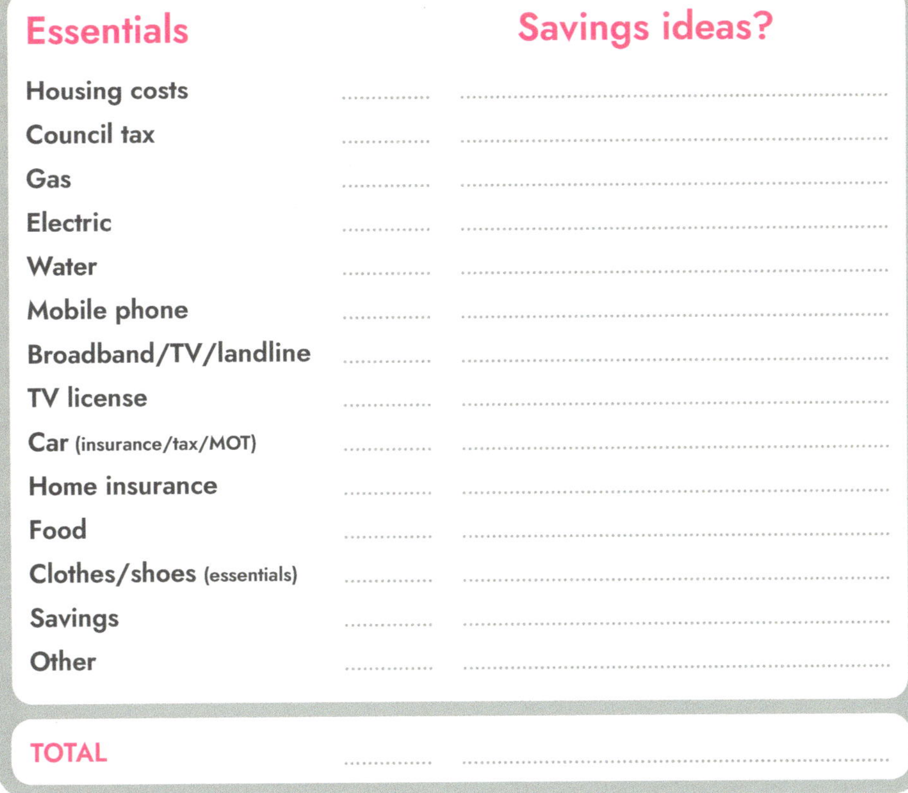

What's coming in?

Salary

Extras

Bank Balance

Total

What's going out?

Essentials   Savings ideas?

Housing costs
Council tax
Gas
Electric
Water
Mobile phone
Broadband/TV/landline
TV license
Car (insurance/tax/MOT)
Home insurance
Food
Clothes/shoes (essentials)
Savings
Other

TOTAL

Are you getting the best interest rates?

Debts...

Credit cards
Loans
Other

TOTAL

The Fun Stuff

Gym
Socialising
Clothes
Holidays
Gifts
Hair/beauty
Hobbies
Other

TOTAL

Day to day costs

Lunch/Food
Travelling
Drinks
Extras

Where are we?

Incomings
Outgoings
What's left

Action plan...

Better With A PLAN | BUDGET PLANNER

What's coming in?

Salary	Extras	Bank Balance	Total

What's going out?

Essentials

Savings ideas?

- Housing costs
- Council tax
- Gas
- Electric
- Water
- Mobile phone
- Broadband/TV/landline
- TV license
- Car (insurance/tax/MOT)
- Home insurance
- Food
- Clothes/shoes (essentials)
- Savings
- Other

TOTAL

Debts...

- Credit cards
- Loans
- Other

TOTAL

Are you getting the best interest rates?

The Fun Stuff

- Gym
- Socialising
- Clothes
- Holidays
- Gifts
- Hair/beauty
- Hobbies
- Other

TOTAL

Day to day costs

- Lunch/Food
- Travelling
- Drinks
- Extras

Where are we?

- Incomings
- Outgoings
- What's left

Action plan...

What's coming in?

Salary	Extras	Bank Balance	Total

Day to day costs

Lunch/Food ....
Travelling ....
Drinks ....
Extras ....

What's going out?

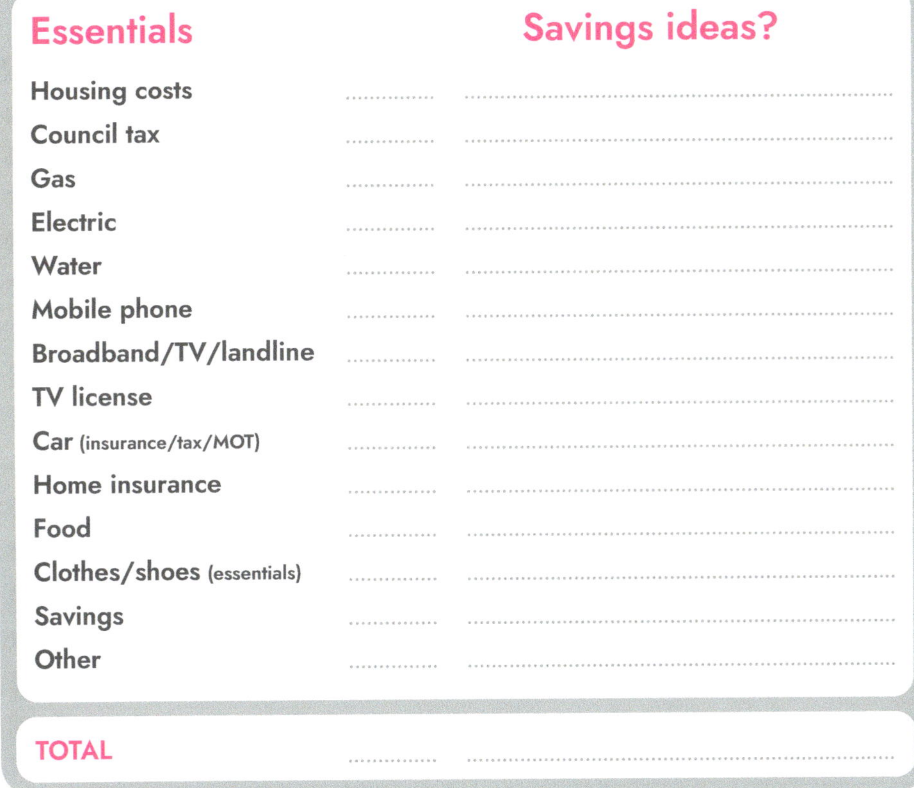

Essentials

Housing costs ....
Council tax ....
Gas ....
Electric ....
Water ....
Mobile phone ....
Broadband/TV/landline ....
TV license ....
Car (insurance/tax/MOT) ....
Home insurance ....
Food ....
Clothes/shoes (essentials) ....
Savings ....
Other ....

Savings ideas?

TOTAL ....

Debts...

Credit cards ....
Loans ....
Other ....

TOTAL ....

The Fun Stuff

Gym ....
Socialising ....
Clothes ....
Holidays ....
Gifts ....
Hair/beauty ....
Hobbies ....
Other ....

TOTAL ....

Where are we?

Incomings ....
Outgoings ....
What's left ....

Action plan...

Better With A PLAN | BUDGET PLANNER

What's coming in?

Salary | Extras | Bank Balance | Total

What's going out?

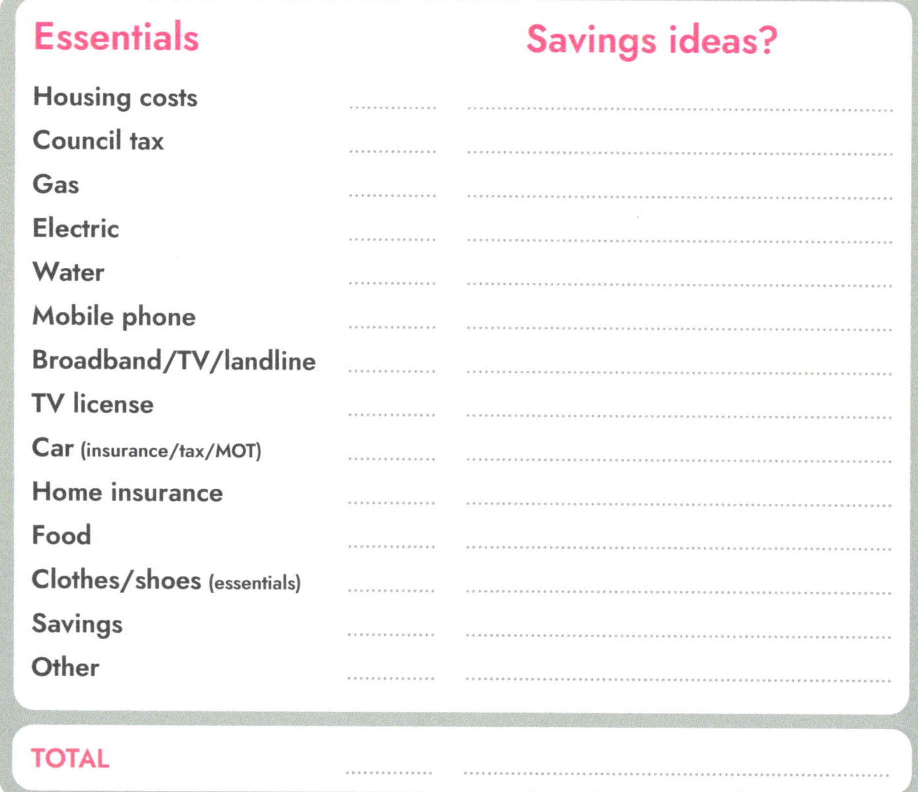

Essentials

Housing costs
Council tax
Gas
Electric
Water
Mobile phone
Broadband/TV/landline
TV license
Car (insurance/tax/MOT)
Home insurance
Food
Clothes/shoes (essentials)
Savings
Other

TOTAL

Savings ideas?

Debts...

Credit cards
Loans
Other

TOTAL

The Fun Stuff

Gym
Socialising
Clothes
Holidays
Gifts
Hair/beauty
Hobbies
Other

TOTAL

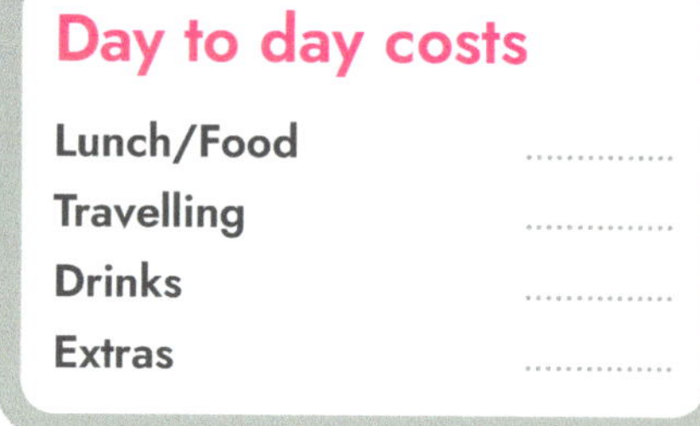

Day to day costs

Lunch/Food
Travelling
Drinks
Extras

Where are we?

Incomings
Outgoings
What's left

Action plan...

Better With A PLAN | BUDGET PLANNER

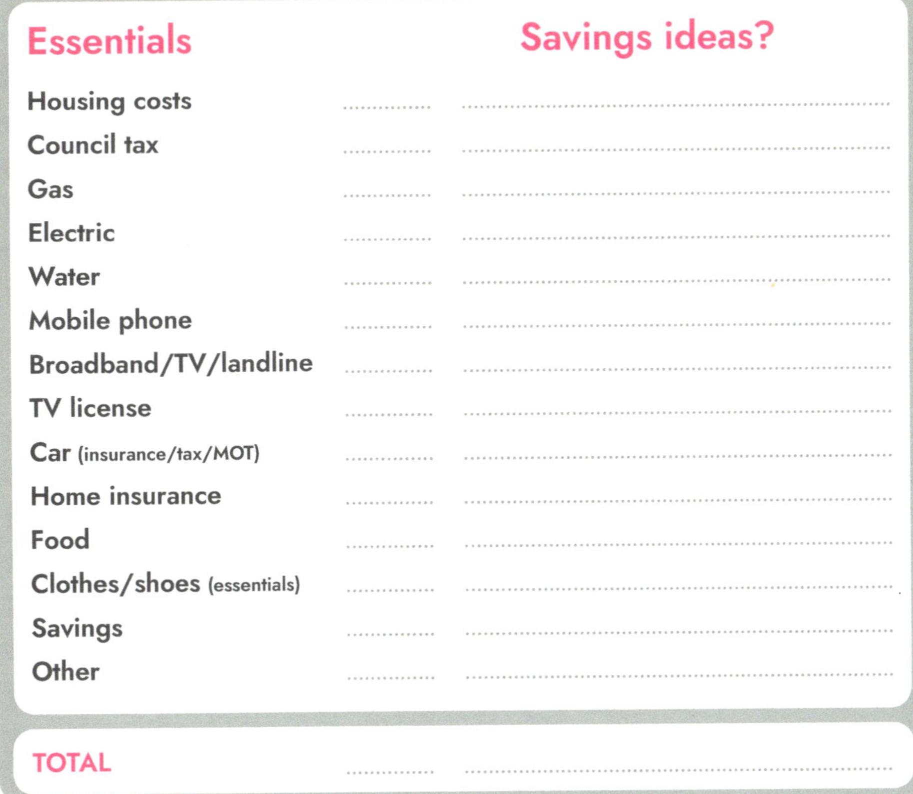

What's coming in?

Salary

Extras

Bank Balance

Total

What's going out?

Essentials

Housing costs
Council tax
Gas
Electric
Water
Mobile phone
Broadband/TV/landline
TV license
Car (insurance/tax/MOT)
Home insurance
Food
Clothes/shoes (essentials)
Savings
Other

TOTAL

Savings ideas?

Day to day costs

Lunch/Food
Travelling
Drinks
Extras

Are you getting the best interest rates?

Debts...

Credit cards
Loans
Other

TOTAL

The Fun Stuff

Gym
Socialising
Clothes
Holidays
Gifts
Hair/beauty
Hobbies
Other

TOTAL

Where are we?

Incomings
Outgoings
What's left

Action plan...

Better With A PLAN | BUDGET PLANNER

What's coming in?

Salary

Extras

Bank Balance

Total

What's going out?

Essentials

Housing costs
Council tax
Gas
Electric
Water
Mobile phone
Broadband/TV/landline
TV license
Car (insurance/tax/MOT)
Home insurance
Food
Clothes/shoes (essentials)
Savings
Other

TOTAL

Savings ideas?

Debts...

Credit cards
Loans
Other

TOTAL

Are you getting the best interest rates?

The Fun Stuff

Gym
Socialising
Clothes
Holidays
Gifts
Hair/beauty
Hobbies
Other

TOTAL

Day to day costs

Lunch/Food
Travelling
Drinks
Extras

Where are we?

Incomings
Outgoings
What's left

Action plan...

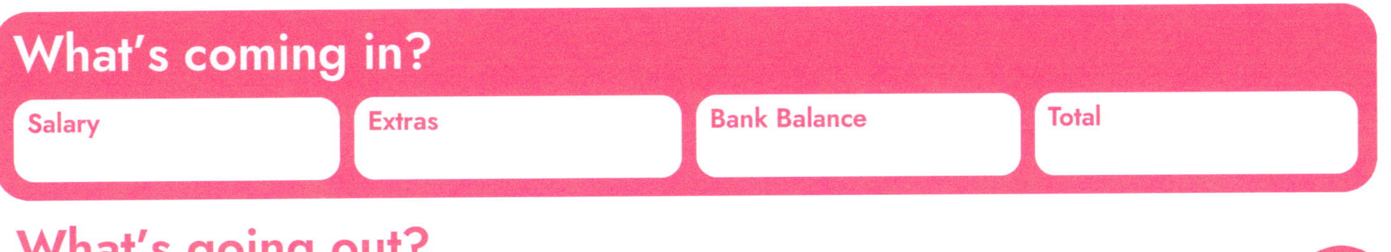

BUDGET PLANNER

What's coming in?

Salary

Extras

Bank Balance

Total

Day to day costs

Lunch/Food
Travelling
Drinks
Extras

What's going out?

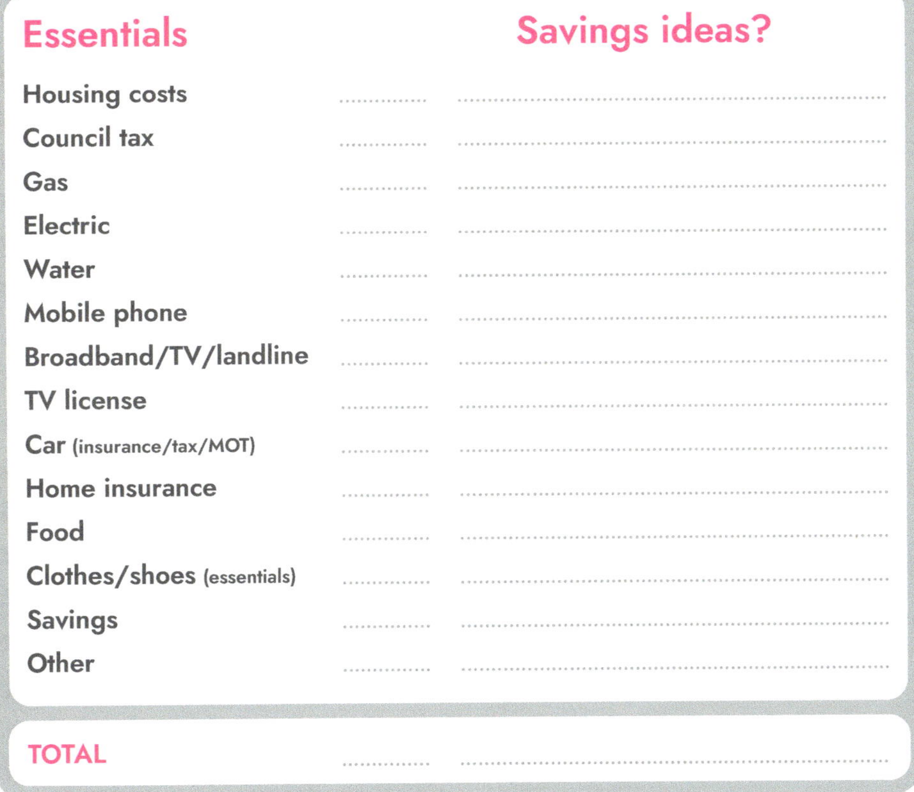

Essentials

Housing costs
Council tax
Gas
Electric
Water
Mobile phone
Broadband/TV/landline
TV license
Car (insurance/tax/MOT)
Home insurance
Food
Clothes/shoes (essentials)
Savings
Other

TOTAL

Savings ideas?

Debts...

Credit cards
Loans
Other

TOTAL

Are you getting the best interest rates?

The Fun Stuff

Gym
Socialising
Clothes
Holidays
Gifts
Hair/beauty
Hobbies
Other

TOTAL

Where are we?

Incomings
Outgoings
What's left

Action plan...

Better With A
PLAN | BUDGET PLANNER

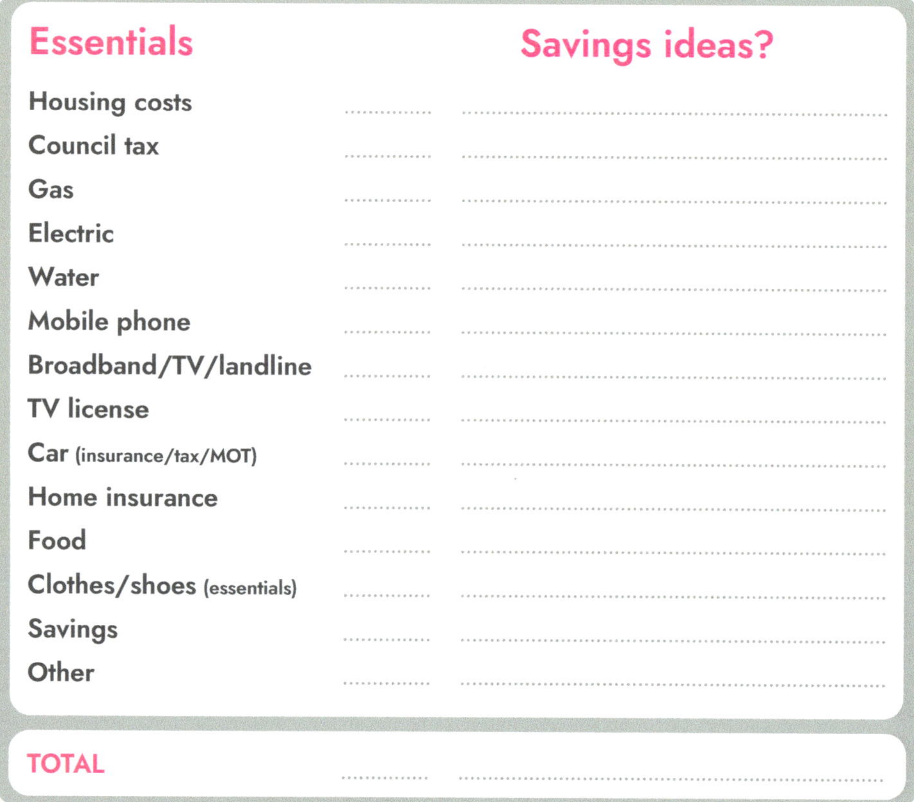

What's coming in?

Salary
Extras
Bank Balance
Total

What's going out?

Essentials   Savings ideas?

Housing costs
Council tax
Gas
Electric
Water
Mobile phone
Broadband/TV/landline
TV license
Car (insurance/tax/MOT)
Home insurance
Food
Clothes/shoes (essentials)
Savings
Other

TOTAL

Debts...

Credit cards
Loans
Other

TOTAL

The Fun Stuff

Gym
Socialising
Clothes
Holidays
Gifts
Hair/beauty
Hobbies
Other

TOTAL

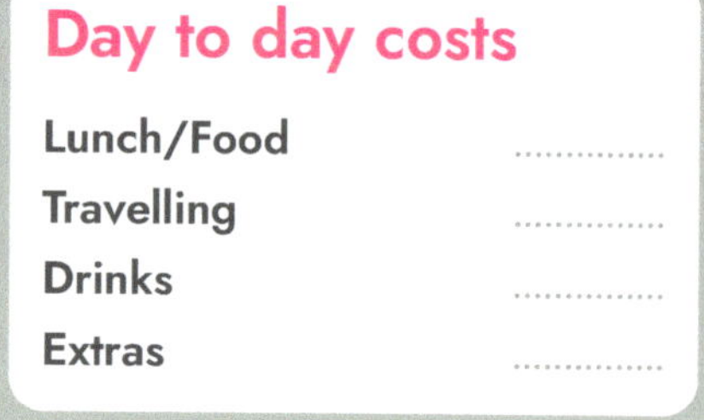

Are you getting the best interest rates?

Day to day costs

Lunch/Food
Travelling
Drinks
Extras

Where are we?

Incomings
Outgoings
What's left

Action plan...

Better With A PLAN | BUDGET PLANNER

What's coming in?

Salary	Extras	Bank Balance	Total

What's going out?

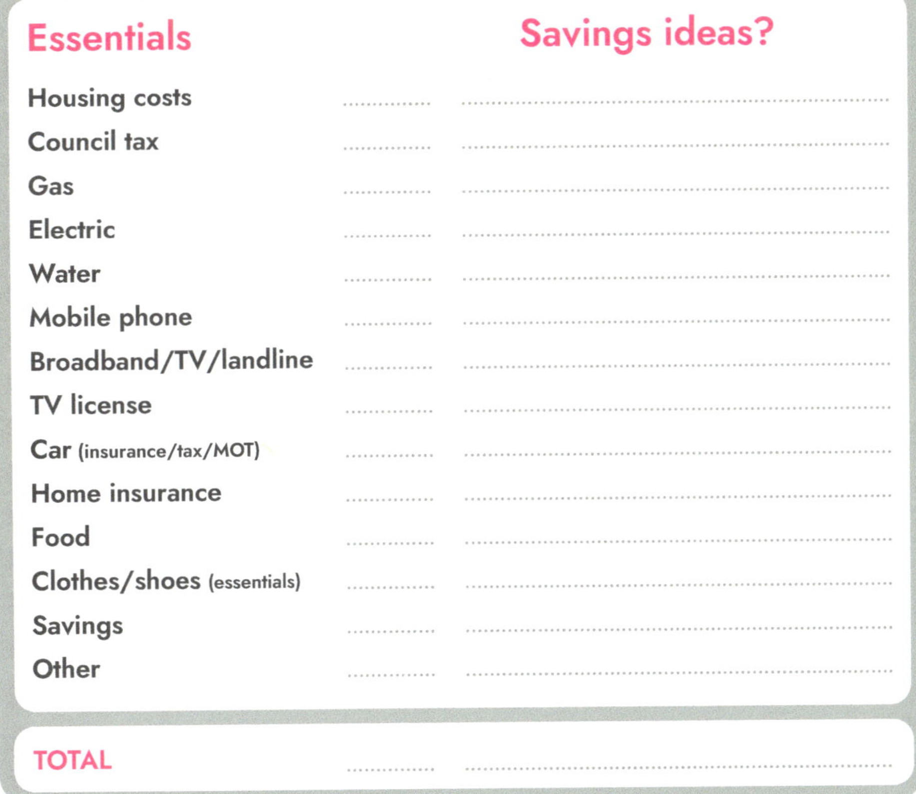

Essentials

	Savings ideas?
Housing costs	
Council tax	
Gas	
Electric	
Water	
Mobile phone	
Broadband/TV/landline	
TV license	
Car (insurance/tax/MOT)	
Home insurance	
Food	
Clothes/shoes (essentials)	
Savings	
Other	

TOTAL

Debts...

Credit cards
Loans
Other

TOTAL

Are you getting the best interest rates?

The Fun Stuff

Gym
Socialising
Clothes
Holidays
Gifts
Hair/beauty
Hobbies
Other

TOTAL

Day to day costs

Lunch/Food
Travelling
Drinks
Extras

Where are we?

Incomings
Outgoings
What's left

Action plan...

BUDGET PLANNER

What's coming in?

Salary

Extras

Bank Balance

Total

What's going out?

Essentials

Housing costs

Council tax

Gas

Electric

Water

Mobile phone

Broadband/TV/landline

TV license

Car (insurance/tax/MOT)

Home insurance

Food

Clothes/shoes (essentials)

Savings

Other

Savings ideas?

TOTAL

Debts...

Credit cards

Loans

Other

TOTAL

Are you getting the best interest rates?

The Fun Stuff

Gym

Socialising

Clothes

Holidays

Gifts

Hair/beauty

Hobbies

Other

TOTAL

Day to day costs

Lunch/Food

Travelling

Drinks

Extras

Where are we?

Incomings

Outgoings

What's left

Action plan...

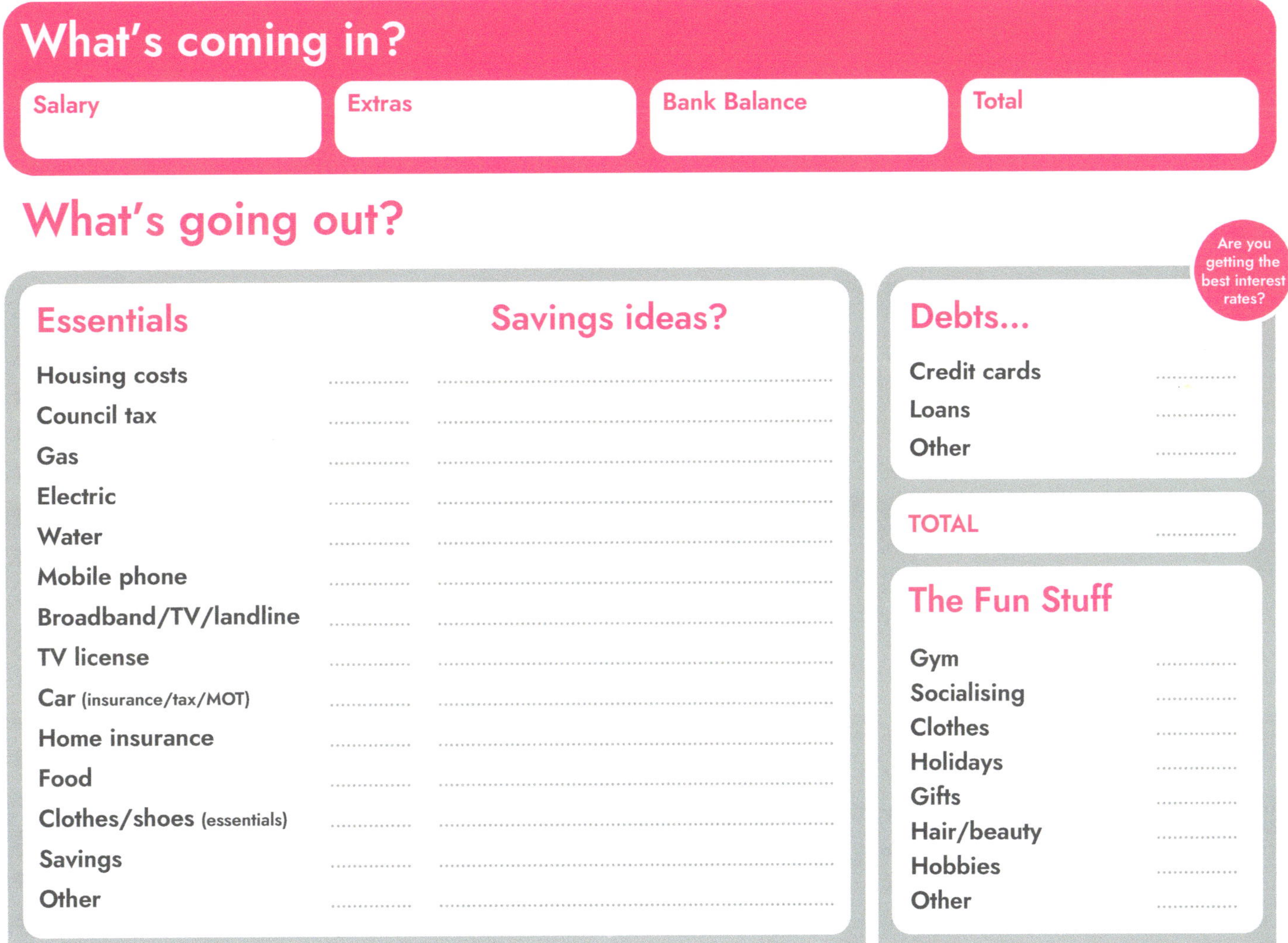

Better With A PLAN | BUDGET PLANNER

What's coming in?

Salary

Extras

Bank Balance

Total

What's going out?

Essentials

Housing costs
Council tax
Gas
Electric
Water
Mobile phone
Broadband/TV/landline
TV license
Car (insurance/tax/MOT)
Home insurance
Food
Clothes/shoes (essentials)
Savings
Other

TOTAL

Savings ideas?

Debts...

Credit cards
Loans
Other

TOTAL

The Fun Stuff

Gym
Socialising
Clothes
Holidays
Gifts
Hair/beauty
Hobbies
Other

TOTAL

Day to day costs

Lunch/Food
Travelling
Drinks
Extras

Where are we?

Incomings
Outgoings
What's left

Action plan...

Better With A PLAN | BUDGET PLANNER

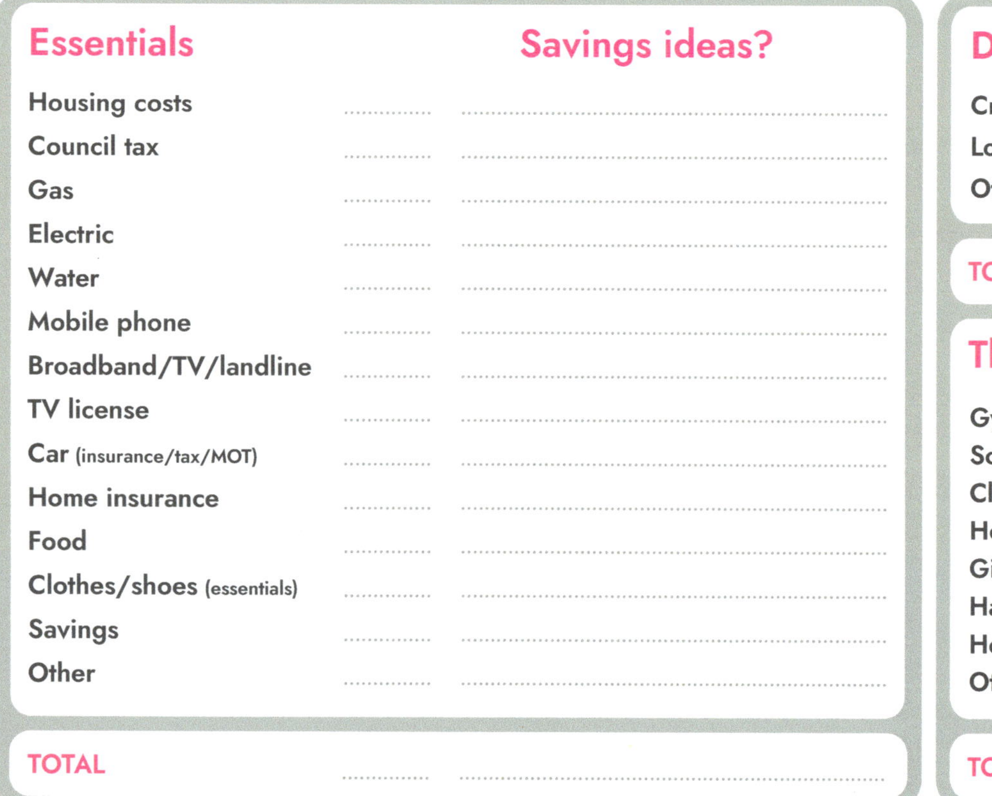

What's coming in?

Salary | Extras | Bank Balance | Total

What's going out?

Essentials

Savings ideas?

Housing costs
Council tax
Gas
Electric
Water
Mobile phone
Broadband/TV/landline
TV license
Car (insurance/tax/MOT)
Home insurance
Food
Clothes/shoes (essentials)
Savings
Other

TOTAL

Debts...

Credit cards
Loans
Other

TOTAL

The Fun Stuff

Gym
Socialising
Clothes
Holidays
Gifts
Hair/beauty
Hobbies
Other

TOTAL

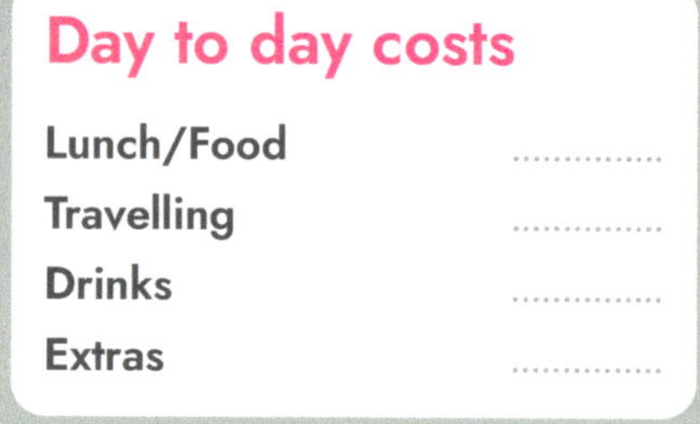

Day to day costs

Lunch/Food
Travelling
Drinks
Extras

Where are we?

Incomings
Outgoings
What's left

Action plan...

Better With A PLAN | BUDGET PLANNER

What's coming in?

Salary	Extras	Bank Balance	Total

What's going out?

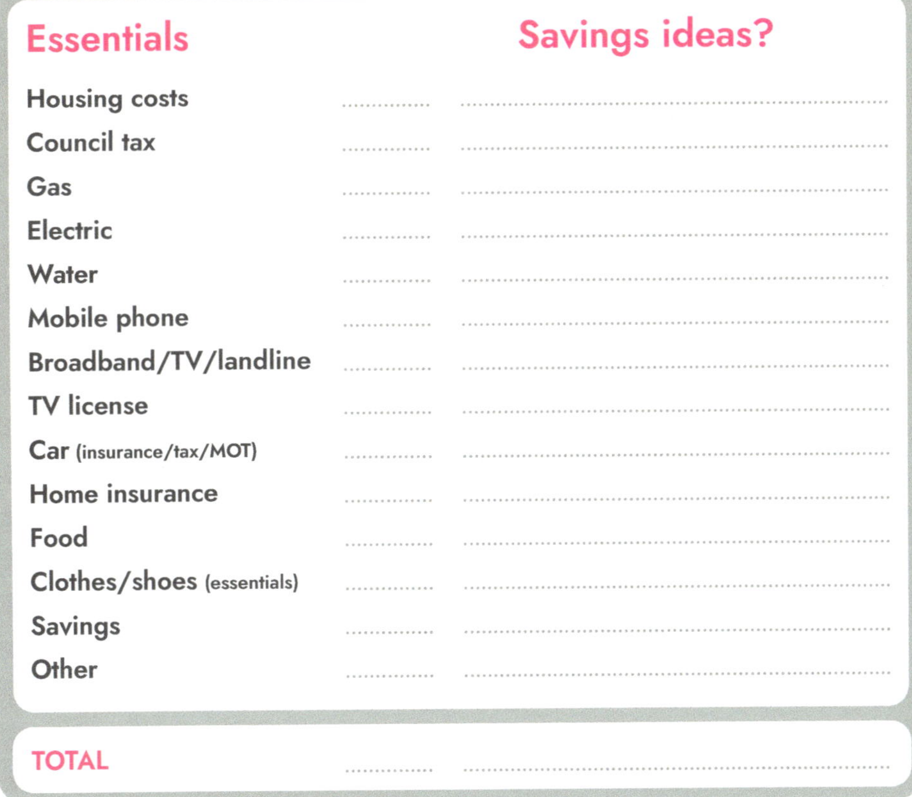

Essentials

		Savings ideas?
Housing costs		
Council tax		
Gas		
Electric		
Water		
Mobile phone		
Broadband/TV/landline		
TV license		
Car (insurance/tax/MOT)		
Home insurance		
Food		
Clothes/shoes (essentials)		
Savings		
Other		

TOTAL

Debts...

Credit cards

Loans

Other

TOTAL

The Fun Stuff

Gym

Socialising

Clothes

Holidays

Gifts

Hair/beauty

Hobbies

Other

TOTAL

Day to day costs

Lunch/Food

Travelling

Drinks

Extras

Are you getting the best interest rates?

Where are we?

Incomings

Outgoings

What's left

Action plan...

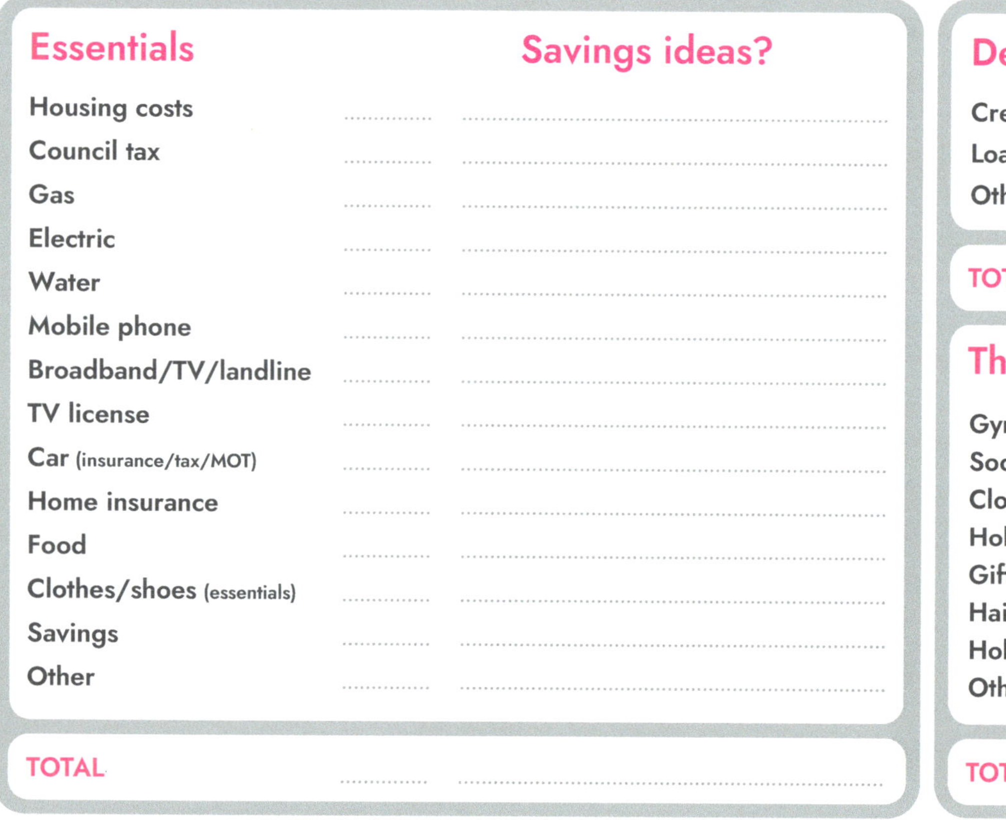

Better With A PLAN | BUDGET PLANNER

What's coming in?

Salary

Extras

Bank Balance

Total

What's going out?

Essentials

Housing costs
Council tax
Gas
Electric
Water
Mobile phone
Broadband/TV/landline
TV license
Car (insurance/tax/MOT)
Home insurance
Food
Clothes/shoes (essentials)
Savings
Other

Savings ideas?

TOTAL

Debts...

Credit cards
Loans
Other

TOTAL

The Fun Stuff

Gym
Socialising
Clothes
Holidays
Gifts
Hair/beauty
Hobbies
Other

TOTAL

Are you getting the best interest rates?

Day to day costs

Lunch/Food
Travelling
Drinks
Extras

Where are we?

Incomings
Outgoings
What's left

Action plan...

BUDGET PLANNER

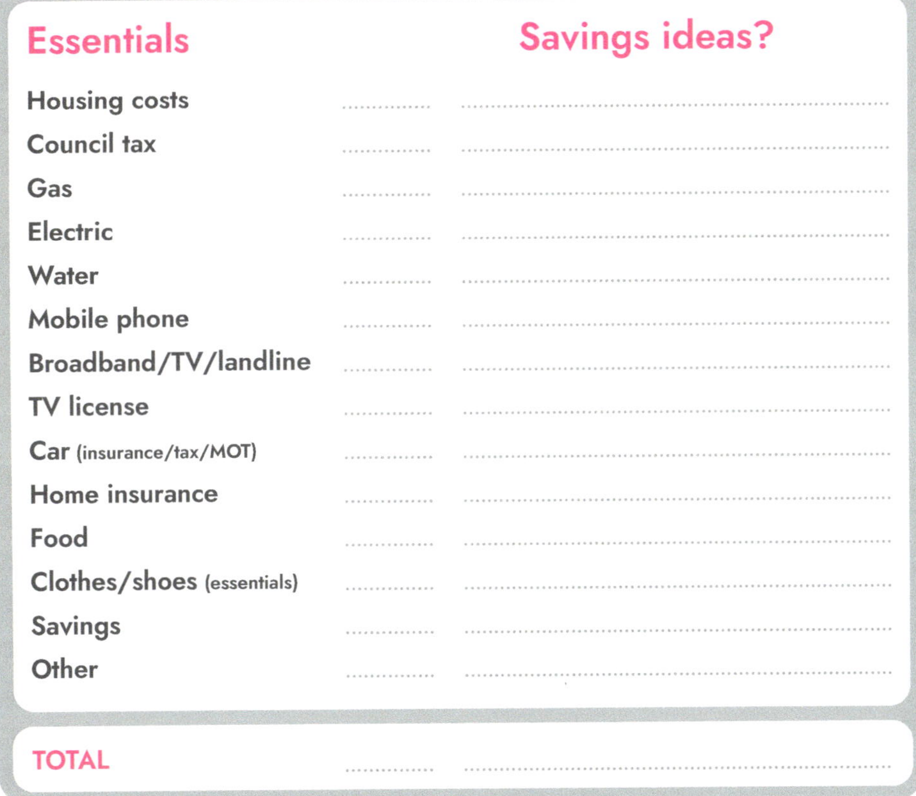

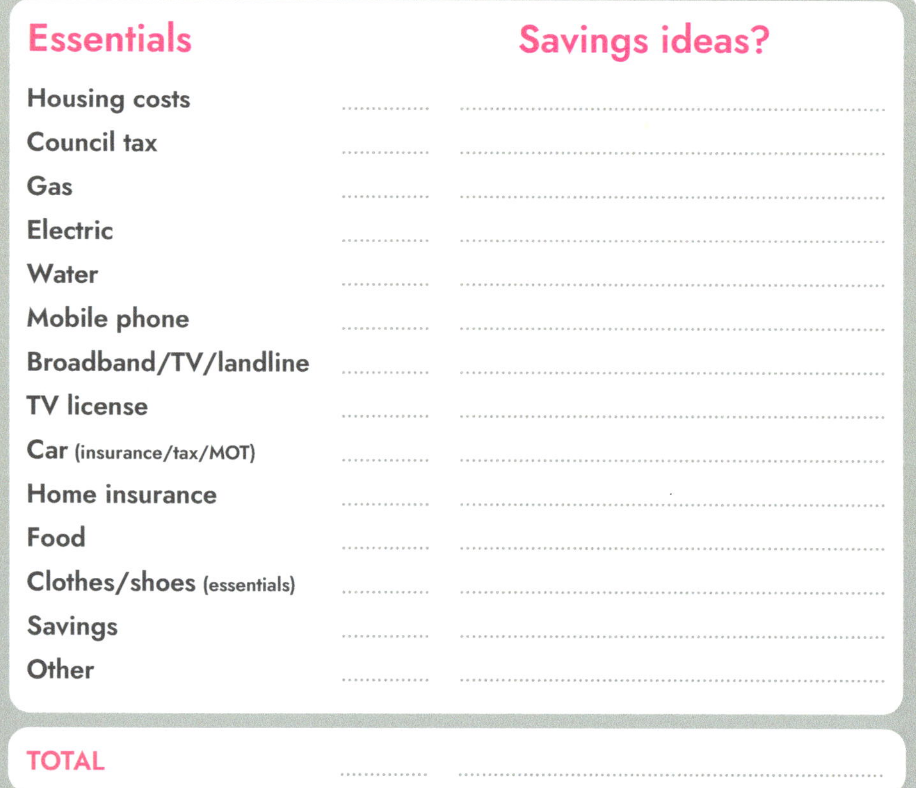

Better With A PLAN | BUDGET PLANNER

What's coming in?

Salary

Extras

Bank Balance

Total

What's going out?

Are you getting the best interest rates?

Essentials

Housing costs
Council tax
Gas
Electric
Water
Mobile phone
Broadband/TV/landline
TV license
Car (insurance/tax/MOT)
Home insurance
Food
Clothes/shoes (essentials)
Savings
Other

Savings ideas?

TOTAL

Debts...

Credit cards
Loans
Other

TOTAL

The Fun Stuff

Gym
Socialising
Clothes
Holidays
Gifts
Hair/beauty
Hobbies
Other

TOTAL

Day to day costs

Lunch/Food
Travelling
Drinks
Extras

Where are we?

Incomings
Outgoings
What's left

Action plan...

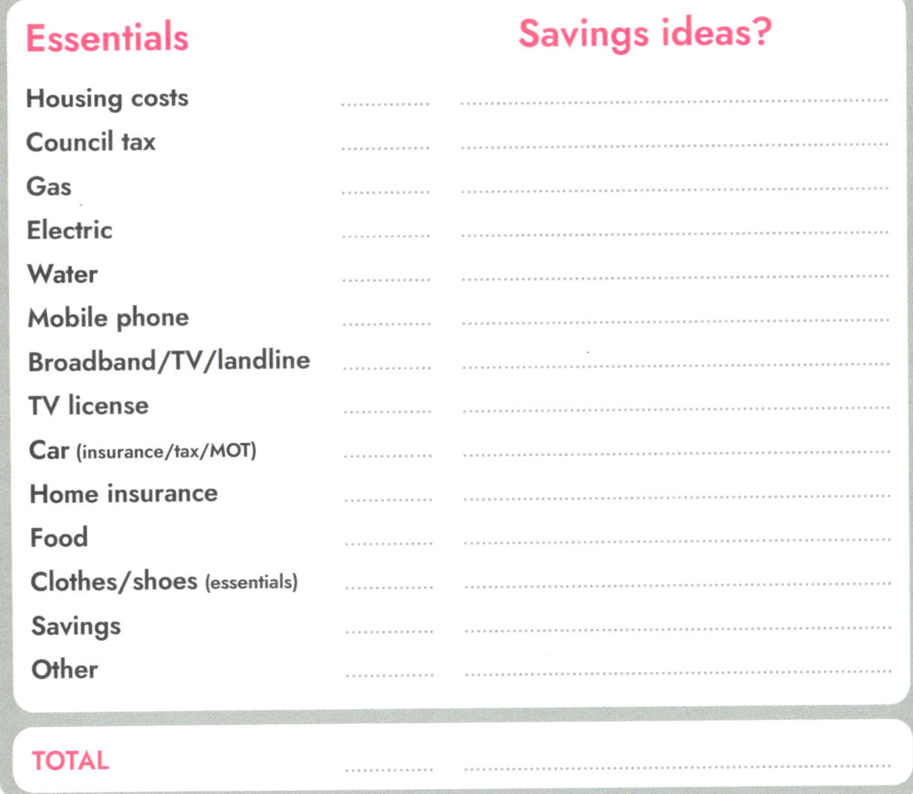

Better With A PLAN | BUDGET PLANNER

What's coming in?

Salary	Extras	Bank Balance	Total

What's going out?

Are you getting the best interest rates?

Essentials · Savings ideas?

Housing costs
Council tax
Gas
Electric
Water
Mobile phone
Broadband/TV/landline
TV license
Car (insurance/tax/MOT)
Home insurance
Food
Clothes/shoes (essentials)
Savings
Other

TOTAL

Debts...

Credit cards
Loans
Other

TOTAL

The Fun Stuff

Gym
Socialising
Clothes
Holidays
Gifts
Hair/beauty
Hobbies
Other

TOTAL

Day to day costs

Lunch/Food
Travelling
Drinks
Extras

Where are we?

Incomings
Outgoings
What's left

Action plan...

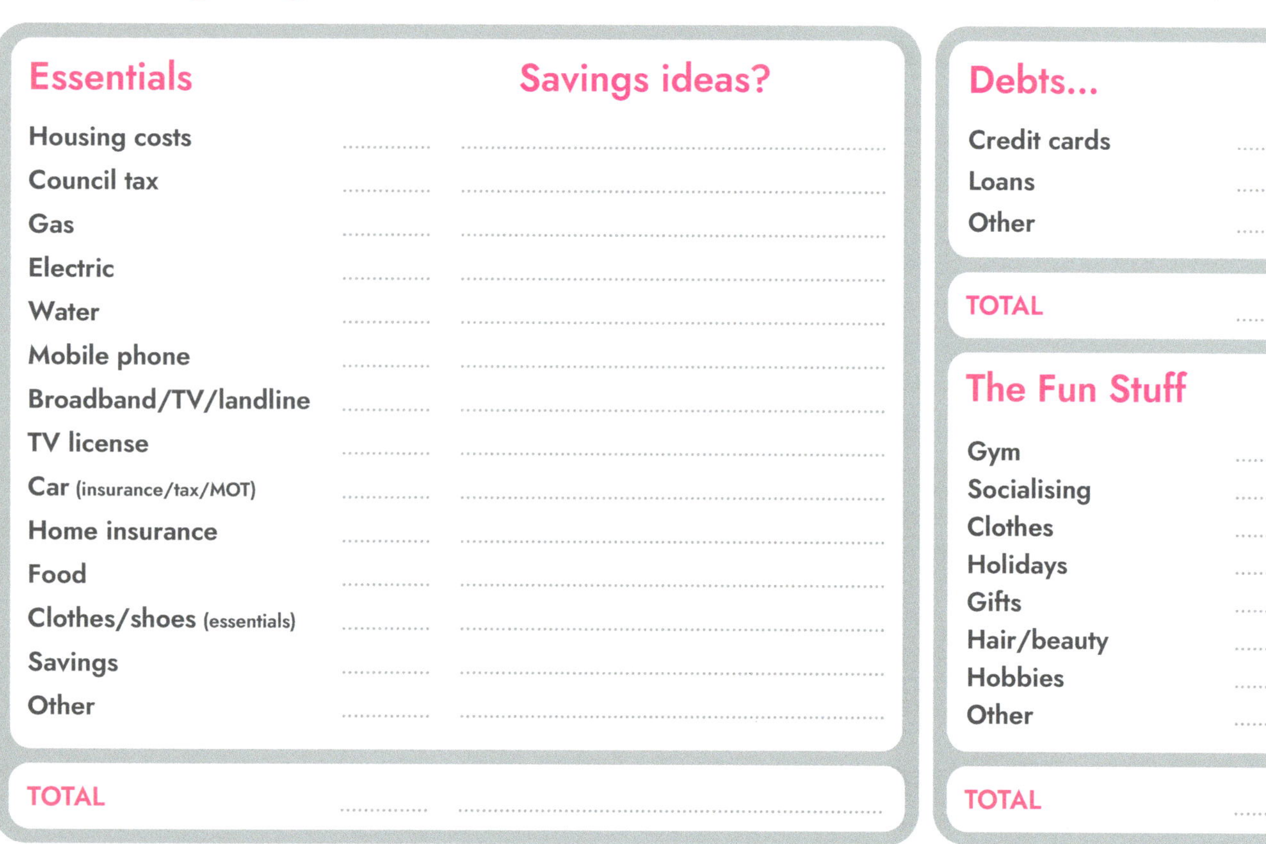

Better With A PLAN | BUDGET PLANNER

What's coming in?

Salary	Extras	Bank Balance	Total

What's going out?

Day to day costs

Lunch/Food
Travelling
Drinks
Extras

Essentials — Savings ideas?

Housing costs
Council tax
Gas
Electric
Water
Mobile phone
Broadband/TV/landline
TV license
Car (insurance/tax/MOT)
Home insurance
Food
Clothes/shoes (essentials)
Savings
Other

TOTAL

Debts...

Are you getting the best interest rates?

Credit cards
Loans
Other

TOTAL

The Fun Stuff

Gym
Socialising
Clothes
Holidays
Gifts
Hair/beauty
Hobbies
Other

TOTAL

Where are we?

Incomings
Outgoings
What's left

Action plan...

PLAN | BUDGET PLANNER

What's coming in?

Salary	Extras	Bank Balance	Total

What's going out?

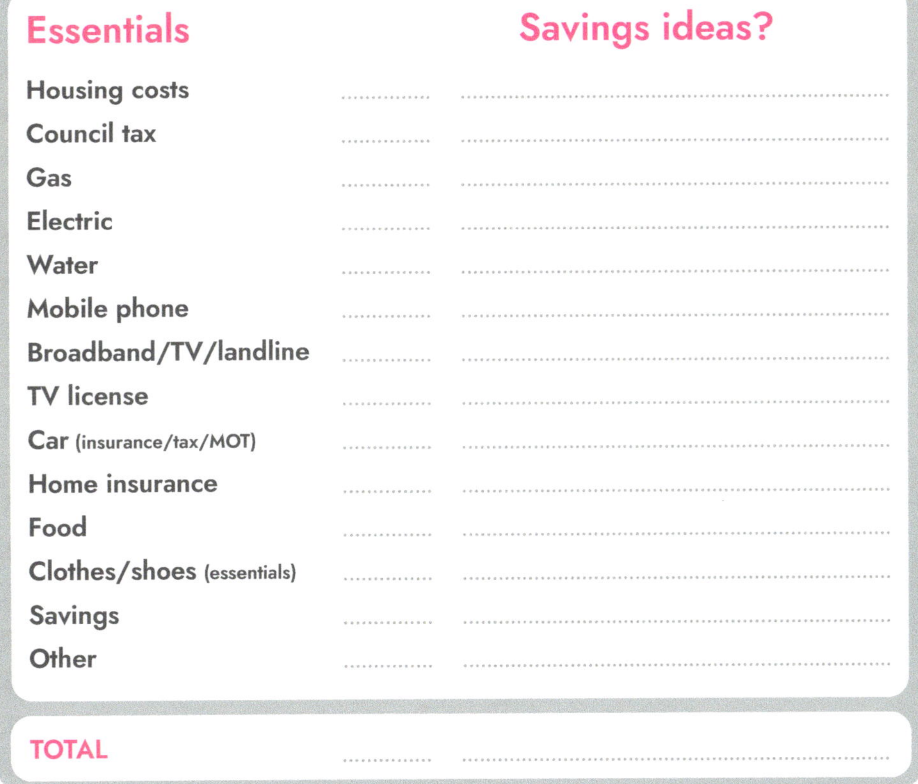

Essentials

Housing costs	Savings ideas?
Council tax	
Gas	
Electric	
Water	
Mobile phone	
Broadband/TV/landline	
TV license	
Car (insurance/tax/MOT)	
Home insurance	
Food	
Clothes/shoes (essentials)	
Savings	
Other	

TOTAL

Debts...

Credit cards
Loans
Other

TOTAL

The Fun Stuff

Gym
Socialising
Clothes
Holidays
Gifts
Hair/beauty
Hobbies
Other

TOTAL

Day to day costs

Lunch/Food
Travelling
Drinks
Extras

Are you getting the best interest rates?

Where are we?

Incomings
Outgoings
What's left

Action plan...

Better With A PLAN | BUDGET PLANNER

What's coming in?

Salary	Extras	Bank Balance	Total

What's going out?

Day to day costs

Lunch/Food ....
Travelling ....
Drinks ....
Extras ....

Essentials — Savings ideas?

Housing costs ....
Council tax ....
Gas ....
Electric ....
Water ....
Mobile phone ....
Broadband/TV/landline ....
TV license ....
Car (insurance/tax/MOT) ....
Home insurance ....
Food ....
Clothes/shoes (essentials) ....
Savings ....
Other ....

TOTAL ....

Debts...

Credit cards ....
Loans ....
Other ....

TOTAL ....

Are you getting the best interest rates?

The Fun Stuff

Gym ....
Socialising ....
Clothes ....
Holidays ....
Gifts ....
Hair/beauty ....
Hobbies ....
Other ....

TOTAL ....

Where are we?

Incomings ....
Outgoings ....
What's left ....

Action plan...

BUDGET PLANNER

What's coming in?

Salary

Extras

Bank Balance

Total

What's going out?

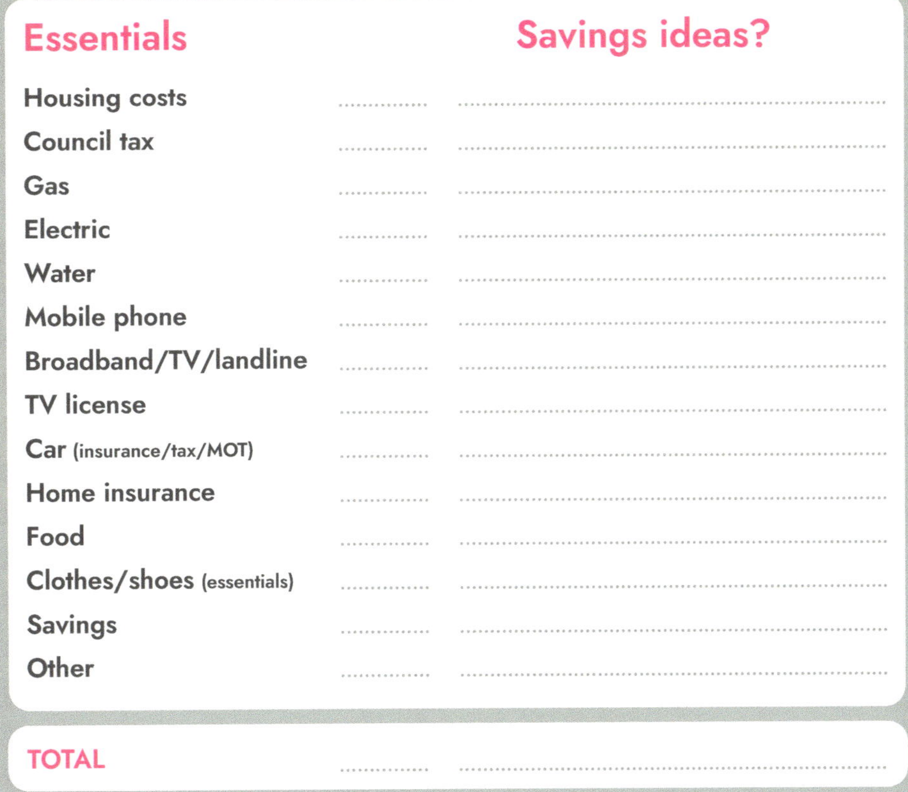

Essentials

Housing costs
Council tax
Gas
Electric
Water
Mobile phone
Broadband/TV/landline
TV license
Car (insurance/tax/MOT)
Home insurance
Food
Clothes/shoes (essentials)
Savings
Other

Savings ideas?

TOTAL

Debts...

Credit cards
Loans
Other

TOTAL

Are you getting the best interest rates?

The Fun Stuff

Gym
Socialising
Clothes
Holidays
Gifts
Hair/beauty
Hobbies
Other

TOTAL

Day to day costs

Lunch/Food
Travelling
Drinks
Extras

Where are we?

Incomings
Outgoings
What's left

Action plan...

Better With A PLAN | BUDGET PLANNER

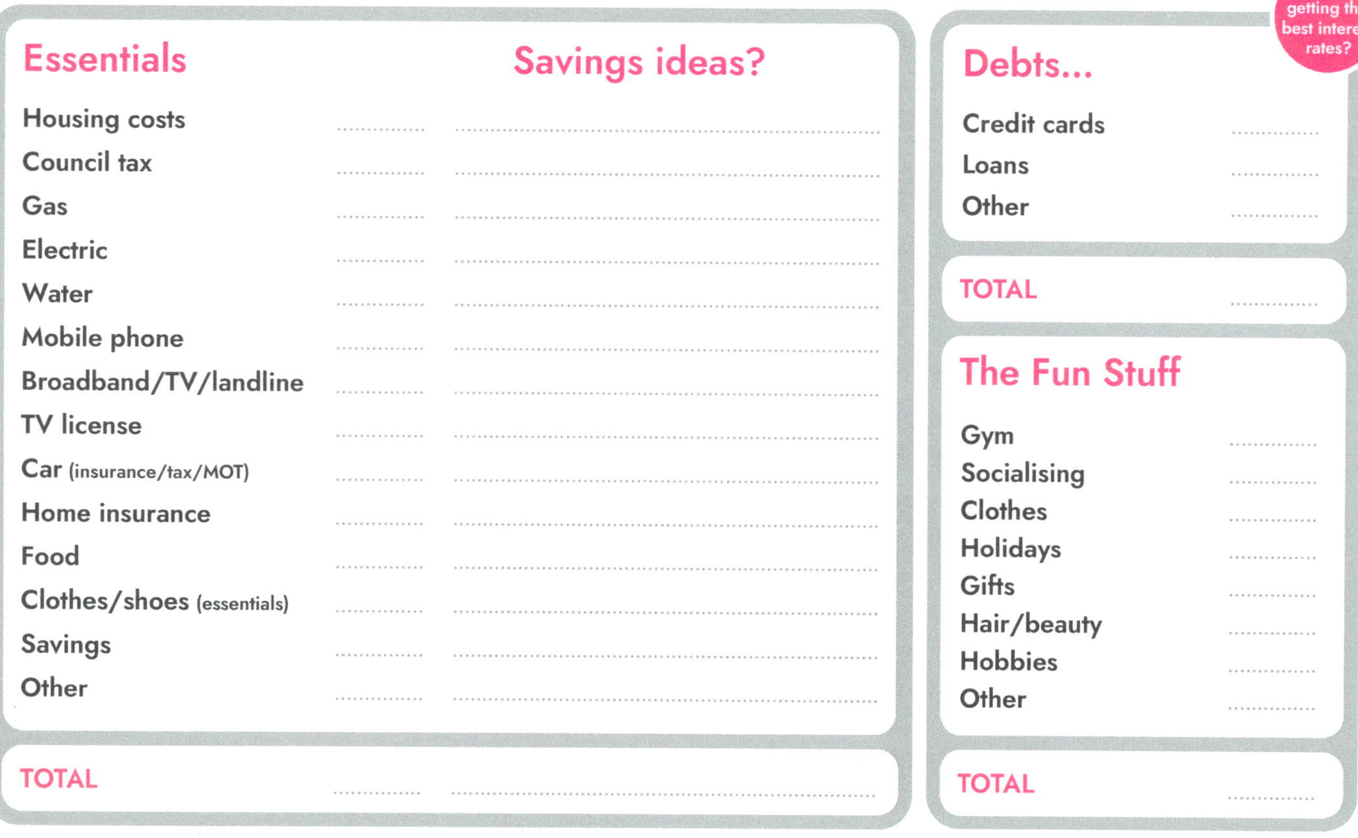

What's coming in?

| Salary | Extras | Bank Balance | Total |

What's going out?

Essentials

Housing costs
Council tax
Gas
Electric
Water
Mobile phone
Broadband/TV/landline
TV license
Car (insurance/tax/MOT)
Home insurance
Food
Clothes/shoes (essentials)
Savings
Other

TOTAL

Savings ideas?

Debts...

Credit cards
Loans
Other

TOTAL

Are you getting the best interest rates?

The Fun Stuff

Gym
Socialising
Clothes
Holidays
Gifts
Hair/beauty
Hobbies
Other

TOTAL

Day to day costs

Lunch/Food
Travelling
Drinks
Extras

Where are we?

Incomings
Outgoings
What's left

Action plan...

Better With A PLAN | BUDGET PLANNER

What's coming in?

Salary

Extras

Bank Balance

Total

What's going out?

Essentials

Housing costs ....
Council tax ....
Gas ....
Electric ....
Water ....
Mobile phone ....
Broadband/TV/landline ....
TV license ....
Car (insurance/tax/MOT) ....
Home insurance ....
Food ....
Clothes/shoes (essentials) ....
Savings ....
Other ....

TOTAL

Savings ideas?

Debts...

Credit cards ....
Loans ....
Other ....

TOTAL ....

The Fun Stuff

Gym ....
Socialising ....
Clothes ....
Holidays ....
Gifts ....
Hair/beauty ....
Hobbies ....
Other ....

TOTAL ....

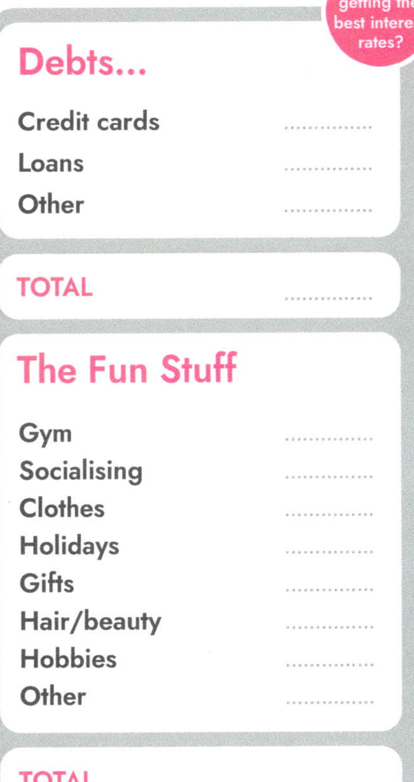

Day to day costs

Lunch/Food ....
Travelling ....
Drinks ....
Extras ....

Where are we?

Incomings ....
Outgoings ....
What's left ....

Action plan...

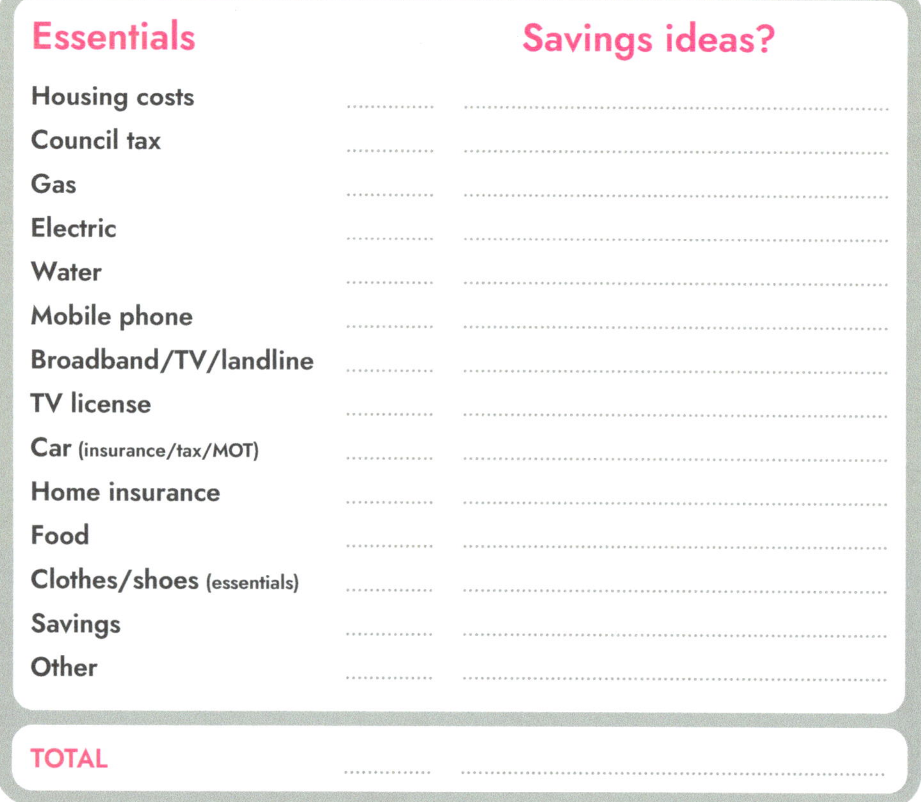

Better With A PLAN | BUDGET PLANNER

What's coming in?

Salary

Extras

Bank Balance

Total

What's going out?

Essentials

Housing costs
Council tax
Gas
Electric
Water
Mobile phone
Broadband/TV/landline
TV license
Car (insurance/tax/MOT)
Home insurance
Food
Clothes/shoes (essentials)
Savings
Other

TOTAL

Savings ideas?

Debts...

Credit cards
Loans
Other

TOTAL

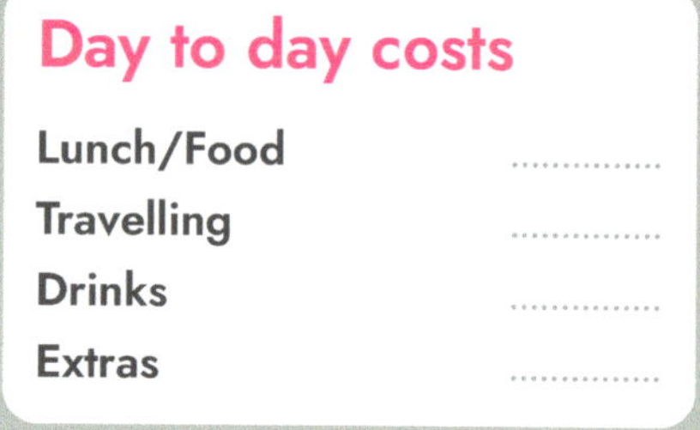

The Fun Stuff

Gym
Socialising
Clothes
Holidays
Gifts
Hair/beauty
Hobbies
Other

TOTAL

Day to day costs

Lunch/Food
Travelling
Drinks
Extras

Where are we?

Incomings
Outgoings
What's left

Action plan...

PLAN | BUDGET PLANNER

What's coming in?

Salary	Extras	Bank Balance	Total

What's going out?

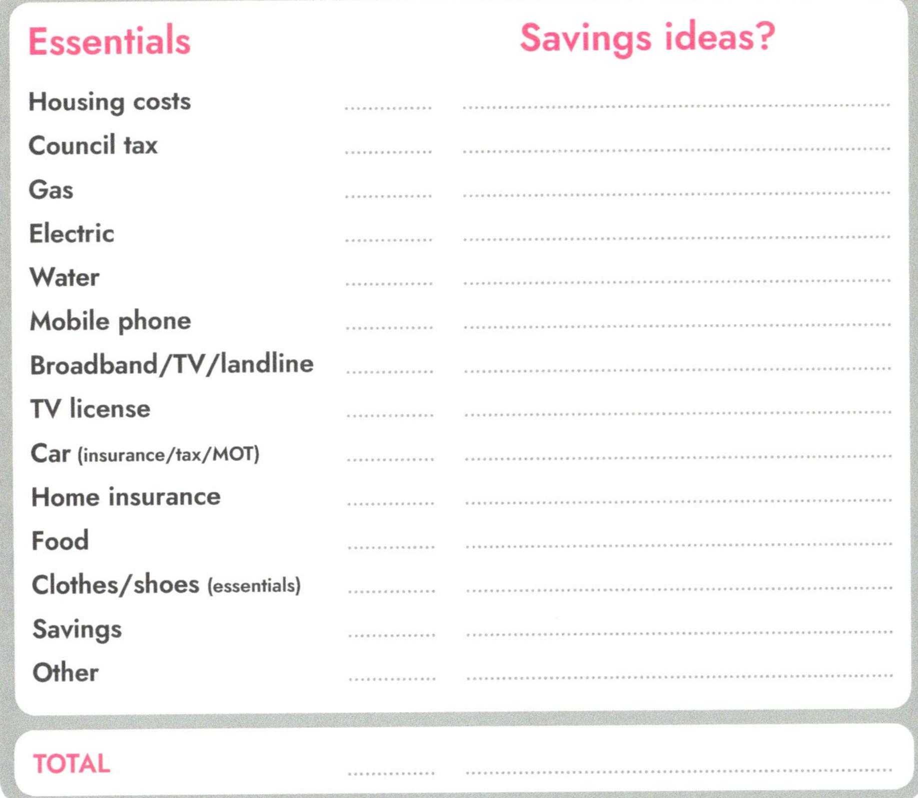

Essentials

Savings ideas?

- Housing costs
- Council tax
- Gas
- Electric
- Water
- Mobile phone
- Broadband/TV/landline
- TV license
- Car (insurance/tax/MOT)
- Home insurance
- Food
- Clothes/shoes (essentials)
- Savings
- Other

TOTAL

Day to day costs

- Lunch/Food ....
- Travelling ....
- Drinks ....
- Extras ....

Are you getting the best interest rates?

Debts...

- Credit cards ....
- Loans ....
- Other ....

TOTAL

The Fun Stuff

- Gym
- Socialising
- Clothes
- Holidays
- Gifts
- Hair/beauty
- Hobbies
- Other

TOTAL

Where are we?

- Incomings ....
- Outgoings ....
- What's left ....

Action plan...

Better With A
PLAN | BUDGET PLANNER

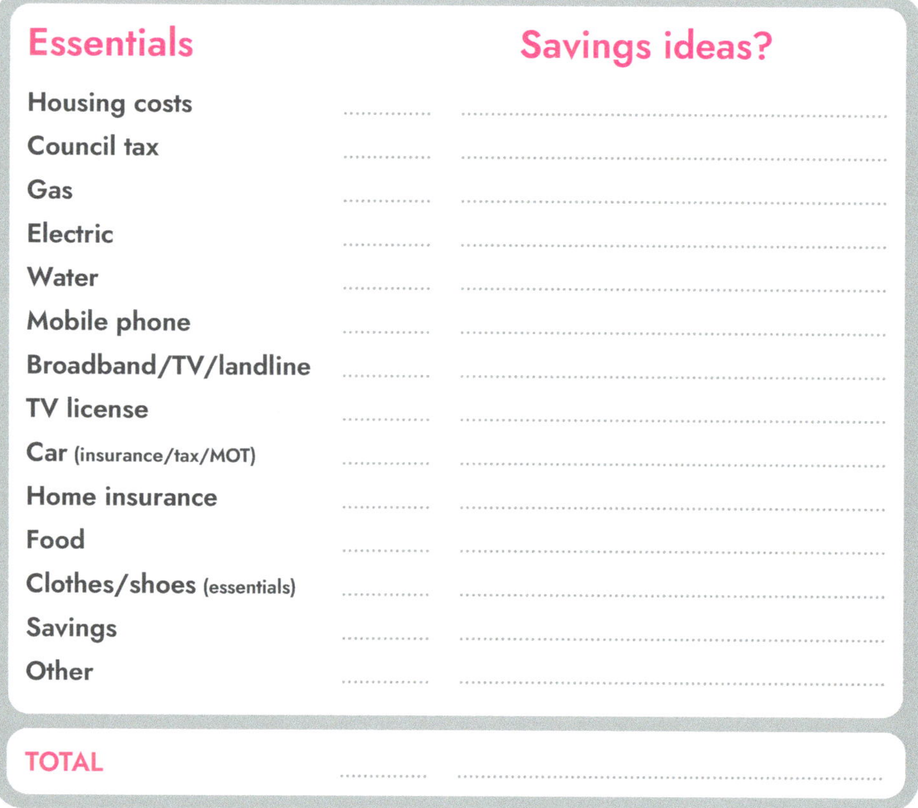

What's coming in?

Salary

Extras

Bank Balance

Total

What's going out?

Essentials

Savings ideas?

Housing costs
Council tax
Gas
Electric
Water
Mobile phone
Broadband/TV/landline
TV license
Car (insurance/tax/MOT)
Home insurance
Food
Clothes/shoes (essentials)
Savings
Other

TOTAL

Are you getting the best interest rates?

Debts...

Credit cards
Loans
Other

TOTAL

The Fun Stuff

Gym
Socialising
Clothes
Holidays
Gifts
Hair/beauty
Hobbies
Other

TOTAL

Day to day costs

Lunch/Food
Travelling
Drinks
Extras

Where are we?

Incomings
Outgoings
What's left

Action plan...

BUDGET PLANNER

What's coming in?

Salary

Extras

Bank Balance

Total

What's going out?

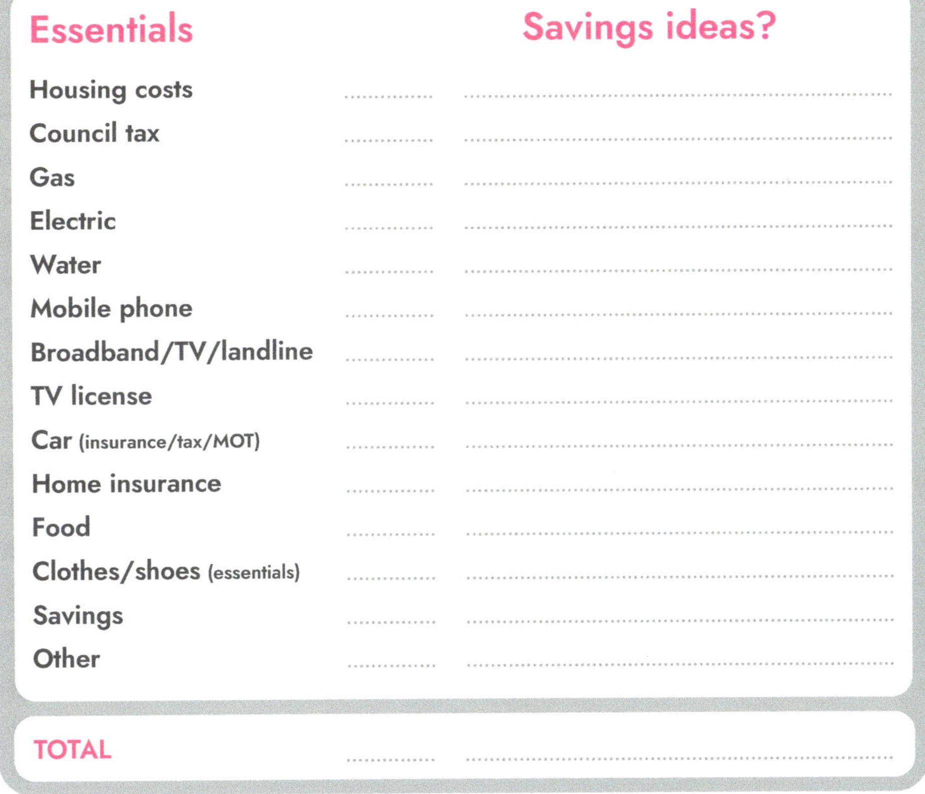

Essentials

Housing costs
Council tax
Gas
Electric
Water
Mobile phone
Broadband/TV/landline
TV license
Car (insurance/tax/MOT)
Home insurance
Food
Clothes/shoes (essentials)
Savings
Other

Savings ideas?

TOTAL

Debts...

Credit cards
Loans
Other

TOTAL

The Fun Stuff

Gym
Socialising
Clothes
Holidays
Gifts
Hair/beauty
Hobbies
Other

TOTAL

Are you getting the best interest rates?

Day to day costs

Lunch/Food
Travelling
Drinks
Extras

Where are we?

Incomings
Outgoings
What's left

Action plan...

Better With A PLAN | BUDGET PLANNER

What's coming in?

Salary

Extras

Bank Balance

Total

What's going out?

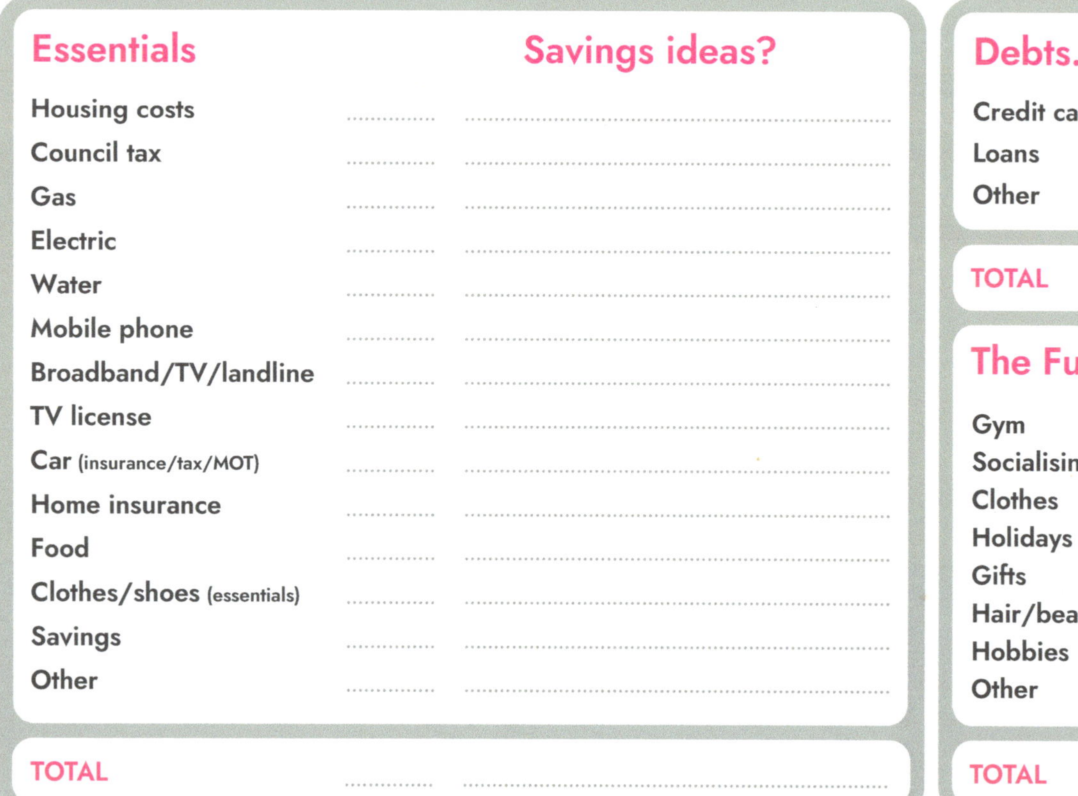

Essentials

Housing costs
Council tax
Gas
Electric
Water
Mobile phone
Broadband/TV/landline
TV license
Car (insurance/tax/MOT)
Home insurance
Food
Clothes/shoes (essentials)
Savings
Other

Savings ideas?

TOTAL

Debts...

Credit cards
Loans
Other

TOTAL

Are you getting the best interest rates?

The Fun Stuff

Gym
Socialising
Clothes
Holidays
Gifts
Hair/beauty
Hobbies
Other

TOTAL

Day to day costs

Lunch/Food
Travelling
Drinks
Extras

Where are we?

Incomings
Outgoings
What's left

Action plan...